THOMSON
URSE TECHNOLOGY

ssional ■ Trade ■ Reference

OPENGL® ES
GAME DEVELOPMENT

DAVE ASTLE
DAVE DURNIL

D1172214

UDES CD-ROM

Premier
Press

© 2004 by Thomson Course Technology PTR. All rights reserved. No part of this book may be reproduced or transmitted in any form or by any means, electronic or mechanical, including photocopying, recording, or by any information storage or retrieval system without written permission from Thomson Course Technology PTR, except for the inclusion of brief quotations in a review.

The Premier Press and Thomson Course Technology PTR logo and related trade dress are trademarks of Thomson Course Technology PTR and may not be used without written permission.

OpenGL is a registered trademark of Silicon Graphics, Inc. BREW and QUALCOMM are registered trademarks of QUALCOMM Incorporated.

All other trademarks are the property of their respective owners.

Important: Thomson Course Technology PTR cannot provide software support. Please contact the appropriate software manufacturer's technical support line or Web site for assistance.

Thomson Course Technology PTR and the author have attempted throughout this book to distinguish proprietary trademarks from descriptive terms by following the capitalization style used by the manufacturer.

Information contained in this book has been obtained by Thomson Course Technology PTR from sources believed to be reliable. However, because of the possibility of human or mechanical error by our sources, Thomson Course Technology PTR, or others, the Publisher does not guarantee the accuracy, adequacy, or completeness of any information and is not responsible for any errors or omissions or the results obtained from use of such information. Readers should be particularly aware of the fact that the Internet is an ever-changing entity. Some facts may have changed since this book went to press.

Educational facilities, companies, and organizations interested in multiple copies or licensing of this book should contact the publisher for quantity discount information. Training manuals, CD-ROMs, and portions of this book are also available individually or can be tailored for specific needs.

ISBN: 1-59200-370-2
Library of Congress Catalog Card Number: 2003098919
Printed in the United States of America

04 05 06 07 08 BH 10 9 8 7 6 5 4 3 2 1

THOMSON

COURSE TECHNOLOGY

Professional ■ Trade ■ Reference

Thomson Course Technology PTR,
a division of Thomson Course Technology
25 Thomson Place
Boston, MA 02210
http://www.courseptr.com

SVP, Thomson Course Technology PTR:
Andy Shafran

Publisher:
Stacy L. Hiquet

Senior Marketing Manager:
Sarah O'Donnell

Marketing Manager:
Heather Hurley

Manager of Editorial Services:
Heather Talbot

Senior Acquisitions Editor:
Emi Smith

Senior Editor:
Mark Garvey

Associate Marketing Managers:
Kristin Eisenzopf and Sarah Dubois

Project Editor/Copy Editor:
Marta Justak

Technical Reviewer:
Aaftab Munshi

Course Technology PTR Market Coordinator:
Elizabeth Furbish

Interior Layout Tech:
Jill Flores

Cover Designer:
Mike Tanamachi

CD-ROM Producer:
Brandon Penticuff

Indexer:
Katherine Stimson

Proofreader:
Gene Redding

For my family and all my best friends.

Dave Durnil

For Lissa, whom I ignored when she told me to stop writing these damn books.

Dave Astle

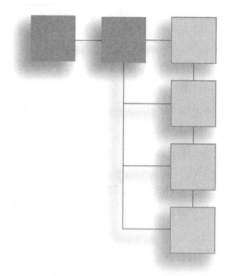

FOREWORD

You say you want a revolution? Well, sometimes the smallest things can create the biggest changes. OpenGL ES originated that way—in a modest 3Dlabs project in 2001 that sought to define a standardized subset of OpenGL for a range of embedded systems. It soon became clear that there was a widespread industry desire for a small footprint, cross platform API with excellent 2D and 3D functionality, particularly as 3D silicon was rapidly becoming both more capable and significantly cheaper, but such an API simply didn't exist in 2001.

As interest quickly grew around 3Dlabs' idea, the search began for a standards body able to create a 3D graphics API for embedded systems that leveraged the proven strengths of OpenGL—an API that has been used by a huge range of applications from games to CAD systems on a wide variety of workstations and PCs. With the support of the OpenGL Architecture Board, the industry body responsible for evolving OpenGL for 10 years, 3Dlabs took the idea of defining a subset of OpenGL to the Khronos Group—an open standards consortium working on OpenGL-related standards. Khronos recognized the opportunity and began to organize to undertake this new project.

Then things started getting really interesting.

At that time, the cell phone industry was also searching for a graphics API to enable the market for 3D gaming on handsets. An early indication of how fast things were about to start developing occurred when Symbian arranged an industry-wide meeting in April 2002, and in a single day, the decision was made to adopt the embryonic OpenGL ES as that standard.

So a small physical platform, the cell phone, began to provide a large commercial momentum that propelled the nascent OpenGL ES into the fast track. In just twelve months the industry's foremost experts in 3D graphics, OpenGL, and embedded systems worked to create the OpenGL ES 1.0 and EGL 1.0 specifications that were publicly released, royalty free, to the industry at Siggraph in July 2003. Six months later Khronos released conformance tests for OpenGL ES—ensuring that products that use the OpenGL ES logo provide consistent levels of quality and functionality that application developers can truly rely on.

OpenGL ES 1.0 immediately gathered strong industry momentum and pushed Khronos membership to over 50 companies. This tremendous success is a testament to what can be achieved when committed companies, some fierce competitors, lay down arms and work together to create a standard to benefit the industry as a whole. The OpenGL ES standard has already spawned a range of software implementations, some that fit within a minute 75 Kbytes, and an array of powerful, but low-power accelerators that are small and cheap enough to fit within cell-phone handsets.

The widespread appeal of OpenGL ES is a result of following the same design principles as the original OpenGL. OpenGL ES is a low-level API that provides just enough abstraction to create cross-platform portability and foster implementation innovation in software and silicon. By staying at a low level, OpenGL ES is able to form the foundation for an unlimited range of applications, games engines, middleware, and higher-level 3D software.

The remarkable thing, even for those working in the midst of the standardization process, is how quickly the cell phone industry is establishing the industry infrastructure for handheld 3D gaming. In one year we have achieved the same level of widespread acceptance for a single 3D API that took almost four years on the PC. Things are likely to continue to develop in "cell phone time," and I believe we are witnessing the beginning of the transformation of cell phones from communication devices into ubiquitous personal computing tools that most of us will eventually use for the bulk of our computing needs. Bringing rich media capabilities, including 3D graphics, onto these devices is one important step in this industry-changing process.

Looking forward, one thing is certain: that innovation will accelerate, and we will soon see OpenGL ES being used in all manner of devices and platforms, including game consoles and set-top boxes, to communicate and entertain. The Khronos Group will continue to develop OpenGL ES to enable the evolving 3D capabilities of embedded platforms, and they have recently delivered the OpenGL ES 1.1 specification at Siggraph 2004 to provide developers access to the increasing capabilities of phones with full 3D acceleration.

The next version of OpenGL ES, OpenGL ES 2.0, is currently being developed by Khronos members for release in 2005 and will bring the power of programmable shaders and the OpenGL Shading Language to embedded platforms—remarkably just one year after OpenGL 2.0 was ratified for desktop machines. By innovating the unique solutions needed to bring programmability to small and diverse platforms, Khronos will unleash enormous computing power in the palm of your hand. The embedded 3D revolution has truly just begun.

And now, by reading this book, you too have become a part of this revolution! The best-designed API is just an academic exercise until it is used by developers to create compelling content. Khronos hopes that you will find using OpenGL ES to be an enjoyable and rewarding experience. It is a growing, evolving API—and so please tell us something of your experiences on the Khronos public forums at **www.khronos.org** so that we may collectively move forward together.

Finally, I would like to take this opportunity to thank everyone who has brought us here, especially all the members of the OpenGL ES Working Group—it is a genuine pleasure and privilege to work with you all. I would also make special mention of Kurt Akeley and the OpenGL ARB that created OpenGL, the solid and trusted foundation for everything we do; Randi Rost at 3Dlabs, who undertook the first design for an OpenGL subset that was the catalyst for OpenGL ES; Shawn Underwood, Jon Leech, and Thomas Tannert of SGI for their support and expert guidance in expanding the reach of OpenGL into new territories; David Blythe of Hi Corporation and Aaftab Munshi of ATI Technologies for their wisdom and efforts as specification editors; Ed Plowman of ARM, Kari Pulli of Nokia, and Bill Pinnell of Symbian, who had the vision to bring OpenGL ES into the cell phone industry; and Elizabeth Riegel at Gold Standard Group for her tireless organization and promotion of Khronos.

But most importantly—thank you to Dave Astle and Dave Durnil. You have created an outstanding book that will play a vital role in educating developers how this API can be effectively used and the opportunities it creates. You have also done it in "cell-phone" time—making this, the first OpenGL ES book, amazingly up-to-the-minute!

I strongly recommend this book to anyone who wishes to be part of the handheld 3D revolution.

Neil Trevett
Senior Vice President Market Development, 3Dlabs
President, Khronos Group; Chairman, OpenGL ES Working Group
neil.trevett@3dlabs.com
August 2004

Acknowledgments

With any major project, it is the ongoing encouragement of colleagues and loved ones that keeps you motivated. So we both would like to personally thank our friends and family for their continued support and understanding.

We hope everyone will enjoy this book. We couldn't have provided this information without the help of some very talented people. So a special thanks to our contributing authors—Mike Street, Devin Maxwell, and Anders Granlund—for taking their time in adding to the overall quality of this book. Their efforts are greatly appreciated. In the same vein, we'd like to thank our co-worker Brian Ellis for his contributions to the EGL chapter.

Overall, we would like to thank everyone at Course Technology for their efforts in publishing this book. As always, they are an outstanding group of people to work with—though they seem to have forgotten how to party.

We would also like to thank QUALCOMM for allowing us to pursue our passion for writing. Thanks to John Boackle, Vice President of Engineering, and David Ligon, Senior Product Manger for 3D Graphics, for their continued support of projects like this.

We would also like to thank Fathammer, Superscape, and Hi Corporation for allowing us to provide information on their 3D mobile gaming engines. Thank you to Arto Astala, CTO, and Ville Vaten, Project Manager, of Fathammer for their very responsive e-mails, detailed information, and screenshots of the Fathammer X-Forge engine. Thanks to Brendan Roberts, Vice President of North American business development for Superscape. We also appreciate the great efforts of Stephane Groud of Superscape for helping us collect information on the Swerve engine. Finally, thank you to Carl Korobkin, President and CEO of Mascot Capsule, Inc. (a division of Hi Corporation), for his efforts in providing details on the V3 and V4 Mascot Capsule engine.

We would like to thank the QUALCOMM QIS Business and Marketing Unit for BREW™, who provided a general overview of the mobile gaming market. Thanks to Mike Yuen, Director of Product Management, for providing the core explanations of how the mobile gaming market works, and Aaron Bernstein, Product Manager, Game Developer Relations, for helping pull this information together. A very special thanks goes to Bella Alabanza, Manager of Marketing Communications, for her tireless efforts in pulling the mobile business chapter together for us.

The Khronos Group richly deserves credit for their support of this book, and of course, for developing and promoting OpenGL ES in the first place. Neil Trevett and Elizabeth Riegel were particularly helpful in promoting and supporting this book.

Last, but certainly not least, we would personally like to thank ATI and our technical editor, Aaftab Munshi. Thanks, Affie, for helping edit the book, for providing information on the ATI 2300 series hardware, and for keeping us up-to-date with the evolving OpenGL ES 1.1 specification.

ABOUT THE AUTHORS

Dave Astle is a senior software engineer at QUALCOMM, where he plays a primary role in the development and optimization of their OpenGL ES implementation. Prior to that, he spent several years developing console games. He is a founder and operator of GameDev.net, the leading online community for game developers. He's a coauthor of the best-selling *OpenGL Game Programming* and *Beginning OpenGL Game Programming*, has contributed to numerous other books as an author and editor, and is a regular speaker at game industry conferences.

Dave Durnil is currently leading engineering efforts focusing on 3D gaming and graphics applications research for QUALCOMM CDMA Technologies next generation hardware. He has extensive knowledge in the areas of 3D graphics development for wireless devices and over 10 years' experience with OpenGL®. Before joining QUALCOMM, he was a lead engineer on the NASA Mars space program.

Contributing Authors

Chapter 4, "A Fixed Point Math Primer"

Michael Street has been programming embedded systems for many years. He wrote low-level 3D game engine code for the Nintendo 64 while working for Angel Studios (now Rockstar San Diego). Games that he developed included *Major League Baseball featuring Ken Griffey, Jr.* and *Virtual Jungle Cruise* for DisneyQuest. He is now a senior engineer at QUALCOMM, developing low-level drivers for OpenGL ES. He is a key component of the 3D graphics software team and continues to work on OpenGL ES for QUALCOMM's product line of 3G wireless chipsets.

Chapter 5, "Developing OpenGL ES Games"

Anders Granlund is a lead programmer in the handheld division of **Climax**. During his five years in the game industry, he has worked on a wide range of hardware, including both console and handheld platforms. He is one of the first game developers to port a commercial console game (*MotoGP2*) to OpenGL ES using ATI IMAGEON 2300 series hardware with the BREW development environment. The port of *MotoGP2* was a major step in the industry as it was another leap forward for gaming on a mobile device by proving that high-quality 3D gaming is now a reality. Leveraging his expertise in the areas of commercial game development, Anders has written articles on working with prerelease hardware and has been a guest speaker for ATI at the Game Developers Conference, talking about OpenGL ES.

CLIMAX

Founded in 1988 by Karl Jeffery, Climax has since gone on to become one of the world's leading interactive software development companies, employing nearly 400 people. Climax continues to expand its head count, in addition to acquiring and opening new studios in other locations across the world.

The Handheld Division started in 2003 and is at the cutting edge of game development for all handheld platforms, working with world leaders such as ATI, Sony, THQ, and Disney, to bring both licensed and original content to new 3D mobile phones, Sony PSP, Nintendo DS and Game Boy Advance, and N-Gage.

Chapter 7, "Audio for Mobile Devices"

Devin Maxwell is a founding owner of the LoudLouderLoudest Music Production Company, and he currently holds the position Director of Development. LoudLouderLoudest is a leading provider of media, sound, and music to the wireless industry. LoudLouderLoudest's original music, sound effects, game audio, wireless film music, ringtones, ringbacks, animated ringtones, and hybrids are found internationally and on all major U.S. carriers. LoudLouderLoudest provides wireless audio services to some of the largest and most prestigious companies in the wireless industry, the music industry, and the games industry.

In addition to his work at LoudLouderLoudest, he is an active composer, engineer, producer, and studio and chamber musician in New York City. He is a member of the Audio Engineering Society, the American Composer's Forum, the International Game Developer's Association, the Game Audio Network Guild, and ASCAP. Devin holds a B.M. in Percussion Performance from the University of Cincinnati College-Conservatory of Music and a dual M.F.A. in Composition and Performance from the California Institute of the Arts.

CONTENTS AT A GLANCE

Contents

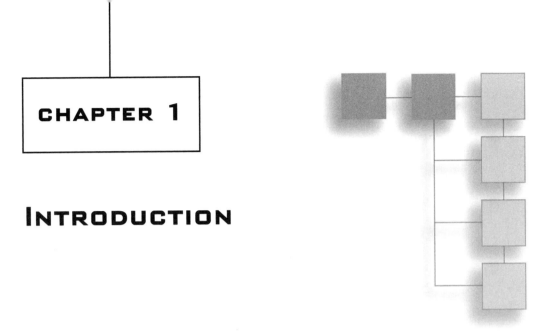

CHAPTER 1

INTRODUCTION

Welcome to *OpenGL ES Game Development*. In this book you'll be learning about 3D game development for cell phones and other embedded devices using OpenGL ES and related libraries. But before we get started, this introduction will provide an overview of the topics that will be covered, as well as providing you with information you'll need to get the most out of this book.

What You'll Learn

While the focus of this book is on OpenGL ES, it also presents a broad range of information covering 3D game development on embedded devices in general.

Chapter 2, "The EGL Interface," describes the native platform graphics interface designed to be used with OpenGL ES.

Chapter 3, "OpenGL ES," provides a comprehensive summary of the differences between OpenGL and OpenGL ES 1.0, as well as highlighting the new features introduced by OpenGL ES.

Chapter 4, "A Fixed Point Math Primer," written by Michael Street, will help you understand and implement efficient and robust math libraries for platforms that don't provide native floating point support.

Chapter 5, "Developing OpenGL ES Games," written by Anders Granlund, describes how the Climax Group ported a game originally developed for Microsoft's Xbox to an embedded device supporting OpenGL ES. This chapter provides valuable tips and insights to other developers moving from PCs or consoles to mobile phones.

Chapter 6, "Limitations of the Medium," offers some tips and tricks for getting the most out of mobile devices so that your games can be the best they can possibly be.

Chapter 7, "Audio for Mobile Devices," by Devin Maxwell, provides a guide to developing quality audio for cell phones.

Chapter 8, "3D Game Engines for Mobile Devices," takes a look at three commercial 3D mobile game engines with support for OpenGL ES: X-Forge, Swerve 2, and Mascot Capsule V4.

Chapter 9, "The Future," looks at the newly announced 1.1 revision of OpenGL ES, as well as providing an idea of how the specification will continue to evolve.

Chapter 10, "The Mobile Business Model," provides an overview of opportunities available in the mobile gaming market for those who are new to it.

What You Should Know

Like most books, this book has some prerequisites, which allow it to focus on the core material rather than devoting time and space to covering topics that are better covered elsewhere.

One of the main topics covered in this book is OpenGL ES. However, not surprisingly, OpenGL ES has a lot in common with OpenGL. Many of our readers may have a good understanding already of OpenGL, as it is a well-established API. So rather than dedicating hundreds of pages to covering OpenGL itself, we'll focus instead on the differences between OpenGL and OpenGL ES, as well as the new functionality added to OpenGL ES. If you're not already familiar with OpenGL, there are several excellent resources listed at the end of Chapter 3.

You should also have some experience developing games on other platforms. Cell phones and similar devices aren't particularly well-suited as a platform for beginning game programmers, so throughout this book we'll be assuming that you have a basic understanding of game development.

The code samples available in the book and on the CD were written in C and C++, so a solid understanding of those languages is recommended as well.

Code Samples

The platforms on which OpenGL ES is available are extremely diverse, which presents a challenge in providing sample code. Although the OpenGL ES code itself should be the same and easily portable across platforms, the rest of the code (for application initialization, event handling, input processing, etc.) won't be. For example, although a BREW-based application should run on any BREW-enabled phone, a great deal of the code would have to be rewritten for the same program to run on other platforms, such as Symbian OS.

For us to provide sample programs for each of the platforms on which OpenGL ES is available is impractical. So instead, we've limited the code printed in the book to short snippets free of any platform-dependent code. The CD included with this book also contains a number of sample programs using OpenGL ES on various platforms. See Appendix A, "Using the CD," for details.

Obtaining OpenGL ES

Since you're reading this book, we expect that you probably already have an OpenGL ES implementation that you're developing for. If not, there are a couple of freely available implementations that you can download and use to experiment.

The first is the OpenGL ES extension for QUALCOMM's BREW SDK. The SDK and extension are available from **www.brewdeveloper.com**. You have to become a registered BREW developer, but doing so is free.

The second is Vincent, an open source OpenGL ES implementation administered by Hans-Martin Will. It is available from **ogl-es.sourceforge.net**.

Other OpenGL ES implementations are likely to become available in the near future. We'd recommend checking the official OpenGL ES Web site at **www.opengles.org** for more information.

Contacting the Authors

The authors have set up a support Web site for this book at **http://glbook.gamedev.net/opengles/**. There you'll find any relevant updates, errata, frequently asked questions, and contact information for the authors.

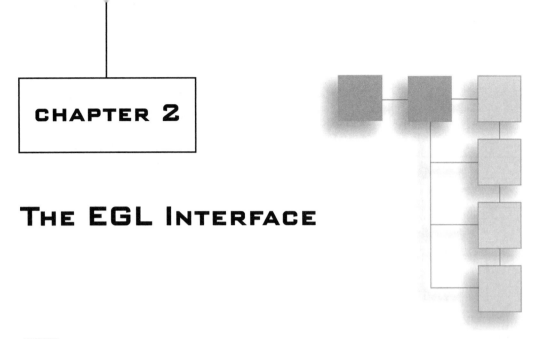

CHAPTER 2

THE EGL INTERFACE

E GL is the interface between OpenGL ES and the underlying native platform window system. This chapter will focus on the EGL API for OpenGL ES and how to use it to create contexts, drawing surfaces, and so on and provide a comparative analysis with other windowing APIs used for OpenGL, such as WGL and GLX. In this chapter we will cover the following information:

- An overview of EGL
- EGL's major components (such as displays, contexts, and configurations)
- Using EGL with BREW and Windows CE
- A comparison of EGL and other OpenGL windowing systems

Introduction to EGL

EGL was designed to work with OpenGL ES and to be platform independent. In this chapter, you'll learn about each EGL API in detail and see the limitations and platform considerations to be aware of when using EGL. OpenGL ES offers extensions for additional functionality and possible platform-specific development, but there still needs to be a layer that allows OpenGL ES to interact with the native windowing system in a platform-independent manner. OpenGL ES is essentially a state machine for a graphics pipeline, and EGL is an outside layer used to keep track of this group of graphics' states and to maintain framebuffers and other rendering surfaces. Figure 2.1 diagrams a typical system layout of EGL.

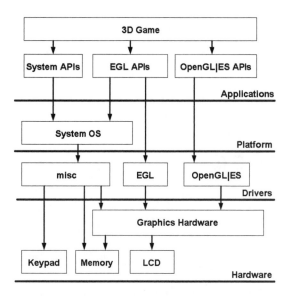

Figure 2.1 A typical system layout of EGL.

The EGL windowing design is based on the popular native interfaces used by OpenGLES for Microsoft Windows (WGL) and UNIX (GLX), though it's most similar to the latter. The states of the OpenGL ES graphics pipeline are stored in a context that EGL maintains. Frame buffers and other drawing surfaces are created, managed, and destroyed by using the EGL APIs. EGL also controls and provides access to the device displays and the possible rendering configurations of the device.

EGL Data Types

EGL includes its own set of data types and also provides support for a set of platform-specific native data types. These native data types will be defined in the EGL system header file. Once you understand the fundamental difference between these data types, working with them is straightforward. For the most part, developers will use abstract data types and avoid using the direct system data types to maintain portability where possible. By using the native types defined in EGL, you'll be able to write EGL code that should work on any EGL implementation. The native EGL types are explained below.

- `NativeDisplayType` refers to the platform display data type that identifies the physical screen on the device on which you are developing.

- `NativeWindowType` refers to the platform windowing data type that identifies the system window.

- `NativePixmapType` refers to a system pixmap (or host memory) data type that can be used as a framebuffer on the platform. This data type is only used for offscreen rendering.

The following code is one possible example of what a `NativeWindowType` might look like. This is only an example and will vary from platform to platform. The whole point of using a native type is to abstract these details away from the developer. For QUALCOMM's native types, they use an IDIB structure as follows:

```
struct IDIB {
  AEEVTBL(IBitmap) *pvt;                // virtual table pointer
  IQueryInterface * pPaletteMap;        // cache for computed palette mapping info
  byte *          pBmp;                 // pointer to top row
  uint32 *        pRGB;                 // palette
  NativeColor     ncTransparent;        // 32-bit native color value
  uint16          cx;                   // number of pixels in width
  uint16          cy;                   // number of pixels in height
  int16           nPitch;               // offset from one row to the next
  uint16          cntRGB;               // number of palette entries
  uint8           nDepth;               // size of pixel in bits
  uint8           nColorScheme;         // IDIB_COLORSCHEME_...(ie. 5-6-5)
  uint8           reserved[6];
};
```

The following sections will go into more detail on the EGL data types. The standard EGL data types are described in Table 2.1.

Table 2.1 EGL Data Types

Data Type	Value
EGLBoolean	EGL_TRUE =1, EGL_FALSE=0
EGLint	System defined int data type
EGLDisplay	System display id or handle
EGLConfig	EGL configuration for a surface
EGLSurface	System window or frame buffer handle
EGLContext	Graphics context for OpenGL ES
NativeDisplayType	The native system display type
NativeWindowType	The native system window buffer type
NativePixmapType	The native system frame buffer

EGL Displays

EGLDisplay is a generic data type for referencing the system's physical screen. For a PC, this display would typically be your monitor handle. On both embedded systems and a PC, it is possible to have multiple physical display devices. In order to use the system's display devices, EGL provides the data type EGLDisplay and a set of APIs to access the displays of the device. Figure 2.2 illustrates what a physical display might look like:

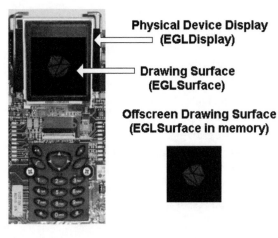

**Physical Device Display
(EGLDisplay)**

**Drawing Surface
(EGLSurface)**

**Offscreen Drawing Surface
(EGLSurface in memory)**

Figure 2.2 A typical system display device.

The following is the function prototype for getting a native display:

```
EGLDisplay eglGetDisplay (Native-
DisplayType display);
```

The *display* parameter is the native system's windowing display ID number. If you just want to get the default display for your system, you can use the parameter *EGL_DEFAULT_DISPLAY*. If the *display* value does not match any native display IDs that are available on your system, then EGL_NO_DISPLAY is returned but no error condition is set. Since no error condition is set for bogus *display* values, you should always check the return type before proceeding.

Note

It is always good practice to check the return value of EGL function calls, since the EGL error condition is not always set when the function call fails.

Here is an example of getting a system display using the EGL API:

```
m_eglDisplay = eglGetDisplay( system.display);
if (m_eglDisplay == EGL_NO_DISPLAY || eglGetError() != EGL_SUCCESS))
    throw error_egl_display;
```

Initialization

Like many windowing APIs, EGL needs to be initialized before it can be actively used, and thus each EGLDisplay needs to be initialized before use. When initializing an EGLDisplay, you can get the version of EGL that is implemented on your system. Knowing the current version number can be very valuable in terms of backward compatibility. Embedded and mobile devices are constantly being released into the market, so you should expect that your code will need to execute on a variety of implementations. By dynamically querying the EGL version number, you can enable additional features or workarounds for newer or older versions of EGL. Developing software that is aware of which set of APIs to call based on the platform configuration will provide the maximum portability for your code.

The following is the function prototype for initializing EGL:

```
EGLBoolean eglInitialize (EGLDisplay dpy, EGLint *major, EGLint *minor);
```

dpy should be a valid `EGLDisplay`. When this function returns, *major* and *minor* will be set to the current EGL version. For example, with EGL 1.0, *major* would be 1 and *minor* would be 0. Passing `NULL` for both major and minor is valid if you're not interested in the version number.

The `eglQueryString()` function is another way to retrieve version information, as well as other information. Since retrieving the version information through `eglQueryString()` would require the parsing of the version string, it is typically easier to get this information by passing pointers to integers into the `eglInitialize()` function. Be aware that you must call `eglInitialize()` on your `EGLDisplay` before calling `eglQueryString()`, or the call will fail and an `EGL_NOT_INITIALIZED` error condition will be set.

The following is the function prototype for getting the EGL version string:

```
const char * eglQueryString (EGLDisplay dpy, EGLint name);
```

The parameter *name* may be `EGL_VENDOR`, `EGL_VERSION`, or `EGL_EXTENSIONS`. This function is most useful for querying the implementation to see what EGL extensions are supported. All EGL extensions are optional, so be sure to query the implementation to verify that any extensions you want to use are supported instead of assuming that the function is present. A `NULL` string is returned if no extensions are supported, and if the *name* parameter is invalid, an `EGL_BAD_PARAMETER` error condition is set.

EGL Configurations

`EGLConfig` is a data type that describes the configuration of an EGL surface. The format of the surface is very important to achieve the correct rendering results. Depending on your platform, the surface configuration may be limited; for example, a device might only support a 16 bit color depth display. Other examples of limitations might include no stencil buffer support or other limited functionality or precision.

The following is the function prototype for getting your system's available EGL configurations:

```
EGLBoolean eglGetConfigs (EGLDisplay dpy, EGLConfig *configs,
                          EGLint config_size, EGLint *num_config);
```

The *configs* parameter will contain a list of all the EGL framebuffer configurations available for your platform. The total number of configurations supported is returned in `num_config`. The actual number of configurations returned in `configs` will depend on the value of `config_size` passed in by the application. If `config_size` < `num_config`, then not all the configurations will be returned. The best way to get all configurations supported by the system is to call `eglGetConfigs` with `NULL` values for `configs`, which will return the total number of supported configurations in `num_config`. Then this can be used to allocate the appropriate `configs` buffer and then call `eglGetConfigs` with this buffer.

The following is an example of how to call the `eglGetConfig()` function:

```
EGLConfig  *configs_list;
EGLint  num_configs;

// Main Display
m_eglDisplay = eglGetDisplay(EGL_DEFAULT_DISPLAY);
if( m_eglDisplay == EGL_NO_DISPLAY || eglGetError() != EGL_SUCCESS )
    return FALSE;

if( eglInitialize( m_eglDisplay, NULL, NULL ) == EGL_FALSE ||
    eglGetError() != EGL_SUCCESS )
    return FALSE;

// find out how many configurations are supported
if ( eglGetConfigs( m_eglDisplay, NULL, 0, &num_configs)
   == EGL_FALSE || eglGetError() != EGL_SUCCESS )
   return FALSE;

configs_list = malloc(num_configs * sizeof(EGLConfig));
if (configs_list == (EGLConfig *)0)
   return FALSE;

// Get Configurations
if( eglGetConfigs( m_eglDisplay, configs_list, num_configs, &num_configs)
    == EGL_FALSE || eglGetError() != EGL_SUCCESS )
    return FALSE;
```

Due to the limitations of current platforms, there are typically only a few configurations available. The configurations supported by the system usually will provide the best performance with the system's hardware. When you are porting your game to multiple platforms where the EGL configurations might differ slightly, we would suggest handling those cases directly as a common porting issue.

Choosing an EGL Configuration

Based on the EGL attributes, you can define a configuration that you would like to find on the system, and it will return the best match for your requirements. Choosing your own configuration is a little misleading, as you can only use the configurations available on your platform. `eglChooseConfig()` will take in configuration requirements that you would like and try to match those closely to a system configuration that is available.

The following is the function prototype for choosing an EGL configuration:

```
EGLBoolean eglChooseConfig(EGLDisplay dpy, const EGLint *attrib_list,
                           EGLConfig *configs, EGLint config_size,
                           EGLint * num_config);
```

The *attrib_list* parameter specifies what attributes to consider when choosing a configuration. The *configs* parameter will contain a list of all the EGL framebuffer configurations available for your platform sorted based on the attribute list. The *config_size* parameter basically specifies how many out of the total number of configurations are available to return in the *configs*. The *num_configs* parameter describes the total number of configurations that were a match.

The following is an example of how to call the eglChooseConfig() function:

```
EGLint      attrs[3] = { EGL_DEPTH_SIZE, 16, EGL_NONE };
EGLint      num_configs;
EGLConfigs *configs_list;

// Get the display device
if ((eglDisplay = eglGetDisplay(EGL_NO_DISPLAY)) == EGL_NO_DISPLAY)
{
    return eglGetError();
}


// Initialize the display
if (eglInitialize(eglDisplay, NULL, NULL) == EGL_FALSE)
{
    return eglGetError();
}
// Obtain the total number of configurations that match
if (eglChooseConfig(eglDisplay, attrs, NULL, 0, &num_configs) == EGL_FALSE)
{
    return eglGetError();
}
configs_list = malloc(num_configs * sizeof(EGLConfig));
if (configs_list == (EGLConfig *)0)
   return eglGetError();

// Obtain the first configuration with a depth buffer of 16 bits
if (!eglChooseConfig(eglDisplay, attrs, &configs_list, num_configs, &num_configs))
{
    return eglGetError();
}
```

If more than one matching configuration is found, then there is a simple sort algorithm applied to try and closely match the configuration you are looking for. Table 2.2 shows what selection and sorting order will be used, based on the attribute values, as well as the complete EGL configuration attributes and default values as laid out in the EGL spec.

Table 2.2 Default Values and Match Criteria for EGL config Attributes

Attributes	Data Type	Default Value	Sort Priority	Selection Order
EGL_BUFFER_SIZE	int	0	3	Smaller value
EGL_RED_SIZE	int	0	2	Larger value
EGL_GREEN_SIZE	int	0	2	Larger value
EGL_BLUE_SIZE	int	0	2	Larger value
EGL_ALPHA_SIZE	int	0	2	Larger value
EGL_CONFIG_CAVET	enum	EGL_DONT_CARE	1 (first)	Exact value
EGL_CONFIG_ID	int	EGL_DONT_CARE	9	Exact value
EGL_DEPTH_SIZE	int	0	6	Smaller value
EGL_LEVEL	int	0	-	Equal value
EGL_NATIVE_RENDERABLE	Boolean	EGL_DONT_CARE	-	Exact value
EGL_NATIVE_VISUAL_TYPE	int	EGL_DONT_CARE	8	Exact value
EGL_SAMPLE_BUFFERS	int	0	4	Smaller value
EGL_SAMPLES	int	0	5	Smaller value
EGL_STENCIL_SIZE	int	0	7	Smaller value
EGL_SURFACE_TYPE	bitmask	EGL_WINDOW_BIT	-	Mask value
EGL_TRANSPARENT_TYPE	enum	EGL_NONE	-	Exact value
EGL_TRANSPARENT_RED_VALUE	int	EGL_DONT_CARE	-	Exactl value
EGL_TRANSPARENT_GREEN_VALUE	int	EGL_DONT_CARE	-	Exact value
EGL_TRANSPARENT_BLUE_VALUE	int	EGL_DONT_CARE	-	Exact value

Attribute Definitions

The EGL attribute definitions from Table 2.2 are described in greater detail in this section.

EGL_ BUFFER_SIZE is the total number of bits used to represent the RGBA values. Each color component size is specified in bit width.

```
EGL_BUFFER_SIZE = EGL_RED_SIZE + EGL_GREEN_SIZE + EGL_BLUE_SIZE + EGL_ALPHA_SIZE
```

The color buffer depth is calculated based on different color schemes. For example, a common color scheme is 4444, which means 4 bits will be used to represent the color red, 4 bits will be used to represent the color green, 4 bits will be used to represent the color blue, and 4 bits will be used to represent the alpha value.

EGL_CONFIG_CAVEAT is used to represent how the configuration may have an effect on the rendering to a drawing surface. Currently, the only values supported for this attribute are the following:

EGL_NONE: There is no side effect when using this configuration.

EGL_SLOW_CONFIG: Rendering may be slower using this configuration.

EGL_NON_CONFORMANT_CONFIG: The OpenGL ES conformance tests may fail if this configuration is used. This may be used by the implementation to offer developers a highly optimized configuration for their platform, but in doing so, some of the OpenGL ES APIs may not be completely conformant.

EGL_CONFIG_ID is used to represent the unique configuration ID.

EGL_DEPTH_SIZE is the total number of bits used to represent the z buffer depth size. The z value stored in the depth buffer is limited to the number of bits used to represent the depth size. A common value for EGL_DEPTH_SIZE is 16 bits.

EGL_LEVEL is used to represent the framebuffer level. Buffer level 0 is the default framebuffer, negative numbers are underlays, and positive numbers are overlays.

EGL_MAX_PBUFFER_WIDTH and EGL_MAX_PBUFFER_HEIGHT are used to represent the maximum width and height of any pbuffer created.

EGL_MAX_PBUFFER_PIXELS is used to specify the total size of any pbuffer created. The total size is predetermined by the system implementation, and it represents how large a pbuffer may be allocated if there is available memory. The max value is not necessarily found just by multiplying the maximum width by the maximum height, since implementations may limit the total amount of memory that can be allocated for one pbuffer to less than that quantity.

EGL_NATIVE_RENDERABLE is used to specify whether the native system rendering APIs can directly render to a drawing surface (or framebuffer). If this attribute is set to EGL_TRUE, then mixing OpenGL ES rendering APIs with native system rendering APIs should be possible. However, native rendering system APIs can't be used with pbuffers simply because pbuffers are allocated by EGL and not available to native system functions.

EGL_NATIVE_VISUAL_ID is used to represent the native system visual or display ID if one should exist. If there are some native functions available that will allow rendering with OpenGL ES rendering APIs, then more than likely you'll need a handle on the native system's display id.

EGL_NATIVE_VISUAL_TYPE is used to represent the native display type based on the system's implementation. Some embedded systems already have a native display and native system APIs for drawing to the system display.

EGL_SAMPLE_BUFFERS is used to represent the number of multisampling buffers available for use.

EGL_SAMPLES is used to represent the number of samples required in multisampling buffers. If there are no sample buffers available, this value will be 0.

EGL_STENCIL_SIZE is used to represent the total number of bits used per pixel in the stencil buffer.

EGL_SURFACE_TYPE is used to specify which drawing surface types are available for the particular configuration. Not all configurations will support all types of rendering, so be sure to check or require that the configuration supports all of the rendering types that you want to use.

The following are the three drawing surfaces made available in EGL:

■ EGL_WINDOW_BIT: This type indicates windows are supported.

■ EGL_PIXMAP_BIT: This type indicates pixmaps (offscreen system buffers) are supported.

■ EGL_PBUFFER_BIT: This type indicates pbuffers are supported.

EGL_TRANSPARENT_TYPE is used to represent whether transparency is available. The two types currently available in EGL are EGL_NONE and EGL_TRANSPARENT_RGB. If transparency is supported, then there will be a red, green, blue value indicating for which values a pixel will be transparent. The ranges of these transparent values are as follows:

■ EGL_TRANSPARENT_RED_VALUE $= 0..(2^{EGL\_RED\_SIZE}-1)$

■ EGL_TRANSPARENT_GREEN_VALUE $= 0..(2^{EGL\_GREEN\_SIZE}-1)$

■ EGL_TRANSPARENT_BLUE_VALUE $= 0..(2^{EGL\_BLUE\_SIZE}-1)$

The sorting of attributes is done in ascending order using the following rules outlined in the EGL spec:

1. EGL_CONFIG_CAVET is the first to be sorted on, where the precedence is EGL_NONE, EGL_SLOW_CONFIG, EGL_NON_CONFORMANT_CONFIG.

2. Use the largest number of RGBA color bits. So out of the color component sizes, the attributes (EGL_RED_SIZE, EGL_GREEN_SIZE, EGL_BLUE_SIZE, EGL_ALPHA_SIZE) with the largest bit widths will be used. If the attribute list that is being used to sort is specified as a color component of 0 bits or EGL_DONT_CARE, then this sort condition is not considered.

3. If the EGL_BUFFER_SIZE that you have specified in your search attribute list is smaller than the one contained in an already existing configuration, then use this existing configuration.

4. If the EGL_SAMPLE_BUFFERS that you have specified in your search attribute list are smaller than the one contained in an already existing configuration, then use this existing configuration.

5. If the EGL_SAMPLES that you have specified in your search attribute list are smaller than the one contained in an already existing configuration, then use this existing configuration.

6. If the EGL_DEPTH_SIZE that you have specified in your search attribute list is smaller than the one contained in an already existing configuration, then use this existing configuration.

7. If the EGL_STENCIL_SIZE that you have specified in your search attribute list is smaller than the one contained in an already existing configuration, then use this existing configuration.

8. If the EGL_NATIVE_VISUAL_TYPE is used, then the actual sort order is unknown, depending on how EGL was implemented on your system.

9. If the EGL_CONFIG_ID that you have specified in your search attribute list is smaller than the one contained in an already existing configuration, then use this existing configuration. This attribute value will be the last value sorted on. EGL guarantees a unique ID ordering.

Table 2.3 shows what a typical default EGL configuration could look like. Depending on the vendor, some of the default values will vary.

Once you have an EGL configuration either from eglGetConfigs() or eglChooseConfig(), the handle to that configuration will remain valid as long as the EGL display associated with your configuration is still valid. If the EGL display is terminated by eglTerminate(), then the EGL configuration handle associated with that display will no longer be valid.

Querying the EGL Configuration

To get the value of an EGL configuration attribute, you can call eglGetConfigAttrib(). The return value for calling this function is as follows: EGL_TRUE if attribute exists, or EGL_FALSE if there is a bad configuration or display parameter. An EGL_BAD_ATTRIBUTE error is set if the attribute value passed does not exist. The attribute value is stored in the *attribute_value* parameter passed into the eglGetConfigAttrib() function.

The following is the function prototype for getting an EGL configuration attribute:

```
EGLBoolean eglGetConfigAttrib(EGLDisplay displayID, EGLConfig* config,
                              EGLint attribute_name,EGLint* attribute_value);
```

The *config* parameter is the EGL configuration to use when querying for attributes. The *attribute_name* is the name of the attribute you are interested in. The *attribute_value* returns the value of the attribute contained in the *config* passed in.

Table 2.3 A Default EGL Configuration

Attributes	Default Value
Red	5
Green	6
Blue	5
Alpha	0
BufferSize	16
ConfigCaveat	EGL_NONE
ConfigID	2
DepthSize	16
Level	0
MaxPBufferWidth	512
MaxPBufferHeight	512
MaxPBufferPixels	320*240
NativeRenderable	EGL_TRUE
NativeVisualID	EGL_NONE
NativeVisualType	EGL_NONE
SampleBuffers	0
Samples	0
StencilSize	0
SurfaceType	EGL_WINDOW_BIT | EGL_PIXMAP_BIT | EGL_PBUFFER_BIT
TransparencyType	EGL_NONE
TransparencyRedValue	0
TransparencyGreenValue	0
TransparencyBlueValue	0

EGL Surfaces and Buffers

An EGLSurface represents a drawing surface available for use by OpenGL ES. There is the potential for both onscreen and offscreen surfaces being available for rendering. For onscreen rendering, OpenGL ES can draw directly to the currently active window's framebuffer memory. For offscreen rendering, *pbuffers* or *pixmaps* are used. Pbuffers are allocated by the EGL implementation and allow the developer to render into an offscreen buffer for later use. Pixmaps use the NativePixmapType to render directly into a buffer allocated by the user, and they do allow for their contents to be directly accessed by native system calls that use the NativePixmapType.

The following is the function prototype for creating an onscreen rendering surface:

```
EGLSurface eglCreateWindowSurface
(EGLDisplay dpy, EGLConfig config,
    NativeWindowType window, const
        EGLint *attrib_list);
```

The *config* parameter is the selected EGL configuration to use when creating an EGL surface. The *window* parameter is just the native window type. For the most part, you don't need to worry about the native window type. Once you declare a NativeWindowType in your application, all you need to do is pass it in to this function. Some EGL implementations will allow you to modify the fields contained in the NativeWindowType, for example, if the platform's EGL implementation allows you to adjust the window size when creating a surface. The *attrib_list* parameter will contain the attributes associated with the EGL surface that is returned.

The following code shows an example of creating an EGL surface:

```
EGLConfig      configs_list;
EGLint     num_configs;
NativeWindowType system_window;
EGLint attrib_list = { EGL_ALPHA_SIZE, 0,
                       EGL_RED_SIZE, 5,
                       EGL_GREEN_SIZE, 6,
                       EGL_BLUE_SIZE, 5,
                       EGL_DEPTH_SIZE, 16,
                       EGL_SURFACE_TYPE, EGL_WINDOW_BIT,
                       EGL_NONE };

// Get the display device
if ((m_eglDisplay = eglGetDisplay(EGL_DEFAULT_DISPLAY)) == EGL_NO_DISPLAY)
{
    return FALSE;
}

// Initialize the display
if (eglInitialize(eglDisplay, NULL, NULL) == EGL_FALSE)
{
    return FALSE;
}

// Choose Configuration
if( eglChooseConfig( m_eglDisplay, attrib_list, &configs_list, 1, , 0, &num_configs)
    == EGL_FALSE || eglGetError() != EGL_SUCCESS)
    return FALSE;
// Create an EGL surface
m_eglSurface = eglCreateWindowSurface(m_eglDisplay, configs_list,
                                      system_window, NULL);
if (m_eglSurface == EGL_NO_SURFACE || eglGetError() != EGL_SUCCESS)
    return FALSE;
```

EGL Pixmap Surfaces

The ability to render to offscreen surfaces is a very useful feature in EGL. These surfaces can then be combined later or used as textures to achieve a variety of effects. EGL makes it simple to use offscreen surfaces; simply create a pixmap or pbuffer surface with `eglCreatePixmapSurface()` or `eglCreatePbufferSurface()`, respectively. Then these surfaces can be rendered into just by making them current with `eglMakeCurrent()`.

The following is the function prototype for creating an EGL pixmap surface:

```
EGLSurface eglCreatePixmapSurface (EGLDisplay dpy, EGLConfig config,
                         NativePixmapType pixmap, const EGLint *attrib_list);
```

The *config* parameter is the selected EGL configuration to use when creating an EGL pixmap surface. The *pixmap* parameter is just the native pixmap type. For the most part you don't need to worry about the native pixmap type. Once you declare a NativePixmapType in your application, all you need to do is pass it in to this function. Some EGL implementations will allow you to modify the fields contained in the NativePixmapType, for example, if the platform's EGL implementation allows you to adjust the pixmap size when creating a surface. The *attrib_list* parameter will contain the attributes associated with the EGL pixmap surface that is returned.

The following is an example of creating an EGL pixmap:

```
EGLConfig configs_list;
EGLint    num_configs;
NativePixmapType system_pixmap;
EGLint attrib_list = { EGL_ALPHA_SIZE, 0,
                       EGL_RED_SIZE, 5,
                       EGL_GREEN_SIZE, 6,
                       EGL_BLUE_SIZE, 5,
                       EGL_DEPTH_SIZE, 16,
                       EGL_SURFACE_TYPE, EGL_PIXMAP_BIT,
                       EGL_NONE };

// Get the display device
if ((m_eglDisplay = eglGetDisplay(NULL)) == EGL_NO_DISPLAY)
{
    return FALSE;
}

// Initialize the display
if (!eglInitialize(eglDisplay, NULL, NULL))
{
    return FALSE;
}

// Choose Configuration
if( eglChooseConfig( m_eglDisplay, attrib_list, &configs_list, 1, &num_configs)
    == EGL_FALSE || eglGetError() != EGL_SUCCESS)
    return FALSE;
```

```
// Create an EGL pixmap surface
m_eglPixmap = eglCreatePixmapSurface(m_eglDisplay, configs_list,
                                     system_pixmap, NULL);
if( m_eglPixmap == EGL_NO_SURFACE || eglGetError() != EGL_SUCCESS)
    return FALSE;
```

EGL Pbuffer Surfaces

A pbuffer is an offscreen rendering surface. Pbuffers are EGL resources and have no associated native window or native window type. It may not be possible to render to pbuffers using APIs other than OpenGL ES and EGL. The pbuffer feature in EGL 1.0 is an optional feature i.e., an implementation is not required to support rendering into a pbuffer and can fail the allocation of the pbuffer surface.

The following is the function prototype for creating an EGL pbuffer surface:

```
EGLSurface eglCreatePbufferSurface (EGLDisplay dpy, EGLConfig config,
                                    const EGLint *attrib_list);
```

The *config* parameter is the selected EGL configuration to use when creating an EGL pbuffer surface. The *attrib_list* parameter will contain the attributes associated with the EGL pixmap surface that is returned.

The following is an example of creating an EGL pbuffer:

```
EGLConfig configs_list;
EGLint     num_configs;
NativePixmapType system_pixmap;
EGLint attrib_list = { EGL_ALPHA_SIZE, 0,
                       EGL_RED_SIZE, 5,
                       EGL_GREEN_SIZE, 6,
                       EGL_BLUE_SIZE, 5,
                       EGL_DEPTH_SIZE, 16,
                       EGL_SURFACE_TYPE, EGL_PBUFFER_BIT,
                       EGL_NONE };

// Get the display device
if ((m_eglDisplay = eglGetDisplay(EGL_NO_DISPLAY)) == EGL_NO_DISPLAY)
{
    return FALSE;
}

// Initialize the display
if (!eglInitialize(eglDisplay, NULL, NULL))
{
    return FALSE;
```

```
}

// Choose Configuration
if( eglChooseConfig( m_eglDisplay, attrib_list, &configs_list, 1, &num_configs)
    == EGL_FALSE || eglGetError() != EGL_SUCCESS)
    return FALSE;

// Create an PBuffer surface
m_eglPBuffer = eglCreatePbufferSurface(m_eglDisplay, configs_list,
                                       NULL);
if( m_ eglPBuffer == EGL_NO_SURFACE || eglGetError() != EGL_SUCCESS)
    return FALSE;
```

A simple example of rendering a motion blur will need to render each frame into an off-screen surface and then combine the frames into the framebuffer for display, with each previous frame using an increasing transparency value or weight. It is important to keep the color buffer formats in mind when rendering offscreen, as eglCopyBuffers() is only required to work when both color buffer formats are the same. In the case of rendering to an offscreen surface to be used as a texture, be sure to pick a color buffer format that is also supported by the OpenGL ES implementation for texturing.

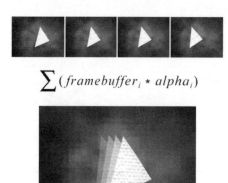

$$\sum (framebuffer_i * alpha_i)$$

Figure 2.3 Simple motions blur effect using offscreen rendering.

More About EGL Surfaces

EGL provides the function eglSwapBuffers() to post the current active surface to the native window surface or display, which will probably be the platform display. Keep in mind that the state of the color buffer in the surface after the call to eglSwapBuffers() is undefined.

The following is the function prototype for swapping the buffers:

```
EGLBoolean eglSwapBuffers (EGLDisplay dpy,
EGLSurface drawing_surface);
```

The *dpy* is the native display of the platform. The native display is usually the LCD panel attached to the device. The *drawing_surface* is the current active surface that you are rendering to and are ready to update the display with.

This function can be used to set a surface as the current display as follows:

```
if( eglSwapBuffers( m_eglDisplay, m_eglSurface ) == EGL_FALSE )
    throw error_egl_swapbuffers;
```

The function `eglCopyBuffers()` is provided as a means to retrieve the contents

of an `EGLSurface` into a native pixmap. The major restriction of `eglCopyBuffers()` is that an EGL implementation is only required to support copying to a native pixmap that has the same number of components and component sizes as the `EGLSurface`. Check the implementation's extension documentation to see if there are any additional conversions between formats supported by the implementation.

The following is the function prototype for copying an `EGLSurface`:

```
EGLBoolean eglCopyBuffers (EGLDisplay dpy, EGLSurface surface,
                           NativePixmapType target);
```

An `EGLSurface` can be copied as follows:

```
if( eglCopyBuffers(m_eglDisplay, m_eglPBuffer, m_sysPixmap) == EGL_FALSE )
    throw error_egl_copy;
```

When using `eglSwapBuffers()` and `eglCopyBuffers()`, keep in mind that the EGL 1.0 specification requires that the `EGLSurface` passed must be current. While this restriction may be lifted in future EGL versions, to ensure compatibility with EGL 1.0, make these calls while the surface is current or they may not take effect.

When rendering to a single surface with a combination of OpenGL ES and your native platform graphics or text APIs, it is important to make use of the synchronization functions provided by EGL to avoid accidentally drawing to the screen out of order. The EGL functions `eglWaitGL()` and `eglWaitNative()` are available for this purpose. These functions will ensure that all writing to the screen buffer has completed before the call returns for OpenGL ES and your native platform, respectively.

The following are the function prototypes for the synchronization functions:

```
EGLBoolean eglWaitGL (void);
```

```
EGLBoolean eglWaitNative (EGLint engine);
```

The *engine* parameter is used to identify the marking engine. A marking engine is any non-OpenGL ES native drawing API, such as GDI on Windows platforms. Valid values for *engine* are implementation-dependent, but all implementations are required to support `EGL_CORE_NATIVE_ENGINE`, which is used to indicate the most common drawing API for the target platform.

For example, if an application were drawing a background with native bitmap calls, rendering a 3D model using OpenGL ES, and finally drawing text using the native platform font API, the program flow would be synchronized as follows:

Draw native bitmapped background

eglWaitNative(EGL_CORE_NATIVE_ENGINE)

Render OpenGL ES scene

eglWaitGL()

Draw text

Since any implementation of eglWaitGL() will have at least an implicit glFinish(), hardware-accelerated implementations will be forced to stall until rendering has completed. For this reason, it is good practice to avoid eglWaitGL() calls unless necessary; similarly, eglWaitNative() can have hidden costs if native routines are accelerated. Keep in mind that not all cases of mixed OpenGL ES and native rendering require synchronization using the EGL constructs. A common example of this is the case where the native rendering is to a small HUD at the top or bottom of the screen. In this case, it is easy to set up OpenGL ES to only render to the non-HUD portion of the screen and to set up native rendering only to affect the HUD region. Since the target rendering areas do not overlap, strict synchronization is not required as correct visual results will not be dependent on draw order between OpenGL ES and the native system for a frame.

EGL Context

The EGL context stores the state information used by the OpenGL ES graphics pipeline. Since the graphics state machine is stored and managed by EGL, you can create and maintain multiple contexts using EGL to switch easily between different types of rendering. Before you can use any OpenGL ES functions, you must first create a graphics context and then make that context current and attach it to a rendering surface for the graphics pipeline to work correctly. From that point on, all states will be stored with that context and will be updated when any OpenGL ES call that affects the current state is executed.

The following is the function prototype for creating an EGL rendering context:

```
EGLContext eglCreateContext (EGLDisplay dpy, EGLConfig config,
                             EGLContext share_list, const EGLint *attrib_list);
```

The *config* parameter is the current EGL configuration that specifies the resources that will be used to create an EGL context. The EGL context contains all the states in EGL, and if you want to share those states among texture objects to be more efficient in using textures, then you should pass in an EGL context for the *share_list* parameter. If you do not want to share the EGL context with other texture objects, then you should pass in *EGL_NO_CONTEXT* as the parameter value. The values contained in the *attrib_list* parameter will be mapped to the EGL context states.

eglCreateContext() should return a handle to an EGL context that has been initialized to the default OpenGL ES values.

The following is the function prototype for querying a value from an EGL context:

```
EGLBoolean eglQueryContext (EGLDisplay dpy, EGLContext ctx, EGLint attribute,
                            EGLint *value);
```

At present, only the configuration ID that was used to create the context can be queried by using the attribute value `EGL_CONFIG_ID`.

It's possible for an application to maintain multiple contexts, and other applications running on the same system may have their own context as well. However, OpenGL ES can have only one active context at any given time, so application developers need to let OpenGL ES know which context to use. This is done through EGL by using `eglMakeCurrent()`:

```
EGLBoolean eglMakeCurrent (EGLDisplay dpy, EGLSurface draw_surface,
                           EGLSurface read_surface, EGLContext ctx);
```

The *draw_surface* parameter is the surface you will be rendering to. The *read_surface* parameter is the surface that you'll be reading from, for example when calling `glReadPixels()`. The *ctx* parameter is the context that is specified to bind with the *draw_surface* and *read_surface*, as well as the current context to use for the process thread. After this function call, the *draw_surface* and *read_surface* are now current and active using the specified context states.

You can query the current context by using the following:

```
EGLContext eglGetCurrentContext (void);
```

When you are done using a context (typically when your application exits), you should destroy it in order to prevent a memory leak. The following is the function prototype for destroying an EGL context:

```
EGLBoolean eglDestroyContext (EGLDisplay dpy, EGLContext ctx);
```

Setting Up EGL

For your application to work properly, you must follow these general steps when setting up EGL. The EGL setup should occur before calling any OpenGL ES APIs. Depending on which platform you are developing, this particular initialization sequence might not always be the case, but should serve as a guideline to the steps required to set up EGL.

The following are the steps required to set up EGL:

1. Get the main native display

   ```
   eglGetDisplay (display);
   ```

2. Initialize EGL

   ```
   eglInitialize (dpy, &major, &minor);
   ```

3. Choose an EGL configuration

```
eglChooseConfig (dpy, attrib_list, &configs, config_size, &num_config);
```

4. Create an EGL window surface

```
eglCreateWindowSurface (dpy, config, window, attrib_list);
```

5. Create an EGL graphics context

```
eglCreateContext (dpy, config, share_list, attrib_list);
```

6. Make an EGL graphics context current

```
eglMakeCurrent (dpy, draw, read, ctx);
```

The following shows an example of this in code:

```
void MYAPP::egl_setup()
{
    EGLConfig myConfig;
    EGLint num_config = 1; // the number of configurations
    EGLint attrib_list = { EGL_ALPHA_SIZE, 0,
                           EGL_RED_SIZE, 5,
                           EGL_GREEN_SIZE, 6,
                           EGL_BLUE_SIZE, 5,
                           EGL_DEPTH_SIZE, 16,
                           EGL_SURFACE_TYPE, EGL_WINDOW_BIT,
                           EGL_NONE };

    // Init State Data
    m_eglDisplay = EGL_NO_DISPLAY;
    m_eglSurface = EGL_NO_SURFACE;
    m_eglContext = EGL_NO_CONTEXT;

    // Get the main native display
    m_eglDisplay = eglGetDisplay(nativeDisplay)
    if ( m_eglDisplay == EGL_NO_DISPLAY || eglGetError() != EGL_SUCCESS )
        throw error_egl_display;

    // Initialize EGL
    if ( eglInitialize( m_eglDisplay, NULL, NULL ) == EGL_FALSE ||
         eglGetError() != EGL_SUCCESS )
        throw error_egl_initialize;

    // Choose an EGL configuration
    eglChooseConfig( m_eglDisplay, attrib_list, &myConfig, 1, &num_config );

    // Create an EGL window Surface
```

```
m_eglSurface = eglCreateWindowSurface( m_eglDisplay, myConfig,
              nativeWindow, NULL );
if( m_eglSurface == EGL_NO_SURFACE || eglGetError() != EGL_SUCCESS )
    throw error_egl_surface;


// Create an EGL graphics context
m_eglContext = eglCreateContext( m_eglDisplay, myConfig,0,0);
if( m_eglContext == EGL_NO_CONTEXT || eglGetError() != EGL_SUCCESS )
    throw error_egl_context;
if( eglMakeCurrent( m_eglDisplay, m_eglSurface, m_eglSurface, m_eglContext )
    == EGL_FALSE || eglGetError() != EGL_SUCCESS )
    throw error_elg_makecurrent
}
```

Cleaning Up EGL

When exiting your application, you must clean up and terminate your EGL setup. This is more important on mobile and embedded devices since resources are very limited and will more than likely not have an OS that cleans up the resources upon termination.

Here are some steps to clean up EGL resources:

1. Set the current context to nothing

    ```
    eglMakeCurrent (EGLDisplay dpy, EGLSurface draw, EGLSurface read,
              EGLContext ctx);
    ```

2. Free any EGL contexts; should be called per context created

    ```
    eglDestroyContext (EGLDisplay dpy, EGLContext ctx);
    ```

3. Free any EGL surfaces; should be called per surface created

    ```
    eglDestroySurface (EGLDisplay dpy, EGLSurface surface);
    ```

4. Terminate any EGL displays; should be called per display initialized

    ```
    eglTerminate (EGLDisplay dpy);
    ```

Note

According to the EGL spec, only Steps 1 and 4 are necessary since all contexts and surfaces associated with each display are freed upon the display's termination. However, it is good practice to explicitly free all resources allocated so that you can have an equal number of create and destroy calls to help prevent memory leaks in other areas of your code by providing a consistent style of allocation and free calls.

The following is a sample routine to clean up EGL resources:

```
void MYAPP::egl_cleanup() {
    eglMakeCurrent( EGL_NO_DISPLAY, EGL_NO_SURFACE, EGL_NO_SURFACE,
                    EGL_NO_CONTEXT);
    eglDestroyContext( m_eglDisplay, m_eglContext );
    eglDestroySurface( m_eglDisplay, m_eglSurface );
    eglTerminate( m_eglDisplay );
}
```

EGL Error Handling

Functions in EGL have no side effects if they fail; this means that if you pass invalid parameters to EGL APIs or call EGL functions out of order, they will return without changing the current state. To retrieve more useful information about why a particular call failed, EGL provides the function eglGetError().

The following is the function prototype for getting the current error status:

```
EGLint eglGetError (void);
```

See Table 2.4 for a complete list of EGL error codes provided by the EGL spec.

Table 2.4 EGL Return Values

EGL Error Codes	Notes
EGL_SUCCESS	Function succeeded.
EGL_NOT_INITIALIZED	EGL is not initialized or could not be initialized for the specified display.
EGL_BAD_ACCESS	EGL cannot access a requested resource (for example, a context is bound in another thread).
EGL_BAD_ALLOC	EGL failed to allocate resources for the requested operation.
EGL_BAD_ATTRIBUTE	An unrecognized attribute or attribute value was passed in an attribute list.
EGL_BAD_CONTEXT	An EGLContext argument does not name a valid EGLContext.
EGL_BAD_CONFIG	An EGLConfig argument does not name a valid EGLConfig.
EGL_BAD_CURRENT_SURFACE	The current surface of the calling thread is a window, pbuffer, or pixmap that is no longer valid.
EGL_BAD_DISPLAY	An EGLDisplay argument does not name a valid EGLDisplay or EGL is not initialized on the specified EGLDisplay.
EGL_BAD_SURFACE	An EGLSurface argument does not name a valid surface (window, pbuffer, or pixmap) configured for OpenGL ES rendering.
EGL_BAD_MATCH	Arguments are inconsistent; for example, an otherwise valid context requires buffers (e.g. depth or stencil) not allocated by an otherwise valid surface.
EGL_BAD_PARAMETER	One or more argument values are invalid.
EGL_BAD_NATIVE_PIXMAP	A NativePixmapType argument does not refer to a valid native pixmap.
EGL_BAD_NATIVE_WINDOW	A NativeWindowType argument does not refer to a valid native window.

The EGL error handling is very straightforward; after calling any EGL function you can get the current error status to verify the EGL function succeeded or get information about why the call failed. See the EGL spec for a complete list of error codes for each function.

The following is a simple exception handling routine for EGL errors:

```
try {
    m_eglDisplay = eglGetDisplay( system.display);
    if (m_eglDisplay == EGL_NO_DISPLAY || eglGetError() != EGL_SUCCESS)
        throw error_egl_display;
[el]
}
catch (EGLint error)
{
    switch(error)
    {
    case error_egl_display:
        logfile.print("ERROR: eglGetDisplay() =
            %s",GetErrorString(eglGetError()));
        break;
    [el]
    }
    // Clean up application and gracefully exit
}
```

EGL Extensions

At the time of this printing, there were no officially defined extensions for EGL. Some likely areas for growth with EGL could be key press event handling and power management. OpenGL ES and EGL were designed to be platform-independent, and EGL is a high-level set of APIs that sits on top of a system-specific implementation that could support key events or other input devices. Defining a standard set of APIs to handle such events would go a long way toward helping the mobile gaming industry. The EGL 1.0 spec alludes to having implementers supply their own platform-specific extension to support power management, event detection, and resource management. So it's possible that there might be quite a few extensions developed in the near future.

The following is the function prototype for querying available EGL extensions:

```
const char * eglQueryString(dpy,EGL_EXTENSIONS)
```

If your system does offer extensions for EGL, then the return value will be a space-delimited string of the available extension names. Usually, these extensions will be well documented by the particular vendor.

The function eglGetProcAddress() can be used to obtain a pointer to a function for your system EGL extensions. This function provides a generic interface to newly added functions and allows the system implementation the capability to create the extension either statically or dynamically, based on different configurations.

The following is the function prototype for getting the address of an extension function:

```
void (*eglGetProcAddress(const char *procname))();
```

By using the *procname* as a null-terminated string parameter, a pointer to the available extension will be returned. According to the EGL 1.0 spec, even if the extensions are unavailable at the time of the function call, a pointer to an EGL extension function will be returned. There could be cases where well-defined and custom extensions that exist on a system might not be accessible until certain conditions or configurations have been met. For example, if the system offered an EGL extension for handling low power mode, then this extension might not be available to call until the system initialization routines have completed or other underlying system-independent software has been executed to return the proper value.

The following is an example of how to query and call an EGL extension. In this example, we simply use a made-up extension name for demonstration purposes only.

```
int (*ext_power_level)();
const char* extensions = eglQueryString(display, EGL_EXTENSIONS );

// Parse extension string to see if the extension we want to use exist
#ifdef EXT_EGL_POWER_LEVEL
if (STRSTR(extensions, "EXT_EGL_POWER_LEVEL") != NULL)
{
    ext_power_level = eglGetProcAddress("EXT_EGL_POWER_LEVEL");
    printf("Current power level of device is at  = %d%\n",ext_power_level());
}
#endif
```

Using EGL with BREW

BREW (Binary Runtime Environment for Wireless) is an independent platform development environment for mobile devices. BREW was developed by QUALCOMM, a company that is a strong leader in the mobile industry. QUALCOMM has adopted the OpenGL ES and EGL standards. To use EGL with BREW, first you need to have a general understanding of the BREW APIs. There is an excellent BREW developer's Web site for more information. This chapter is only focusing on EGL and not BREW, so for more information please download the BREW SDK:

http://www.brewdeveloper.com

Steps to Using EGL with BREW

1. Create a BREW interface to EGL.

```
if( ISHELL_CreateInstance(pMe->a.m_pIShell, AEECLSID_EGL,
    (void **)&pMe->m_pIEGL) == SUCCESS )
{
    IEGL_Init( pMe->m_pIEGL );
}
else
{
    return FALSE;
}
```

2. Create and initialize an EGL display.

```
pMe->m_eglDisplay = eglGetDisplay( pMe->a.m_pIDisplay );
if( pMe->m_eglDisplay == EGL_NO_DISPLAY || eglGetError() != EGL_SUCCESS )
{
    return FALSE;
}
if( eglInitialize( pMe->m_eglDisplay, NULL, NULL ) == EGL_FALSE ||
    eglGetError() != EGL_SUCCESS )
{
    return FALSE;
}
```

3. Choose an EGL configuration.

```
eglChooseConfig( pMe->m_eglDisplay, attrib_list, &myConfig, 1, &ncfg );
```

4. Create an EGL window surface.

```
IBitmap *pIBitmapDDB;
IDIB *pDIB;
if( IDISPLAY_GetDeviceBitmap(p->a.m_pIDisplay, &pIBitmapDDB) != SUCCESS )
{
    return FALSE;
}
if( IBITMAP_QueryInterface(pIBitmapDDB, AEECLSID_DIB, (void**)&pDIB) != SUCCESS)
{
    return EFAILED;
}
pMe->m_eglSurface = eglCreateWindowSurface(pMe->m_eglDisplay, myConfig,
                                           pDIB, params);

IDIB_Release( pDIB );
```

```
        IBITMAP_Release( pIBitmapDDB );

        if( pMe->m_eglSurface == EGL_NO_SURFACE || eglGetError() != EGL_SUCCESS )
        {
            return FALSE;
        }
```

5. Create an EGL context.

```
        pMe->m_eglContext = eglCreateContext( pMe->m_eglDisplay, myConfig, 0, 0 );
        if( pMe->m_eglContext == EGL_NO_CONTEXT || eglGetError() != EGL_SUCCESS )
        {
            return FALSE;
        }
        6) Make the window and context current
        if( eglMakeCurrent( pMe->m_eglDisplay, pMe->m_eglSurface, pMe->m_eglSurface,
        pMe->m_eglContext ) == EGL_FALSE || eglGetError() != EGL_SUCCESS)
        {
            return FALSE;
        }
```

Using EGL with Windows CE

Windows CE is an operating system that can be found on a variety of embedded systems, including many portable devices. The following will be an overview of how to use EGL with Windows CE, not about programming for Windows CE in general. To get more information about Windows CE, visit Microsoft's MSDN Web page:

http://msdn.microsoft.com/embedded/default.aspx

Steps to Using EGL with Windows CE

1. Create and initialize an EGL display.

```
        pMe->m_eglDisplay = eglGetDisplay( NULL );
        if( pMe->m_eglDisplay == EGL_NO_DISPLAY || eglGetError() != EGL_SUCCESS )
        {
            return FALSE;
        }
        if( eglInitialize( pMe->m_eglDisplay, NULL, NULL ) == EGL_FALSE ||
            eglGetError() != EGL_SUCCESS )
        {
            return FALSE;
        }
```

2. Choose an EGL configuration.

```
eglChooseConfig( pMe->m_eglDisplay, attrib_list, &myConfig, 1, &ncfg );
```

3. Create an EGL window surface.

```
pMe->m_eglSurface = eglCreateWindowSurface(pMe->m_eglDisplay, myConfig,
                                           hwnd, params);

if( pMe->m_eglSurface == EGL_NO_SURFACE || eglGetError() != EGL_SUCCESS )
{
    return FALSE;
}
```

4. Create an EGL context.

```
pMe->m_eglContext = eglCreateContext( pMe->m_eglDisplay, myConfig, 0, 0 );
if( pMe->m_eglContext == EGL_NO_CONTEXT || eglGetError() != EGL_SUCCESS )
{
    return FALSE;
}
```

5. Make the window and context current.

```
if( eglMakeCurrent( pMe->m_eglDisplay, pMe->m_eglSurface, pMe->m_eglSurface,
pMe->m_eglContext ) == EGL_FALSE || eglGetError() != EGL_SUCCESS )
{
    return FALSE;
}
```

Comparing EGL with Other Windowing APIs

In this section, you'll learn about the differences between EGL and two other popular OpenGL windowing APIs: GLX for UNIX and WGL for Windows.

Comparing EGL with GLX

Another common windowing standard is GLX, which is the interface used to connect OpenGL to the X Window System on UNIX-based platforms. The X Windowing System is very portable across all UNIX platforms, and there have been some ports of GLX to mobile devices, but again a more condensed set of windowing APIs is needed to work more efficiently with mobile devices.

Table 2.5 shows the GLX functions and their EGL equivalents. This can be used as a rough guide to ease porting from GLX to EGL.

Table 2.5 GLX vs. EGL Comparison

GLX Functions	EGL Functions	Notes
glXChooseVisual	eglChooseConfig	Chooses configuration, based on requirements specified
glXCreateContext	eglCreateContext	Creates a new context
glXCreateGLXPixmap	eglCreatePixmap	Creates an offscreen pixmap rendering surface
glXDestroyContext	eglDestroyContext	Destroys a context
glXDestroyGLXPixmap	eglDestroySurface	Destroys an offscreen pixmap rendering surface (note that the egl version can destroy any surface)
glXGetConfig	eglGetConfig	Returns configurations
glXGetCurrentContext	eglGetCurrentContext	Retrieves the currently used context
glXGetCurrentDrawable	eglGetCurrentSurface	Retrieves the currently used surface
glXMakeCurrent	eglMakeCurrent	Sets a surface and context current (note that the egl version also requires a display and a read surface)
glXQueryVersion	eglQueryString	Retrieves the versioning information
glXSwapBuffers	eglSwapBuffers	Swaps the specified buffer when using screen buffers
glXWaitGL	eglWaitGL	Waits for the GL engine to complete rendering
glXGetClientString	eglQueryString	Queries for available extensions
glXWaitX	eglWaitNative	Waits for any native rendering to complete

Comparing EGL with WGL

Another common windowing standard, which is known as "wiggle," is Microsoft's windowing APIs for OpenGL. Since WGL is available only on Microsoft platforms, it doesn't lend itself to being a standard windowing API for all mobile devices. Because EGL was designed for use on mobile devices, it uses the most commonly needed functions from WGL and GLX to provide a smaller subset of windowing APIs for mobile devices.

Table 2.6 shows WGL/Win32 functions and their EGL equivalents. This table can be used as a rough guide to ease porting from Windows to EGL

Table 2.6 WGL vs. EGL Comparison

WGL Functions	EGL Functions	Notes
`ChoosePixelFormat`	`eglChooseConfig`	Chooses configuration based on requirements specified
`wglCreateContext`	`eglCreateContext`	Creates a new context
`CreateDIBitmap/CreateDibSection`	`eglCreatePixmap`	Creates an offscreen pixmap
`wglDeleteContext`	`eglDestroyContext`	Destroys a context
`DeleteObject`	`eglDestroySurface`	Destroys a rendering surface
`DescribePixelFormat`	`eglCotConfigAttrib`	Describes a configuration
`wglGetCurrentContext`	`eglGetCurrentContext`	Retrieves the currently used context
`wglGetCurrentDC`	`eglGetCurrentSurface`	Retrieves the currently used surface
`wglMakeCurrent`	`eglMakeCurrent`	Sets a surface and context current (note that the EGL version also requires a display and a read surface)
`GetVersion`	`eglQueryString`	Retrieves the versioning information
`SwapBuffers`	`eglSwapBuffers`	Swaps the specified buffer when using double buffering
`wglGetProcAddress`	`eglGetProcAddress`	Queries for an extension function pointer

Summary

In this chapter we covered the EGL APIs in depth. The EGL windowing APIs have several components. consisting of configuration, context state, display, and surfaces. The examples in this chapter illustrated how to use EGL with BREW and Windows CE environments. For reference, a basic comparison of EGL with GLX and WGL standard windowing APIs was explained.

CHAPTER 3

OpenGL ES

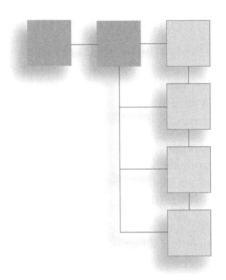

I n this chapter, you'll learn the details of the OpenGL ES APIs.

OpenGL ES 1.0 is based on the OpenGL 1.3 specification. However, OpenGL ES is not a mere subset of OpenGL. There are some important differences that must be understood in order to work effectively with OpenGL ES. In this chapter, we'll cover the following information:

- The history of OpenGL ES
- An overview of the OpenGL ES 1.0 specification and the profiles it defines
- The differences between OpenGL ES and OpenGL
- Which new features OpenGL ES adds

Tip

Throughout this book, you'll learn about OpenGL ES in the context of someone who already knows OpenGL. Thus, we'll be focusing on the similarities and differences, rather than covering OpenGL ES from the ground up. If you do not already know OpenGL, there are several books listed in the "Recommended Reading" section at the end of the chapter.

Note

This chapter is written based on the OpenGL ES 1.0 specification. As this book goes to press, the OpenGL ES 1.1 specification will be in the process of being released. We'll cover the additions to OpenGL ES 1.1 in Chapter 9, "The Future."

Introducing OpenGL ES

Until recently, gaming and graphics APIs on small devices such as cell phones and PDAs were a mess. Many devices included proprietary APIs, often designed by people with very little background in games or graphics. To develop games for these devices, you had to either pick a small number of them to develop for or plan on spending a lot of time porting code.

Fortunately, at SIGGRAPH in 2002, members of the Khronos Group—a special interest group dedicated to leveraging OpenGL-based technology in new ways—looked at this situation and, recognizing that these devices would soon become popular and viable gaming platforms, decided to do something about it.

Taking the OpenGL 1.3 specification as a basis, members of the Khronos Group began to identify a subset of OpenGL that would retain its power and flexibility but enable it to be implemented on devices with limited power and memory. They removed redundant APIs, eliminated functionality that was rarely used, grudgingly gave up a few useful features that were simply impractical on the target devices, and added the option to use fixed point numbers instead of floats on some implementations. Major players in the world of wireless joined Khronos to contribute to the effort, and finally, after a year of hard work, the 1.0 specification for OpenGL for Embedded Systems, or OpenGL ES, was released in San Diego, California, at SIGGRAPH 2003.

Since its launch, support for OpenGL ES has grown quickly, with most of the major cell phone and PDA manufacturers adding support for it, initially with software-only implementations. Soon after this book is published, the first cell phones offering hardware acceleration for OpenGL ES will be available. Finally, there is a standard API for game development on a wide range of wireless devices, and with it will come an exciting new era of mobile gaming.

The potential for OpenGL ES isn't limited to cell phones and PDAs. It will also appear in set top boxes, which represent a very large market. It is also very likely that it will be supported in future game consoles as well. It's clear that OpenGL ES is quickly establishing itself as the standard graphics API for a wide range of devices.

Tip

Throughout this chapter, we'll be referring frequently to both OpenGL and OpenGL ES. To avoid confusion, any reference to "OpenGL" will indicate core OpenGL, specifically version 1.3. All references to OpenGL ES will use the "ES" designation.

OpenGL ES 1.0 Specification and Profiles

OpenGL ES is designed to run on a wide range of embedded devices, and the designers recognized that the needs and capabilities of each of these devices would vary greatly. To address this, they introduced the concept of *profiles*. A profile defines both the subset of OpenGL used by the implementation and the features unique to OpenGL ES. Presently, there are two profiles: the Common profile and the Common Lite profile, described in the following sections.

Both the Common and Common Lite profile support fixed point vertex attributes and command parameters using a 32 bit two's complement signed representation with 16 bits to the right of the binary point (fraction bits).

The Common profile retains the same range and precision requirements as specified in section 2.1.1 of the OpenGL 1.3 specification.

The Common Lite profile is a fixed point profile, and therefore the precision and dynamic range requirements have been simplified. Fixed point computations must be accurate to within $+/-2^{-15}$. The maximum representable magnitude for a fixed point number used to represent positional or normal coordinates must be at least 2^{15}; the maximum representable magnitude for colors or texture coordinates must be at least 2^{10}. The maximum representable magnitude for all other fixed-point values must be at least 2^{15}. $x \times 0 = 0 \times x = 0$. $1 \times x = x \times 1 = x$. $x + 0 = 0 + x = x$. $0^0 = 1$. Fixed point computations may lead to overflows or underflows. The results of such computations are undefined but must not lead to GL interruption or termination.

OpenGL versus OpenGL ES

OpenGL is a powerful, flexible API, initially designed for high-end workstations, but now suitable for PCs. Because it is an open standard contributed to by many leading entities in the graphics world, it was the natural choice when a common graphics API for embedded devices was needed.

However, OpenGL itself isn't suitable for most embedded platforms. Modifications were needed to allow it to be used on low-power, relatively limited capability devices. This required many compromises, but in the end, the Khronos Group was able to deliver a specification that retained a great deal of OpenGL's power while limiting the memory and processing requirements necessary for a compliant implementation.

The changes made in creating OpenGL ES can be broken down into several main areas:

- **Removal of redundant APIs.** For the sake of flexibility, OpenGL includes many different functions that do essentially the same thing. For instance, `glColor()` comes in more than 30 different variations, each differing only in the number and types of parameters. OpenGL ES removes many of these APIs, leaving behind the most common and general-purpose versions.

- **Removal of redundant functionality.** OpenGL sometimes includes multiple ways to do a single thing. For example, geometry can be specified using either immediate mode (i.e., `glBegin()`/`glEnd()`) or vertex arrays. In these cases, OpenGL ES retains the most efficient method and drops the rest.

- **Limitation of expensive features.** A lot of the functionality in OpenGL comes with a high implementation cost, especially for software-based solutions. In many cases, this can't be avoided; texturing, for example, is expensive, but it would be difficult to promote OpenGL ES as a full-featured game API if it didn't support texturing. There are, however, a number of expensive features that are useful but not strictly mandatory. OpenGL ES either removes these features or makes them optional. For example, OpenGL ES 1.0 implementations are required to support the APIs for multitexturing, but they do not have to support more than one texture unit. As OpenGL ES evolves, it's expected that some of these features will be made mandatory.

- **Removal of data types.** Since floating point operations are limited on even the most powerful embedded devices, double-precision floating point values have been removed from OpenGL ES. Because a number of OpenGL 1.3 functions only accept doubles, these functions have been modified to accept single-precision floating point numbers instead.

- **New versions of existing APIs supporting smaller data types.** Recognizing the storage space and bandwidth limitations on embedded devices, OpenGL ES defines several new APIs that accept smaller data types than those supported in OpenGL 1.3. For example, some functions that only accept integer or short values in OpenGL 1.3 will accept bytes in OpenGL ES 1.0.

- **Removal of the ability to retrieve dynamic state.** The ability to query any OpenGL state at any time is useful but can be challenging to implement, especially in multilayered systems. Since this ability was not considered critical, only the static state can be queried in OpenGL ES.

- **No GLU.** The OpenGL Utility library contains quite a bit of helpful functionality, but the most useful functions it offers are simply wrappers on top of OpenGL. There is currently no specification available for an OpenGL ES version of GLU, although vendors are free to provide similar libraries.

- **New APIs supporting fixed point.** Many embedded devices don't include floating point support in hardware. They may support pseudo-floats in software, but operations using them are typically quite slow. For this reason, OpenGL ES supports fixed point APIs and data types in the Common Lite subprofile.

The following sections will look at the differences between OpenGL and OpenGL ES in detail.

Geometry Specification

OpenGL 1.3 provides two different ways to send geometric data down the pipeline. The first is the `glBegin()`/`glEnd()` model, often called *immediate mode*. Using this approach, you might specify a triangle as follows:

```
glBegin(GL_TRIANGLES);
  glVertex3f(-2.0, 0.5, 0.0);
  glVertex3f(0.0, 4.0, -2.0);
  glVertex3f(1.5, 2.5, -0.5);
glEnd();
```

The second way to specify geometry is to define arrays containing the geometric data and then pass those arrays to OpenGL. These are called *vertex arrays*. Converting the previous code snippet to vertex arrays would look something like this:

```
GLfloat vertices[] = { -2.0, 0.5, 0.0, 0.0, 4.0, -2.0, 1.5, 2.5, -0.5 };
glVertexPointer(3, GL_FLOAT, 0, vertices);
glDrawArrays(GL_TRIANGLES, 0, 3);
```

For simple geometry, there is little difference between the two approaches, but for any real data, the overhead of the function calls in immediate mode will start to make a difference in performance, making vertex arrays the better choice.

OpenGL ES uses the vertex array mechanism, with a few functions from immediate mode, to allow you to specify vertex attributes that may not change frequently, depending on your application. These functions are:

```
glNormal3f(GLfloat x, GLfloat y, GLfloat z);
glMultiTexCoord4f(GLenum texture, GLfloat s, GLfloat t, GLfloat r, GLfloat q)
glColor4f(GLfloat r, GLfloat g, GLfloat b, GLfloat a);
```

Although vertex arrays are supported, OpenGL ES does not support the full set of vertex array functions or parameters present in OpenGL 1.3. These functions are listed in Table 3.1, along with a summary of support for immediate mode functions.

Table 3.1 Geometry Specification Functions

Function	Notes
glBegin()	Not supported.
glEnd()	Not supported.
glEdgeFlag[v]()	Not supported.
glVertex{234}{sifd}[v]()	Not supported.
glNormal3f()	Supported.
glNormal3{bsifd}[v]()	Not supported.
glTexCoord{1234}{sifd}[v]()	Not supported.
glMultiTexCoord4f()	Supported.
glMultiTexCoord{1234}{sifd}[v]()	Not supported.
glColor4f()	Supported.
glColor{34}{bsifd ub us ui}[v]()	Not supported.
glIndex{sifd ub}[v]()	Not supported.
glVertexPointer()	Supported. Type cannot be GL_INT or GL_DOUBLE, but support for GL_BYTE has been added.
glNormalPointer()	Supported. Type cannot be GL_INT or GL_DOUBLE, but support for GL_BYTE has been added.
glColorPointer()	Supported. Type cannot be GL_INT or GL_DOUBLE, but support for GL_UNSIGNED_BYTE has been added. In addition, the alpha value must be included with all colors; there is no support for specifying only the RGB values.
glIndexPointer()	Not supported.
glTexCoordPointer()	Supported. Type cannot be GL_INT or GL_DOUBLE, but support for GL_BYTE has been added. Also, because there is no support for 1D textures, at least 2 texture coordinates must be provided per vertex.
glEdgeFlagPointer()	Not supported.
glInterleavedArrays()	Not supported.
glArrayElement()	Not supported.
glDrawArrays()	GL_POINTS, GL_LINES, GL_LINE_LOOP, GL_LINE_STRIP, GL_TRIANGLES, GL_TRIANGLE_STRIP, and GL_TRIANGLE_FAN are supported. GL_QUADS, GL_QUAD_STRIP, and GL_POLYGON are not supported.
glDrawElements()	GL_POINTS, GL_LINES, GL_LINE_LOOP, GL_LINE_STRIP, GL_TRIANGLES, GL_TRIANGLE_STRIP, and GL_TRIANGLE_FAN are supported. GL_QUADS, GL_QUAD_STRIP, and GL_POLYGON are not supported. Type must either be GL_UNSIGNED_BYTE or GL_UNSIGNED_SHORT (not GL_UNSIGNED_INT).
glDrawRangeElements()	Not supported.
glEnableClientState()	Valid for all supported attributes.
glDisableClientState()	Valid for all supported attributes.

Tip

For performance reasons, it may be advantageous to use the GL_SHORT data type for vertex arrays. Shorts offer precision that is adequate for most uses, while taking up half the space and bandwidth of fixed point values.

The only catch with doing this is that shorts aren't scaled at all, so this can be unintuitive for people used to working with floating point values. This problem can be easily solved by using the modelview and texture matrix to scale vertex positions and texture coordinates. Using this method, you can effectively treat shorts as half precision floating point values, with whatever distribution of integer and fractional bits you choose. For example, to use an S7.8 format for texture coordinates, you'd just set the texture matrix to scale each component by 1/256.

As in OpenGL, vertex arrays must be individually enabled or disabled by attribute using glEnableClientState()/glDisableClientState(). Each attribute is disabled by default.

Note

Due to the fact that OpenGL ES 1.0 only supports the fill polygon mode, support for edge flags is not necessary.

Note

OpenGL ES only supports RGBA mode; it does not include any support for indexed color.

Transformations

Transformations are an essential part of any 3D application, so very little functionality was removed in this area. However, many of the transformation functions in OpenGL operate on double-precision floats, and some of them don't have single-precision alternatives. Because the Common profile only supports single-precision floating point values, these functions had to be modified. For the Common Lite profile, these are replaced by fixed point variants.

The full list of functions related to transformations is shown in Table 3.2.

Materials and Lighting

Most of the functionality related to lighting was retained in OpenGL ES, although a few functions were removed and some restrictions were placed on existing functions.

glShadeModel() was kept without modification. It can still be used with either GL_FLAT or GL_SMOOTH.

Table 3.2 OpenGL ES Transformation Functions

Function	Notes
API	Differences.
glTranslatef()	Supported.
glTranslated()	Not supported.
glRotatef()	Supported.
glRotated()	Not supported.
glScalef()	Supported.
glScaled()	Not supported.
glFrustum()	Modified to accept GLfloats instead of GLdoubles.
glOrtho()	Modified to accept GLfloats instead of GLdoubles.
glMatrixMode()	Supports GL_MODELVIEW, GL_PROJECTION, and GL_TEXTURE, but not GL_COLOR.
glLoadIdentity()	Fully supported.
glLoadMatrixf()	Fully supported.
glLoadMatrixd()	Not supported.
glLoadTransposeMatrix{fd}()	Not supported.
glMultMatrixf()	Fully supported.
glMultMatrixd()	Not supported.
glMultTransposeMatrix{fd}()	Not supported.
glPushMatrix()	Supported, with a minimum stack depth of 16 for the modelview matrix and 2 for both the projection and texture matrix.
glPopMatrix()	Fully supported.
glEnable()/glDisable	GL_NORMALIZE and GL_RESCALE_NORMAL.
glViewport()	Fully supported.
glDepthRange()	Modified to accept GLFLOATS instead of GLDOUBLES.

OpenGL ES implementations are required to support at least 8 lights, just as in OpenGL. The performance cost of using more than a few lights may be more significant in OpenGL ES than it is in OpenGL. glLightf()/glLightfv() are included and fully supported, but glLighti()/glLightiv() have been removed, since they do not provide anything that isn't possible with the floating point versions.

Materials are supported, but it is not possible to have separate materials for both the front and back faces of polygons. Thus, all calls to glMaterialf()/glMaterialfv() must be made using GL_FRONT_AND_BACK. glMateriali()/glMaterialiv() are not included for the same reasons that glLighti()/glLightiv() aren't included.

Color material is supported in a limited way. glColorMaterial() is normally used to change which components of the material are changed along with the current color. By default, color material modifies the diffuse and ambient components. Since this is by far the most common usage of color material, it is the only mode supported, and the `glColorMaterial()` API has been removed. Color material can thus be enabled for the diffuse and ambient components by calling `glEnable(GL_COLOR_MATERIAL)`.

OpenGL ES only provides limited control over the lighting model using `glLightModelf()`/ `glLightModelfv()` (the integer versions of `glLightModel()` aren't supported). The application can change the global ambient color (`GL_LIGHT_MODEL_AMBIENT`) and can select either one- or two-sided lighting (`GL_LIGHT_MODEL_TWO_SIDE`), but it can't enable secondary color (`GL_LIGHT_MODEL_COLOR_CONTROL`) or enable a local viewer (`GL_LIGHT_MODEL_LOCAL_VIEWER`).

Table 3.3 provides a summary of the differences between OpenGL 1.3 and OpenGL ES in regards to lighting.

Table 3.3 Lighting Differences

Function	Notes
`glShadeModel()`	Fully supported.
`glMaterialf[v]()`	Supported, but only with `face = GL_FRONT_AND_BACK`.
`glMateriali[v]()`	Not supported.
`glLightf[v]()`	Fully supported.
`glLighti[v]()`	Not supported.
`glLightModelf[v]()`	Supports `GL_LIGHT_MODEL_AMBIENT` and `GL_LIGHT_MODEL_TWO_SIDE`. Does not support `GL_LIGHT_MODEL_COLOR_CONTROL` or `GL_LIGHT_MODEL_LOCAL_VIEWER`.
`glColorMaterial()`	Not supported.
`glEnable()/glDisable()`	Supports `GL_LIGHTING`, `GL_LIGHT0` to `GL_LIGHT7` and `GL_COLOR_MATERIAL`.

Clipping and Culling

Clipping is a necessary part of any rendering engine, so it is included in OpenGL ES. However, the ability to specify user-defined clip planes is not supported.

Face culling is an important phase of the OpenGL graphics pipeline, since it helps avoid spending cycles rasterizing something that won't be visible anyway. This is especially important for early OpenGL ES implementations, since rasterization is likely to take up a significant portion of the limited processing power available on OpenGL ES devices.

The functions related to culling are listed in Table 3.4.

Table 3.4 Clipping and Culling Support

Function	Notes
glClipPlane()	Not supported.
glFrontFace()	Fully supported.
glCullFace()	Fully supported.
glEnable()/glDisable()	Supports GL_CULL_FACE. Doesn't support GL_CLIP_PLANE{0-5}.

Points, Lines, and Polygons

OpenGL provides a great deal of flexibility in regards to how primitives are drawn. You can change the size of points and lines, enable antialiasing, render using a stipple pattern, and so on. Although this flexibility is useful, for many applications it is not needed, and some of it is redundant. For example, polygons (including quads and triangles) can be drawn filled (the default), as lines tracing their outline, or as points at each vertex. This is useful for things like drawing a model in wireframe mode. However, in most cases the same results can be obtained by using lines instead of polygons.

Since almost all functionality in this area adds a cost at the already expensive rasterization stage, much of it has been dropped or made optional in OpenGL ES.

For points, the point size can be changed, but implementations are not required to support any size other than 1. Similarly, point smoothing is supported, but if an implementation only supports the default point size, then point smoothing has no effect. You can determine the range of supported point sizes by calling glGetIntegerv() with GL_ALIASED_POINT_SIZE_RANGE and GL_SMOOTH_POINT_SIZE_RANGE.

Lines are similar to points. The line width can be changed, but implementations only needs to support the default width of 1, and line smoothing only needs to be available if widths other than 1 are supported. In addition, stippling for lines is not supported. You can determine the range of supported line widths by calling glGetIntegerv() with GL_ALIASED_LINE_WIDTH_RANGE and GL_SMOOTH_LINE_WIDTH_RANGE.

Polygons (which only include triangles, triangle strips, and triangle fans—quads, quad strips, and polygons aren't supported in OpenGL ES) can only be drawn in fill mode. Polygon stippling and polygon smoothing are not supported. Polygon offset is supported, but only for fill mode (not surprisingly, since fill mode is the only option).

OpenGL ES support for primitive rendering modes is summarized in Table 3.5.

Table 3.5 Primitive Rendering Modes

Function	Notes
glPointSize()	Supported, but support for sizes other than 1 is optional.
glLineWidth()	Supported, but support for widths other than 1 is optional.
glLineStipple()	Not supported.
glPolygonStipple()	Not supported.
glPolygonOffset()	Fully supported.
glPolygonMode()	Not supported.
glEnable()/glDisable()	GL_POINT_SMOOTH and GL_LINE_SMOOTH are supported but have no effect unless point and line sizes other than 1 are supported. GL_POLYGON_OFFSET_FILL is supported, but GL_POLYGON_OFFSET_LINE and GL_POLYGON_OFFSET_POINT are not. GL_LINE_STIPPLE, GL_POLYGON_STIPPLE, and GL_POLYGON_SMOOTH are not supported.

Imaging

In addition to its well-established capabilities as a 3D API, OpenGL provides powerful imaging capabilities. This includes the ability to draw images to the display directly, with a wide range of filtering and histogram options, and much more.

Although all of this functionality is useful, the implementation cost is quite high since it requires a separate path from the standard 3D pipeline. Furthermore, it's unlikely that the applications being developed for embedded systems will need extensive imaging support. Finally, the most common imaging operations can be achieved by using textures with screen-aligned quads. As a result, almost all of the imaging APIs have been removed in OpenGL ES. In fact, the only remaining function is glPixelStorei(), since it is necessary to modify pixel alignment for glReadPixels() and the texture functions.

Table 3.6 provides a summary of the imaging functions in OpenGL ES.

Texturing

There's no questioning that textures play a major role in the quality of 3D graphics. Practically every surface in a modern game has at least one texture applied to it—and often three or four. However, textures don't come for free. They require potentially very expensive memory fetches and calculations to be performed per pixel.

Because texturing is a very desirable but costly feature to have, this is one area in which quite a few compromises had to be made when designing OpenGL ES. Some functionality was removed completely, one major feature was made optional, and restrictions were imposed on almost all remaining functionality.

Table 3.6 Imaging Functions

Function	Notes
glPixelStorei()	Supported for GL_PACK_ALIGNMENT and GL_UNPACK_ALIGNMENT, but nothing else.
glPixelStoref()	Not supported.
glBitmap()	Not supported.
glDrawPixels()	Not supported.
glPixelZoom()	Not supported.
glPixelTransfer()	Not supported.
glPixelMap()	Not supported.
glColorTable()	Not supported.
glColorSubTable()	Not supported.
glColorTableParameter()	Not supported.
glCopyColorTable()	Not supported.
glCopyColorSubTable()	Not supported.
glConvolutionFilter1D()	Not supported.
glConvolutionFilter2D()	Not supported.
glCopyConvolutionFilter1D()	Not supported.
glCopyConvolutionFilter2D()	Not supported.
glSeparableFilter2D()	Not supported.
glConvolutionParameter()	Not supported.
glHistogram()	Not supported.
glResetHistogram()	Not supported.
glMinmax()	Not supported.
glResetMinmax()	Not supported.
glEnable()/glDisable()	Not supported: GL_COLOR_TABLE, GL_POST_CONVOLUTION_COLOR_TABLE, GL_POST_COLOR_MATRIX_COLOR_TABLE, GL_HISTOGRAM, and GL_MINMAX.

Removed Texturing Features

Due to the limited amount of memory on most typical OpenGL ES devices, support for 3D textures would be impractical. Even a modestly sized 64×64×64 16 bit texture would consume over 500KB of memory, which is larger than many applications.

Cube maps are a useful feature, but implementation costs and memory requirements are high, so they have been removed from OpenGL ES. A number of cube map-based techniques can be accomplished using only 2D textures (e.g., sphere maps or dual paraboloid environment maps).

One-dimensional texture support has been removed as well. One-dimensional textures can be simulated by using 2D textures with a height of 1, so this is an area in which redundancy was removed without reducing functionality.

Automatic texture coordinate generation (aka *texgen*) is useful for effects such as reflections and projective textures, but the implementation cost is fairly high. In addition, at least some techniques that make use of texgen can be achieved by having the game generate the texture coordinates. So texgen was removed from OpenGL ES, though it will likely appear in future revisions to the specification.

Texture borders are not supported. This means that `texturewrapmode GL_CLAMP` is the same as `GL_CLAMP_TO_EDGE`, so `GL_CLAMP` was dropped. `GL_CLAMP_TO_BORDER` was removed for the same reason.

Although mipmapping is supported, the ability to control the level of detail via clamping and setting the minimum and maximum LOD is not included.

Due to the significant complexity involved with the `GL_COMBINE` texture environment mode, it is not supported in OpenGL ES 1.0.

Finally, OpenGL ES does not include the ability to set texture priorities or to create proxy textures.

Optional Texturing Features

Multitexturing is obviously an extremely useful feature for games. Modern graphics hardware on PCs and consoles can offer multitexturing easily, since years of evolution have produced extremely efficient texturing operations. But on software-based OpenGL ES implementations, texturing with only a single texture is very expensive. Multitexturing is much worse. Each supported texture layer requires:

- A set of texture coordinates. These will need to be interpolated, with an expensive perspective correction calculation being performed per-pixel.
- Memory to store the texture.
- A texel lookup per-pixel—four texels if bilinear filtering is used.
- If bilinear filtering is used, the weighted average of four texels must be calculated.
- If mipmapping is used, an expensive LOD calculation must be performed.

In addition, the results of each texture layer must be combined according to the texture environment.

The cost of multitexturing is thus too high to require it of a software-based implementation. However, if hardware is present, then these costs are reduced dramatically. So multitexturing was made optional. Implementations are required to support all of the APIs related to multitexturing, but they don't have to support more than one texture layer. To determine the number of texture layers available, the following can be used:

```
glGetIntegerv(GL_MAX_TEXTURE_UNITS, &numTexUnits);
```

When multitexturing is not available, multipass rendering might provide a viable alternative (which is yet another reason to make multitexturing optional).

What's Left

The remaining texturing features are supported by OpenGL ES, although not without some restrictions. Fortunately, the restrictions aren't so onerous that they present a problem for most applications.

You'll find that 2D textures are supported, as is the ability to update a portion of an existing image via glTexSubImage2D(). However, only the most common formats and data types are supported, as shown in Table 3.7. The internal format of a texture must always be the same as the external format; in other words, you can't cause OpenGL ES to convert the format you provide into something else internally. Finally, texture borders are not supported, so the border size must always be zero.

Table 3.7 Texturing Formats and Types

Format	Data Types
GL_RGBA	GL_UNSIGNED_BYTE (4 bytes/texel), GL_UNSIGNED_SHORT_5_5_5_1 (2 bytes/texel), GL_UNSIGNED_SHORT_4_4_4_4 (2 bytes/texel)
GL_RGB	GL_UNSIGNED_BYTE (3 bytes/texel), GL_UNSIGNED_SHORT_5_6_5 (2 bytes/texel)
GL_LUMINANCE_ALPHA	GL_UNSIGNED_BYTE (2 bytes/texel) GL_LUMINANCE GL_UNSIGNED_BYTE (1 byte/texel)
GL_ ALPHA	GL_UNSIGNED_BYTE (1 byte/texel)

The ability to copy from the color buffer to a texture is supported, including updating just a portion of a texture, although there are restrictions on the formats that can be used with this operation. Specifically, it is not possible to add color components, but it is possible to remove them. So an RGB color buffer can be used to create a luminance texture, but it can't be used to create an RGBA texture. Table 3.8 summarizes these restrictions.

Table 3.8 Copy Texture Formats

Color Buffer Format	Texture Format
GL_RGBA	GL_RGBA, GL_RGB, GL_LUMINANCE_ALPHA, GL_LUMINANCE, GL_ALPHA
GL_RGB	GL_RGB, GL_LUMINANCE
GL_LUMINANCE_ALPHA	GL_LUMINANCE_ALPHA, GL_LUMINANCE, GL_ALPHA
GL_LUMINANCE	GL_LUMINANCE_ALPHA
GL_ALPHA	GL_ALPHA

Compressed textures are included, but the only compressed format that must be supported is paletted textures via the mandatory OES_compressed_paletted_texture extension, discussed later in the chapter. It is not possible to have OpenGL ES automatically compress a texture for you, although this feature (or other compressed formats) may be available via vendor-specific extensions.

Texture objects are supported, as they are a vital mechanism for managing more than one texture in an efficient manner.

Only the GL_REPEAT and GL_CLAMP_TO_EDGE texture wrap modes are supported, since they are the most commonly used. All texture filtering modes are supported, including mipmapping.

Other than GL_COMBINE (which was discussed earlier), all texture environment modes are supported.

Table 3.9 provides a convenient list of the texturing support present in OpenGL ES.

Fog

Fog is used by many games and other applications, so it is fully supported in OpenGL ES, other than modes related to indexed color. It's worth noting that applications have the option of calculating fog either per-vertex or per-pixel (or both, in which case the mode can be changed via glHint()). Per-pixel fog is more accurate, but is considerably more expensive, so most OpenGL ES implementations will only support per-vertex fog. The inaccuracy of per-vertex fog is typically only noticeable when drawing large triangles with rapidly changing depth values (i.e., ones that are nearly parallel to the viewing direction).

Fog support in OpenGL ES is listed in Table 3.10.

Per-Fragment Operations

Per-fragment operations include blending, depth buffer operations, stencil buffer operations, multisampling, alpha testing, scissoring, logic ops, and dithering. Most of these features are supported in OpenGL ES, but not without some caveats.

Basic blending is supported, including all OpenGL 1.3 blend factors. However, the ability to change the blend equation to something other than the default (add) and the ability to set a blend color are not included, since these are primarily used for imaging (although they can be useful in games).

All depth buffer, stencil buffer, and multisample buffer operations are supported; however, an OpenGL ES implementation doesn't actually have to supply any of these buffers. The presence of each can be determined using EGL. In practice, it would be unusual for an implementation to not at least support a depth buffer. Support for stencil and multisample buffers may be less common.

Table 3.9 Texturing Support

Function	Notes
glTexImage1D()	Not supported.
glTexSubImage1D()	Not supported.
glCopyTexImage1D()	Not supported.
glCopyTexSubImage1D()	Not supported.
glTexImage2D()	Supported with restrictions: The internal format and format must match and meet the requirements listed in Table 3.7, the border size must be 0, proxy textures cannot be used, and cube maps cannot be used.
glTexSubImage2D()	Supported with restrictions: The internal format and format must match and meet the requirements listed in Table 3.7.
glCopyTexImage2D()	Supported with restrictions: The color buffer format and texture format must meet the requirements listed in Table 3.8, and the border size must be 0.
glCopyTexSubImage2D()	Supported with restrictions: The color buffer format and texture format must meet the requirements listed in Table 3.8.
glTexImage3D()	Not supported.
glTexSubImage3D()	Not supported.
glCopyTexImage3D()	Not supported.
glCopyTexSubImage3D()	Not supported.
glCompressedTexImage1D()	Not supported.
glCompressedTexSubImage1D()	Not supported.
glCompressedTexImage2D()	Supported, but only with the OES_compressed_paletted_texture format, and subject to the other restrictions on 2D textures.
glCompressedTexSubImage2D()	Supported, but undefined for the paletted texture format, so this will be useful only if the vendor has provided other compressed formats.
glCompressedTexImage3D()	Not supported.
glCompressedTexSubImage3D()	Not supported.
glClientActiveTexture()	Supported, but there may be only one texture unit.
glActiveTexture()	Supported, but there may be only one texture unit.
glTexParameterf()	Supports GL_NEAREST and GL_LINEAR for the magnification filter, GL_NEAREST, GL_LINEAR, GL_NEAREST_MIPMAP_NEAREST, GL_NEAREST_MIPMAP_LINEAR, GL_LINEAR_MIPMAP_NEAREST, GL_LINEAR_MIPMAP_LINEAR for the minification filter, and GL_REPEAT and GL_CLAMP_TO_EDGE for s and t wrap modes. GL_TEXTURE_BORDER_COLOR, GL_TEXTURE_MIN_LOD, GL_TEXTURE_MAX_LOD, GL_TEXTURE_BASE_LEVEL, GL_TEXTURE_MAX_LEVEL, GL_TEXTURE_WRAP_R, and GL_TEXTURE_PRIORITY are not supported. GL_MIRROR and GL_CLAMP_TO_BORDER wrap modes are not supported.
glTexParameteri()	Not supported.

continued

glTexParameter{if}v()	Not supported.
glTexEnvf[v]()	Supported with the exception of GL_COMBINE and related states.
glTexEnvi[v]()	Not supported.
glGenTextures()	Fully supported.
glDeleteTextures()	Fully supported.
glBindTexture()	Supports GL_TEXTURE_2D but not GL_TEXTURE_1D, GL_TEXTURE_3D, or GL_TEXTURE_CUBE_MAP.
glAreTexturesResident()	Not supported.
glPrioritizeTextures()	Not supported.
glTexGen()	Not supported.
glEnable()/glDisable()	Supports GL_TEXTURE_2D. Does not support GL_TEXTURE_1D, GL_TEXTURE_3D, GL_TEXTURE_CUBE_MAP, GL_TEXTURE_GEN_S, GL_TEXTURE_GEN_T, GL_TEXTURE_GEN_R, or GL_TEXTURE_GEN_Q.

Table 3.10 Fog Support

Functions	Notes
glFogf[v]()	Supported other than GL_FOG_INDEX.
glFogi[v]()	Not supported.
glEnable()/glDisable()	Supports GL_FOG.

Alpha test, scissoring, and logic ops are all fully supported. Dithering is supported, though an implementation is free to ignore this state.

Color index mode isn't supported for any of these operations.

Table 3.11 summarizes support for per-fragment features available in OpenGL ES.

Framebuffer Operations

Framebuffer operations are those that affect the entire screen, and they include clears, color masking, controlling which buffer to draw to, and accumulation buffer operations.

Clears are obviously essential, so they are supported for all existing buffers; of course, depth and stencil buffer clears are meaningless if those buffers aren't available. The ability to set the values with which to clear is supported, too.

OpenGL ES also includes the option to mask out any of the red, green, blue, or alpha channels when writing to the color buffer.

Applications are required to always write to the default buffer, so the ability to change the draw buffer isn't supported.

Table 3.11 Per-Fragment Features

Functions	Notes
glBlendFunc()	Fully supported.
glBlendEquation()	Not supported.
glBlendColor()	Not supported.
glDepthFunc()	Supported.
glDepthMask()	Supported, but see glDepthFunc().
glStencilFunc()	Supported, but implementations aren't required to support a stencil buffer.
glStencilOp()	Supported, but see glStencilFunc().
glStencilMask()	Supported, but see glStencilFunc().
glSampleCoverage()	Supported, but implementations aren't required to support a multisample buffer.
glAlphaTest()	Fully supported.
glScissor()	Fully supported.
glLogicOp()	Fully supported.
glEnable()/glDisable()	Supports GL_MULTISAMPLE, GL_DEPTH_TEST, GL_STENCIL_TEST, GL_MULTISAMPLE, GL_SAMPLE_COVERAGE, GL_SAMPLE_ALPHA_TO_COVERAGE, GL_SAMPLE_ALPHA_TO_ONE, GL_ALPHA_TEST, GL_SCISSOR_TEST, GL_COLOR_LOGIC_OP, GL_DITHER. Does not support GL_INDEX_LOGIC_OP.

The accumulation buffer is expensive to implement, and it is generally too slow to be practical in interactive applications, so it is not supported.

glReadBuffer

It is possible to read from the color buffer (but not the depth or stencil buffer) using glReadPixels(), though it does not support the full range of formats offered by OpenGL. Implementations are only required to support two formats and type combinations. One combination is always GL_RGBA and GL_UNSIGNED_BYTE. The other varies by implementation and can be determined using the mandatory OES_read_format extension described later in the chapter. Because only the default buffer can be read from, there is no need for glReadBuffer().

It's not possible to directly copy from one portion of the color buffer to the other, but the same results can be achieved by reading the entire framebuffer and then copying the needed portions into a texture (though this will be slower).

The support for whole framebuffer operations present in OpenGL ES is summarized in Table 3.12.

Table 3.12 Supported Framebuffer Operations

Functions	Notes
glClear()	Fully supported.
glClearColor()	Fully supported.
glClearDepth()	Fully supported.
glClearStencil()	Fully supported.
glClearIndex()	Not supported.
glColorMask()	Fully supported.
glIndexMask()	Not supported.
glDrawBuffer()	Not supported.
glReadBuffer()	Not supported.
glAccum()	Not supported.
glClearAccum()	Not supported.
glReadPixels()	Supported with restrictions. Only the color buffer can be read from, and the number of format/type combinations supported is reduced to 2.
glCopyPixels()	Not supported.

State Querying

As mentioned earlier in the chapter, OpenGL ES generally does not support the querying of dynamic state. This is due to the fact that the implementation may operate asynchronously, so retrieving dynamic state would require the current state to be shadowed, which would increase the memory requirements. Static state, on the other hand, does not have this restriction, and is required for the programmer to be able to determine implementation-dependent values, such as the maximum texture size.

Of the various generic glGet() functions, only glGetIntegerv() is supported, since it is sufficient to return all of the static states that can be queried in OpenGL ES. These states are listed in Table 3.13.

All of the states associated with glGetString()—namely, the vendor, version, renderer, and extension string—are static, so it is fully supported. The version string for OpenGL ES 1.0 implementations will always take on the form "OpenGL ES-CM 1.0" for Common profiles and "OpenGL ES-CL 1.0" for Common Lite profiles.

The ability to determine whether an error has occurred is essential for debugging and creating robust applications, so glGetError() is supported, though the error GL_TABLE_TOO_LARGE can't be generated by any functions present in OpenGL ES.

It's not possible to query whether or not a specific state is enabled. Although this is a convenient feature to have, the application can easily track this on its own.

Table 3.13 Queryable States

State
GL_ALIASED_LINE_WIDTH_RANGE
GL_ALIASED_POINT_SIZE_RANGE
GL_ALPHA_BITS
GL_BLUE_BITS
GL_COMPRESSED_TEXTURE_FORMATS
GL_DEPTH_BITS
GL_GREEN_BITS
GL_MAX_ELEMENTS_INDICES
GL_MAX_ELEMENTS_VERTICES
GL_MAX_LIGHTS
GL_MAX_MODELVIEW_STACK_DEPTH
GL_MAX_PROJECTION_STACK_DEPTH
GL_MAX_TEXTURE_SIZE
GL_MAX_TEXTURE_STACK_DEPTH
GL_MAX_TEXTURE_UNITS
GL_MAX_VIEWPORT_DIMS
GL_NUM_COMPRESSED_TEXTURE_FORMATS
GL_RED_BITS
GL_SMOOTH_LINE_WIDTH_RANGE
GL_SMOOTH_POINT_SIZE_RANGE
GL_STENCIL_BITS
GL_SUBPIXEL_BITS
GL_IMPLEMENTATION_COLOR_READ_FORMAT_OES*
GL_IMPLEMENTATION_COLOR_READ_TYPE_OES*

*—Part of the OES_read_format extension

OpenGL includes a large number of functions to query states related to a specific feature, such as glGetLight() or glGetMaterial(). Since these are considered dynamic states that can usually be tracked by the application, these functions are not included.

Table 3.14 lists the support for OpenGL ES state query functions.

Everything Else

OpenGL ES does not support the ability to push or pop attributes to save and restore state. These values can easily be tracked by the application.

Evaluators, selection, and feedback are not frequently used, especially in games, and when needed can be accomplished through alternate means, so they are not supported.

Table 3.14 State Query Support

Functions	Notes
glGetString()	Fully supported.
glGetError()	Supported.
glIsEnabled()	Not supported.
glGetIntegerv()	Supported for values in Table 3.13.
glGetBooleanv()	Not supported.
glGetDoublev()	Not supported.
glGetFloatv()	Not supported.
glGetLight{if}[v]()	Not supported.
glGetMaterial{if}[v]()	Not supported.
glGetClipPlane()	Not supported.
glGetPolygonStipple()	Not supported.
glGetPixelMap()	Not supported.
glGetColorTableParameter()	Not supported.
glGetColorTable()	Not supported.
glGetConvolutionFilter()	Not supported.
glGetSeparableFilter()	Not supported.
glGetConvolutionParameter()	Not supported.
glGetHistogram()	Not supported.
glGetHistogramParameter()	Not supported.
glGetMinmax()	Not supported.
glGetMinmaxParameter()	Not supported.
glGetTexImage()	Not supported.
glGetCompressedTexImage()	Not supported.
glGetTexParemeter()	Not supported.
glGetTexLevelParemeter()	Not supported.
glGetTexEnv()	Not supported.
glGetTexGen()	Not supported.
glIsTexture()	Not supported.
glGetMap{ifd}()	Not supported.

Display lists are extremely useful and widely used for performance gains, but they are also expensive and complicated to implement correctly, so they were not included in OpenGL ES.

Flush and finish operations are supported, though as with OpenGL, it's recommended that you avoid their use. EGL provides better mechanisms for synchronization.

The ability to give OpenGL hints for features that may have speed-quality tradeoff options is supported, but as always, the implementation is free to ignore them.

OpenGL ES does not support the direct drawing of rectangles; however, this can be accomplished through other means. Since drawing pixels and bitmaps isn't supported, there is no need for the ability to set the raster position.

All of these features are summarized in Table 3.15.

Other OpenGL Features

OpenGL has evolved considerably since 1.3, adding many features in 1.4 and 1.5 that weren't even considered for OpenGL ES 1.0. For convenience, those features are listed here so that you'll know not to expect them in an OpenGL ES 1.0 implementation (they may be available as extensions). See Chapter 9 for a more detailed discussion of these features.

The following features were added in OpenGL 1.4:

- Texture crossbar
- LOD bias
- Texture mirrored repeat
- Automatic mipmap generation
- Depth textures
- Shadows
- Fog coordinates
- Multiple draw arrays
- Point parameters
- Separate blend functions
- Blend squaring
- Secondary color
- Stencil wrap
- Window raster position

The following features were added in OpenGL 1.5:

- Buffer objects
- Occlusion queries
- Shadow functions

Table 3.15 Miscellaneous Features

Functions	Notes
glPushAttrib()	Not supported.
glPopAttrib()	Not supported.
glPushClientAttrib()	Not supported.
glPopClientAttrib()	Not supported.
glMap1{fd}()	Not supported.
glMap2{fd}()	Not supported.
glEvalCoord{12}{fd}[v]()	Not supported.
glMapGrid1{fd}()	Not supported.
glMapGrid2{fd}()	Not supported.
glEvalMesh1()	Not supported.
glEvalMesh2()	Not supported.
glEvalPoint1()	Not supported.
glEvalPoint2()	Not supported.
glInitNames()	Not supported.
glLoadName()	Not supported.
glPushName()	Not supported.
glPopName()	Not supported.
glRenderMode()	Not supported.
glSelectBuffer()	Not supported.
glFeedbackBuffer()	Not supported.
glPassThrough()	Not supported.
glNewList()	Not supported.
glEndList()	Not supported.
glCallList()	Not supported.
glCallLists()	Not supported.
glListBase()	Not supported.
glGenLists()	Not supported.
glIsList()	Not supported.
glDeleteLists()	Not supported.
glFlush()	Fully supported.
glFinish()	Fully supported.
glHint()	Supported except for GL_POLYGON_SMOOTH_HINT and GL_TEXTURE_COMPRESSION_HINT, since these features aren't included in OpenGL ES.
glRect()	Not supported.
glRasterPos()	Not supported.

OpenGL ES Extensions

OpenGL ES defines several new extensions that either modify OpenGL 1.3 or add functionality not previously present in OpenGL. Each of these extensions will be explained in this section.

Generally speaking, extensions are optional, but because OpenGL ES has to modify some fundamental behavior of OpenGL, most of the extensions listed here aren't optional. Extensions can be grouped into either core additions or profile extensions. Some profile extensions are required for all OpenGL ES implementations, and other profile extensions are optional. The differences between these groups are important and are described in the following sections.

Interestingly, because OpenGL ES extensions are written against the OpenGL 1.3 specification, in some cases, they modify functionality that does not exist in OpenGL ES. Therefore, a full OpenGL implementation that supports these extensions would have to do more than an OpenGL ES implementation. These additions will be covered with each extension, but it will be noted that they aren't included in OpenGL ES to avoid confusion.

Core Additions

Core additions are, as the name implies, part of the core library, and their functions and tokens don't include the suffix normally used by OpenGL ES extensions. These extensions don't have to appear in the GL_EXTENSIONS string, though an implementation may choose to provide this for portability. If so, then entry points to the functions—with an extension suffix—will be available via eglGetProcAddress(). Note that if an implementation chooses to do this, it still has to provide static bindings for the functions.

There are three core additions in OpenGL ES 1.0: OES_byte_coordinates, OES_single_precision, and OES_fixed_point.

OES_byte_coordinates

Earlier in this chapter, we mentioned that OpenGL ES allows the byte data type to be used in several ways that aren't available in OpenGL. Specifically, bytes can be used to represent vertex and texture coordinate data. This allows for a more compact representation of data that can help compensate for the limited bandwidth and memory available on mobile devices. Of course, this also leads to a loss in precision, but this may be acceptable for some purposes.

The availability of bytes in vertex arrays is exposed through the OES_byte_coordinates extension, which is a core addition. The only two OpenGL ES functions affected are glVertexPointer() and glTexCoordPointer(). Both of these functions are extended to accept GL_BYTE as the *type* parameter.

Byte coordinates are treated in the same way as their short and integer counterparts. In other words, internally they are effectively mapped to floating point values without any scaling or biasing, so a value of 24 is equivalent to 24.0.

OES_fixed_point

Although some embedded systems provide native support for floating point values, most do not, especially cell phones, where the power requirements for an FPU are too high. However, noninteger values are critical to 3D graphics, so OpenGL ES provides the option for implementations to support them via the OES_fixed_point core addition.

This extension adds a number of things to OpenGL ES. First, it adds two new types, GLfixed and GLclampx. These types are effectively 32 bit integers treated as fixed point value in an S15.16 format (see Chapter 4 for a detailed discussion of fixed point math).

Second, the glVertexPointer(), glColorPointer(), glNormalPointer(), and glTexCoordPointer() functions are extended to accept GL_FIXED as the *type* parameter, indicating an array of type GLfixed.

Finally, functions that accept *GLfloat* or *GLdouble* parameters are modified to accept *GLfixed* instead. These functions are suffixed with an "x", even if the original function was not suffixed with an "f" or "d". A complete list of these functions is shown in Table 3.16.

OES_single_precision

OpenGL ES does not support double-precision floating point values, since most of the platforms it is available on do not support this type natively. However, there are a number of OpenGL functions that only accept double-precision floating point parameters. This addition modifies those functions to accept single-precision floating point values.

This is a core addition, but only for Common profiles.

This addition adds the following functions:

```
void glDepthRangef(GLclampf n, GLclampf f);
void glFrustumf(GLfloat l, GLfloat r, GLfloat b, GLfloat t, GLfloat n, GLfloat f);
void glOrthof(GLfloat l, GLfloat r, GLfloat b, GLfloat t, GLfloat n, GLfloat f);
void glClearDepthf(GLclampf depth);
```

It also adds the following functions, although these functions are not present in OpenGL ES 1.0. They are, however, included in OpenGL ES 1.1 (see Chapter 9):

```
GLvoid glClipPlanef(GLenum plane, const GLfloat* equation);
GLvoid glGetClipPlanef(GLenum plane, GLfloat* equation);
```

Table 3.16 Fixed Point Functions

Function

```
void glNormal3x (GLfixed nx, GLfixed ny, GLfixed nz);
void glMultiTexCoord4x(GLenum texture, GLfixed s, GLfixed t, GLfixed r, GLfixed q);
void glColor4x(GLfixed r, GLfixed g, GLfixed b, GLfixed a);
void glDepthRangex(GLclampx n, GLclampx f);
void glLoadMatrixx(const GLfixed m[16]);
void glMultMatrixx(const GLfixed m[16]);
void glRotatex(GLfixed angle, GLfixed x, GLfixed y, GLfixed z);
void glScalex(GLfixed x, GLfixed y, GLfixed z);
void glTranslatex(GLfixed x, GLfixed y, GLfixed z);
void glFrustumx(GLfixed l, GLfixed r, GLfixed b, GLfixed t, GLfixed n, GLfixed f);
void glOrthox(GLfixed l, GLfixed r, GLfixed b, GLfixed t, GLfixed n, GLfixed f);
void glMaterialx[v](GLenum face, GLenum pname, GLfixed param);
void glLightx[v](GLenum light, GLenum pname, GLfixed * params);
void glLightModelx[v](GLenum pname, GLfixed param);
void glPointSizex(GLfixed size);
void glLineWidthx(GLfixed width);
void glPolygonOffsetx(GLfixed factor, GLfixed units);
void glTexParameterx[v](GLenum target, GLenum pname, GLfixed param);
void glTexEnvx[v](GLenum target, GLenum pname, GLfixed param);
void glFogx[v](GLenum pname, GLfixed param);
void glSampleCoverage(GLclampx value, GLboolean invert);
void glAlphaFuncx(GLenum func, GLclampx ref);
void glClearColorx(GLclampx red, GLclampx green, GLclampx blue, GLclampx alpha);
void glClearDepthx(GLclampx depth);
```

Required Extensions

Required extensions must be included in the GL_EXTENSIONS string, use extension suffixes, and make their function entry points available through eglGetProcAddress(). In addition, if the core library makes static bindings available, then required extension functions must be included in the static bindings as well. In this case, the extension suffix will be used still.

OpenGL ES 1.0 includes two required extensions: OES_read_format and OES_compressed_paletted_texture.

OES_read_format

As mentioned previously in the chapter, in OpenGL ES, glReadPixels() has been severely restricted, allowing for only two format/type combinations. In addition to the GL_RGBA/GL_UNSIGNED_BYTE combination that all implementations must support, implementations must also provide a second combination. The choice of the format and type is left to the vendor. The format and type combination chosen will typically be the one that offers the best performance.

The required OES_read_format extension allows developers to query the implementation to find out what these values are. This is done by passing GL_IMPLEMENTATION_COLOR_READ_FORMAT_OES and GL_IMPLEMENTATION_COLOR_READ_TYPE_OES to glGetIntegerv(). These two values can be any of the values normally supported by glReadPixels().

The following code shows an example of using this extension:

```
GLint preferredReadFormat;
GLint preferredReadType;

glGetIntegerv(GL_IMPLEMENTATION_COLOR_READ_FORMAT_OES, &preferredReadFormat);
glGetIntegerv(GL_IMPLEMENTATION_COLOR_READ_TYPE_OES, &preferredReadType);
```

OES_compressed_paletted_texture

To help cope with devices that have a limited amount of storage space, OpenGL ES allows the use of paletted textures. These textures are to be used with the compressed texture APIs. Unlike normal textures, which use a buffer of data directly representing the color values at each texel, paletted textures consist of a palette of limited size (either 16 or 256 entries) and indices into that palette at each texel.

The OES_compressed_paletted_texture extension is required for both Common and Common Lite profiles.

Note

Although OpenGL ES implementations are required to support paletted textures, they do not have to directly support them internally. So the implementation may take the paletted texture and convert it into a full RGBA texture internally. There are several implications of this. The first is that, although using paletted textures will reduce the amount of storage space required by your game, they may have no impact on the runtime memory usage or bandwidth consumed when passing texture data down the pipeline. The second is that updating a portion of a paletted texture using glCompressedTexSubImage2D() isn't supported, since doing so would require that the implementation keep a copy of the palette around. The third is that it may be more expensive to create a paletted texture because the implementation may have to unpack it. These trade-offs should be taken into account when deciding whether or not to use paletted textures.

Paletted textures are created by using glCompressedTexImage2D():

```
void glCompressedTexImage2D(GLenum target, GLint level, GLenum internalformat,
                            GLsizei width, GLsizei height, GLint border,
                            GLsizei imageSize, const GLvoid *data);
```

target must always be GL_TEXTURE_2D.

The *level* parameter is used a bit differently than in most texture functions. It must always be either zero or a negative value. If the value is 0, then the texture contains only one level (i.e., it is not mipmapped). If it is negative, then the number of mip levels contained in data is the absolute value of *level* plus 1. So if *level* is −5, then the number of mip levels is 6.

internalformat is also used differently than typical texture functions. Rather than describing the desired internal texture format, it is used to describe the format of the paletted texture. Valid values for *internalformat* and their associated meanings are listed in Table 3.17. These values will also be returned when querying glGet() with GL_NUM_COMPRESSED_TEXTURE_FORMAT and GL_COMPRESSED_TEXTURE_FORMAT.

Table 3.17 Paletted Texture Formats

Function	Notes
GL_PALETTE4_RGB8_OES	16 entry palette of 24 bit RGB values
GL_PALETTE4_RGBA8_OES	16 entry palette of 32 bit RGBA values
GL_PALETTE4_R5_G6_B5_OES	16 entry palette of 16 bit RGB values in 565 format
GL_PALETTE4_RGBA4_OES	16 entry palette of 16 bit RGBA values in 4444 format
GL_PALETTE4_RGB5_A1_OES	16 entry palette of 16 bit RGBA values in 5551 format
GL_PALETTE8_RGB8_OES	256 entry palette of 24 bit RGB values
GL_PALETTE8_RGBA8_OES	256 entry palette of 32 bit RGBA values
GL_PALETTE8_R5_G6_B5_OES	256 entry palette of 16 bit RGB values in 565 format
GL_PALETTE8_RGBA4_OES	256 entry palette of 16 bit RGBA values in 4444 format
GL_PALETTE8_RGB5_A1_OES	256 entry palette of 16 bit RGBA values in 5551 format

width and *height* are the width and height of the texture image. If the texture contains mip levels, these dimensions are for the base level.

border must always be 0.

imageSize is the total size of *data*, in bytes.

data contains the palette data, followed by the indices into the palette, possibly for multiple mipmap levels. An example of how this might look for a 64×64 GL_PALETTE8_RGB8_OES mipmapped texture is shown in Figure 3.1.

Figure 3.1 Memory layout of 64×64 mipmapped texture using the GL_PALETTE8_RGB8_OES format.

For GL_PALETTE8_XXX textures, indices are 8 bit values. For GL_PALETTE4_XXX textures, indices are 4 bit values, with two texel indices packed into a single byte. In this case, the first texel occupies the 4 high bits, and the second texel occupies the 4 low bits, as shown in Figure 3.2.

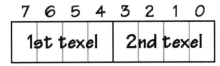

Figure 3.2 4 bit index data format.

The following code illustrates how to set up a 4×4 mipmapped texture using a checkerboard pattern. Since only three colors are needed, a 16-entry palette with the RGB8 format is used.

```
const GLsizei TEXTURE_SIZE = 59; // 16-entry palette * 3 bytes per entry = 48 +
                                 // mip level 0: 4x4 4-bit entries      = 8 +
                                 // mip level 1: 2x2 4-bit entries      = 2 +
                                 // mip level 2: 1x1 4-bit entries      = 1
                                 // Total bytes                         = 59

GLubyte textureData[] = {
  /* palette */
  255, 0, 0,   // red
  0, 0, 255,   // blue
  128, 0, 128, // fuscia (for mip level 2)
  0, 0, 0, 0, 0, 0, 0, 0, 0, 0, 0, 0,
  0, 0, 0, 0, 0, 0, 0, 0, 0, 0, 0, 0,
  0, 0, 0, 0, 0, 0, 0, 0, 0, 0, 0, 0, 0, 0,
  /* indices */
  0, 0x11, 0, 0x11, 0x11, 0, 0x11, 0, // mip level 0 - 0 = RR, 0x11 = BB
  0x01, 0x10,                         // mip level 1 - 0x01 = RB, 0x10 = BR
  0x20 };                             // mip level 2 - 0x01 = fuscia

glCompressedTexImage2D(GL_TEXTURE_2D, -2, GL_PALETTE4_RGB8_OES, 4, 4, 0,
                       TEXTURE_SIZE, textureData);
```

Optional Extensions

When present, optional extensions must be included in the GL_EXTENSIONS string. Like required extensions, they use extension suffixes and make their function entry points available through eglGetProcAddress(). Optional extension functions may be available as static bindings, but this is not required.

OES_query_matrix

Of all the OpenGL ES 1.0 extensions, this is the only one that is optional in both profiles. As mentioned, generally it's not possible in OpenGL ES to query dynamic state. However, it's often desirable to obtain the current modelview or projection matrix. This extension makes doing so possible.

Although OpenGL supports retrieving the current contents of any matrix stack by using the `glGet()` functions, this extension provides a method that is more powerful and flexible. Since a Common Lite profile can implement and store matrices internally in a higher precision format than s15.16, it may not be possible to return the matrix data back as fixed point (overflow/underflow issues arise). To allow an implementation to report its internal representation as accurately as possible without requiring support for floats, the following function has been added:

```
GLbitfield glQueryMatrixxOES(GLfixed mantissa[16], GLint exponent[16]);
```

This retrieves the contents of the top of the currently active matrix stack. The matrix is stored in *mantissa* in `GLfixed` (S15.16) format. The values returned in *exponent* represent the unbiased exponents applied to the matrix components. The two arrays can be used together to determine a close approximation of the internal representation of matrix component *i* as follows:

component i = mantissa[i] $\times$ $2^{\text{exponent}[i]}$

If the implementation uses `GLfixed` values internally, the values in *exponent* will be 0.

The return value of this function can be used to report invalid matrix values. This is only possible if the implementation tracks overflow, which isn't a requirement. If it doesn't, then the return value will always be zero. Otherwise, if the ith component of the matrix is an invalid value (e.g., NaN or Inf), the ith bit in the return value will be set.

The following code illustrates how to use `glQueryMatrixxOES()` to retrieve the current modelview matrix. This simplified version assumes that the internal representation is `GLfixed` (and thus, that exponent contains only zeros). It also assumes that `eglGetProcAddress()` returns successfully.

```
typedef GLbitfield (APIENTRY * PFNGLQUERYMATRIXXOESPROC)
    (GLfixed mantissa[16], GLint exponent[16]);
...
PFNGLQUERYMATRIXXOESPROC glQueryMatrixxOES =
    (PFNGLQUERYMATRIXXOESPROC)eglGetProcAddress("glQueryMatrixxOES");

glMatrixMode(GL_MODELVIEW);
```

```
GLfixed mantissa[16];
GLint exponent[16];

if (glQueryMatrixxOES(mantissa, exponent) != 0)
{
    // matrix contains invalid values
}
```

The following code illustrates how to use both *mantissa* and *exponent* to extract the full precision and range of the internal representation. Assume that powi() is an integer-based power function:

```
#define FIXED16_TO_FLOAT(f) (GLfloat(f)/65536.0f)
...
GLfixed mantissa[16];
GLint exponent[16];
GLfloat modelview[16];

if (glQueryMatrixxOES(mantissa, exponent) != 0)
{
    // matrix contains invalid values
}
for (int i = 0; i < 16; ++i)
{
    // multiplying the mantissa by the exponent can easily cause overflow
    // in fixed point, so it's first converted to float
    modelview[i] = FIXED16_TO_FLOAT(mantissa[i]) * powi(2, exponent[i]);
}
```

Samples

The CD for this book contains a number of sample applications to serve as a starting point to developing your own OpenGL ES applications. See Appendix A, "Using the CD," for information on using these samples.

Recommended Reading

The following books and documents are recommended to gain a better understanding of OpenGL and OpenGL ES.

OpenGL Programming Guide, 4th Edition

Woo, Neider, Davis, Shreiner, Addison-Wesley, 2003

The so-called Red Book is the definitive source for information about programming for

OpenGL. The latest version is written for OpenGL 1.4 and provides comprehensive coverage of all the OpenGL features that were used in OpenGL ES.

Beginning OpenGL Game Programming

Astle, Hawkins, Course Technology PTR, 2004

This book provides concise but complete coverage of the OpenGL features that are useful for game developers. The book was written for OpenGL 1.5, and it is intended for people with limited game and graphics programming experience.

Summary

You've now learned how OpenGL ES came to be and what its intended uses are. You've seen both a high-level and detailed description of the differences between OpenGL ES 1.0 and OpenGL 1.3. You've also seen the new features added in OpenGL ES to address specific concerns of embedded devices. Assuming you have some understanding of OpenGL, you should now be ready to start developing your own OpenGL ES applications.

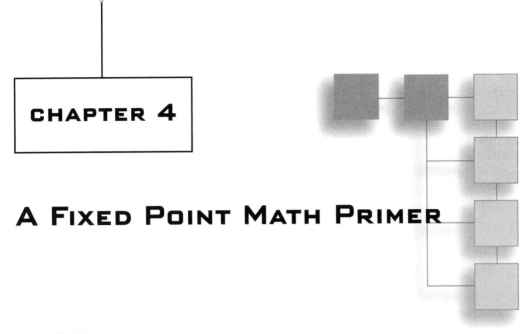

CHAPTER 4

A FIXED POINT MATH PRIMER

by Michael Street

With the standard constraints of low memory footprints, less CPU speed, and very low power consumption requirements, floating point processors have yet to make their way into standard mobile platforms. While this will be changing in the next few years with 3D graphics hardware providing floating point support for the graphics pipeline, for the time being, using fixed point math is essential for 3D games. This chapter will cover the basics of fixed point math needed for developing 3D games on platforms where floating point processor units are not yet feasible. Even on systems that do support floating point operations, there still can be a performance increase when using fixed point math; however, the main trade-off between fixed and floating point operations is always precision.

In this chapter, we'll cover the following information:

- An overview of fixed point math
- Understanding the Q factor
- How to develop fixed point math functions

Introduction

Math…it's hard to get very far in 3D graphics programming without it. It takes a long time to learn and even a longer time to master. However, you're probably accustomed to performing 3D operations using floating point math. Well, now it's time to turn back to the days before floating point math was built into the hardware of your processor or came as a co-processor plugged into your motherboard. OpenGL ES is intended to run on machines with much tighter power constraints, so some goodies like floating point math have been sacrificed to allow for greater battery life.

Floating point in software is just too slow to produce a decent frame rate for real-time game programmers' needs. So what's the alternative? You guessed it, fixed point math. Fixed point math is a technique that uses integer arithmetic to give you noninteger results. Don't worry; we're going to take you step-by-step through the things you need to know. I am not a mathematician, so I will try to explain this topic in a straightforward manner focused primarily on what's important for use with OpenGL ES.

Principles of Fixed Point Mathematics

In arithmetic, fractional values can be approximated by using two integers, known as the *mantissa* and the *exponent*. The pair represents the fraction:

$$m2^{-e}$$

where m is the mantissa and e is the exponent. The exponent can be thought of as the number of bits to the left that the binary point needs to be shifted into the mantissa. Table 4.1 shows some examples of how to represent numbers in this format.

Table 4.1 Mantissa/Exponent Representation

Mantissa (m)	Exponent (e)	Binary	Decimal
11001000	0	11001000.	200
11001000	1	1100100.0	100
11001000	2	110010.00	50
11001000	5	110.01000	6.25
11001000	8	.11001000.	0.78125

In floating point arithmetic, the exponent is a variable and is encoded into the floating point number itself. In fixed point, the exponent is determined either at the compile time or algorithmically (e.g., normalizing), and the mantissa alone is stored in a standard integer variable.

In fixed point, the letter Q is usually used to denote the exponent of a fixed point number. For example, a Q16 value would refer to a fixed point value with an exponent of 16. We will refer to fixed point exponents as Q factors from this point on.

Changing Q Factors

Changing from one Q factor to another is a very simple operation and just requires a simple shift operation. Increasing a Q factor requires shifting the difference between the new Q factor and the old to the left, while decreasing a Q factor requires a shift to the right. Table 4.2 shows some examples of converting the same number between various Q factors.

Table 4.2 Q Factor Conversion

Mantissa (m)	Old Q	New Q	Operation	Old Value	New Value
00001100	0	4	val <<=4;	00001100. (12)	1100.0000 (12)
00001100	2	1	val >>=1;	000011.00 (3)	0000011.0 (3)
00001100	5	2	val >>=3;	000.01100 (.375)	000000.01 (.25)
00001100	5	8	val <<=3;	000.01100 (.375)	.01100000 (.375)
00001100	8	5	val >>=3;	.00001100 (.047)	000.00001 (.031)

Note that in the third and fifth rows of the table, bits are lost as a result of the shift operation, resulting in a loss of precision. Care must be taken when considering Q factors that either the loss of precision is not critical or that there are enough bits available in the resulting value to avoid the loss of precision.

Addition and Subtraction

To add and subtract two fixed point values, it is necessary first to convert both values to the same Q factor (see the previous section). The appropriate Q factor is up to the programmer but should take into account the number of bits available in the variables used and the limits of the input values to avoid overflow or underflow. After the values are converted, all that is required is to add or subtract the mantissas.

As an example, consider the addition of the Q4 value of .3125 (0000.0101 in binary) to the Q1 value of 20.5 (0010100.1 in binary) using unsigned bytes.

Converting 20.5 to Q4 would result in loss of the most significant bit, while converting .3125 to Q1 would result in loss of all significant bits, resulting in zero. There are two things that can be done here: One is counting the number of leading zeros in both values and using the smallest result in determining the Q factor to use. In this case, 20.5 has two leading zeros, which when shifted out to the left would result in a Q3 value. Converting .3125 to Q3 would still incur a loss of one significant bit, changing it from .3125 in Q4 to .25 in Q3. This may be acceptable in some cases where accuracy is not required, but it is a problem in many cases. The other solution is to use larger variables for the calculation; in this case, we could promote the variables to 16 bit integers, and then we would have the extra bits to convert 20.5 to Q4, do the addition, and obtain the result 20.8125 or 000000010100.1101 in 16 bits.

The following code snippets illustrate how to add two different fixed point values.

```
int16 q16val = (int16) (.5 * (1<<16));  // .5 in Q16
int16 q10val = (int16) (.8 * (1<<10));  // .8 in Q10
// Convert both input values to Q14 and add them
int16 q14result = (q10val << 4) + (q16val >> 2);
```

Multiplication

When multiplying two fixed point numbers, the resulting Q factor will be the sum of the two input values' Q factors. Care must be taken to ensure that the resultant value (and any intermediate values) can be stored in the number of bits available to the result variable.

Let's look at a couple of examples. The first is multiplying the Q1 value of 20.5 (0000.0101 in binary) by the Q4 value of .3125. The result, 6.40625, will be a Q5 (4+1) value:

```
0.3125 * 20.5 = 6.40625               // floating point
0000.0101 * 0010100.1 = 110.01101     // binary
5 * 41 = 205                          // integer
```

For the second example, we'll use the Q5 value of 6.40625 and the Q3 value of 4.625. The result of 29.62890625 will have a Q factor of 8 (5+3).

```
6.40625 * 4.625 = 29.62890625                      // floating point
110.01101 * 00100.101 = 11101.10100001 (> 8 bits)  // binary
205 * 37 = 7585                                     // integer
```

Notice that this result will not fit in 8 bits, so the result must be stored in at least a 16 bit value. Even if you intended to shift the result back to a Q3 value (thereby sacrificing the least significant bits), resulting in an 8 bit Q3 value of 11101.101 or 29.625, the intermediate result would still need to be stored in a larger variable that can contain the Q8 value before the shift.

The following snippet shows an example of multiplying two fixed point numbers while preventing overflow in the intermediate result.

```
int16 q16val = (int16)( .6 * (1 << 16)); // .6 in Q16
int16 q14val = (int16)(-1.2 * (1 << 14)); // -1.2 in Q14
int32 q14result = ((int32)q14val*q16val)>>16;  // Result in Q14
/* Note that q14val is cast to an int32 to contain the temporary multiplication
result which is in Q30 before the shift down by 16 to Q14 */
```

As further examples of fixed point multiplication, the following two functions have been provided for multiplying two 4×4 matrices and multiplying a 4×4 matrix by a vector. These functions operate on fixed point values with a Q factor of 16, which is the Q factor for all OpenGL ES fixed point APIs.

```
/*===========================================
FUNCTION    matMultFx

DESCRIPTION
    Multiplies the 4X4 fixed point matrices specified by the parameters a and b
    and returns the result in the 4X4 matrix specified by the parameter c.

    Note: Function loops are unrolled for performance.

DEPENDENCIES
    None

RETURN VALUE
    None

SIDE EFFECTS
===========================================*/

#define Q_FACTOR 16

typedef struct
{
    int32 m[4][4];
} M4Fx;

void matMultFx(M4Fx *c, M4Fx *a, M4Fx *b)
{
    c->m[0][0] = (int32)(((((int64)a->m[0][0] * b->m[0][0]) >> Q_FACTOR)) +
                         ((((int64)a->m[0][1] * b->m[1][0]) >> Q_FACTOR)) +
                         ((((int64)a->m[0][2] * b->m[2][0]) >> Q_FACTOR)) +
                         ((((int64)a->m[0][3] * b->m[3][0]) >> Q_FACTOR))
                        );

    c->m[0][1] = (int32)(((((int64)a->m[0][0] * b->m[0][1]) >> Q_FACTOR)) +
                         ((((int64)a->m[0][1] * b->m[1][1]) >> Q_FACTOR)) +
                         ((((int64)a->m[0][2] * b->m[2][1]) >> Q_FACTOR)) +
                         ((((int64)a->m[0][3] * b->m[3][1]) >> Q_FACTOR))
                        );
```

```
c->m[0][2] = (int32)(((((int64)a->m[0][0] * b->m[0][2]) >> Q_FACTOR)) +
                      ((((int64)a->m[0][1] * b->m[1][2]) >> Q_FACTOR)) +
                      ((((int64)a->m[0][2] * b->m[2][2]) >> Q_FACTOR)) +
                      ((((int64)a->m[0][3] * b->m[3][2]) >> Q_FACTOR))
                     );

c->m[0][3] = (int32)(((((int64)a->m[0][0] * b->m[0][3]) >> Q_FACTOR)) +
                      ((((int64)a->m[0][1] * b->m[1][3]) >> Q_FACTOR)) +
                      ((((int64)a->m[0][2] * b->m[2][3]) >> Q_FACTOR)) +
                      ((((int64)a->m[0][3] * b->m[3][3]) >> Q_FACTOR))
                     );

c->m[1][0] = (int32)(((((int64)a->m[1][0] * b->m[0][0]) >> Q_FACTOR)) +
                      ((((int64)a->m[1][1] * b->m[1][0]) >> Q_FACTOR)) +
                      ((((int64)a->m[1][2] * b->m[2][0]) >> Q_FACTOR)) +
                      ((((int64)a->m[1][3] * b->m[3][0]) >> Q_FACTOR))
                     );

c->m[1][1] = (int32)(((((int64)a->m[1][0] * b->m[0][1]) >> Q_FACTOR)) +
                      ((((int64)a->m[1][1] * b->m[1][1]) >> Q_FACTOR)) +
                      ((((int64)a->m[1][2] * b->m[2][1]) >> Q_FACTOR)) +
                      ((((int64)a->m[1][3] * b->m[3][1]) >> Q_FACTOR))
                     );

c->m[1][2] = (int32)(((((int64)a->m[1][0] * b->m[0][2]) >> Q_FACTOR)) +
                      ((((int64)a->m[1][1] * b->m[1][2]) >> Q_FACTOR)) +
                      ((((int64)a->m[1][2] * b->m[2][2]) >> Q_FACTOR)) +
                      ((((int64)a->m[1][3] * b->m[3][2]) >> Q_FACTOR))
                     );

c->m[1][3] = (int32)(((((int64)a->m[1][0] * b->m[0][3]) >> Q_FACTOR)) +
                      ((((int64)a->m[1][1] * b->m[1][3]) >> Q_FACTOR)) +
                      ((((int64)a->m[1][2] * b->m[2][3]) >> Q_FACTOR)) +
                      ((((int64)a->m[1][3] * b->m[3][3]) >> Q_FACTOR))
                     );

c->m[2][0] = (int32)(((((int64)a->m[2][0] * b->m[0][0]) >> Q_FACTOR)) +
                      ((((int64)a->m[2][1] * b->m[1][0]) >> Q_FACTOR)) +
                      ((((int64)a->m[2][2] * b->m[2][0]) >> Q_FACTOR)) +
                      ((((int64)a->m[2][3] * b->m[3][0]) >> Q_FACTOR))
                     );
```

```
c->m[2][1] = (int32)(((((int64)a->m[2][0] * b->m[0][1]) >> Q_FACTOR)) +
                    (((((int64)a->m[2][1] * b->m[1][1]) >> Q_FACTOR)) +
                    (((((int64)a->m[2][2] * b->m[2][1]) >> Q_FACTOR)) +
                    (((((int64)a->m[2][3] * b->m[3][1]) >> Q_FACTOR))
                    );

c->m[2][2] = (int32)(((((int64)a->m[2][0] * b->m[0][2]) >> Q_FACTOR)) +
                    (((((int64)a->m[2][1] * b->m[1][2]) >> Q_FACTOR)) +
                    (((((int64)a->m[2][2] * b->m[2][2]) >> Q_FACTOR)) +
                    (((((int64)a->m[2][3] * b->m[3][2]) >> Q_FACTOR))
                    );

c->m[2][3] = (int32)(((((int64)a->m[2][0] * b->m[0][3]) >> Q_FACTOR)) +
                    (((((int64)a->m[2][1] * b->m[1][3]) >> Q_FACTOR)) +
                    (((((int64)a->m[2][2] * b->m[2][3]) >> Q_FACTOR)) +
                    (((((int64)a->m[2][3] * b->m[3][3]) >> Q_FACTOR))
                    );

c->m[3][0] = (int32)(((((int64)a->m[3][0] * b->m[0][0]) >> Q_FACTOR)) +
                    (((((int64)a->m[3][1] * b->m[1][0]) >> Q_FACTOR)) +
                    (((((int64)a->m[3][2] * b->m[2][0]) >> Q_FACTOR)) +
                    (((((int64)a->m[3][3] * b->m[3][0]) >> Q_FACTOR))
                    );

c->m[3][1] = (int32)(((((int64)a->m[3][0] * b->m[0][1]) >> Q_FACTOR)) +
                    (((((int64)a->m[3][1] * b->m[1][1]) >> Q_FACTOR)) +
                    (((((int64)a->m[3][2] * b->m[2][1]) >> Q_FACTOR)) +
                    (((((int64)a->m[3][3] * b->m[3][1]) >> Q_FACTOR))
                    );

c->m[3][2] = (int32)(((((int64)a->m[3][0] * b->m[0][2]) >> Q_FACTOR)) +
                    (((((int64)a->m[3][1] * b->m[1][2]) >> Q_FACTOR)) +
                    (((((int64)a->m[3][2] * b->m[2][2]) >> Q_FACTOR)) +
                    (((((int64)a->m[3][3] * b->m[3][2]) >> Q_FACTOR))
                    );

c->m[3][3] = (int32)(((((int64)a->m[3][0] * b->m[0][3]) >> Q_FACTOR)) +
                    (((((int64)a->m[3][1] * b->m[1][3]) >> Q_FACTOR)) +
                    (((((int64)a->m[3][2] * b->m[2][3]) >> Q_FACTOR)) +
                    (((((int64)a->m[3][3] * b->m[3][3]) >> Q_FACTOR))
                    );
}
```

```
/*========================================
FUNCTION    matVec4MultFx

DESCRIPTION
  Multiply the 4x4 fixed point matrix b by the four element fixed point
  vector c and return the resulting four element fixed point vector in a.

DEPENDENCIES
  None

RETURN VALUE
  None

SIDE EFFECTS

========================================*/

#define Q_FACTOR   16

void matVec4MultFx(V4Fx *a, M4Fx *b, V4Fx *c)
{
    int64 temp; // temp will be in Q32
    temp =  ((int64)b->m[0][0] * c->X) +
            ((int64)b->m[0][1] * c->Y) +
            ((int64)b->m[0][2] * c->Z) +
            ((int64)b->m[0][3] * c->W);
    a->X = (int32)(temp >> Q_FACTOR);  // Shift down to Q16 for final answer
    // Note that we do not shift down Q_FACTOR till after all of the additions are
complete

    temp =  ((int64)b->m[1][0] * c->X) +
            ((int64)b->m[1][1] * c->Y) +
            ((int64)b->m[1][2] * c->Z) +
            ((int64)b->m[1][3] * c->W);
    a->Y = (int32)(temp >> Q_FACTOR);

    temp =  ((int64)b->m[2][0] * c->X) +
            ((int64)b->m[2][1] * c->Y) +
            ((int64)b->m[2][2] * c->Z) +
            ((int64)b->m[2][3] * c->W);
    a->Z = (int32)(temp >> Q_FACTOR);

    temp =  ((int64)b->m[3][0] * c->X) +
```

```
            ((int64)b->m[3][1] * c->Y) +
            ((int64)b->m[3][2] * c->Z) +
            ((int64)b->m[3][3] * c->W);
    a->W = (int32)(temp >> Q_FACTOR);
}
```

Division

Division is similar to multiplication in that the two input variables' Q factors are sub-tracted but a bit differently in that you consider the resultant Q factor when determining the first value's Q factor. Since negative Q factors are nonsequential, the first Q factor should be equal to the desired result Q factor plus the second value's Q factor. In other words, if you require a Q4 result and both input values are Q3, you need to convert the first value to a Q7 value and then perform the integer divide. You may need to promote the first value to a larger variable in order to contain the Q7 value without losing the most significant bits.

As an example, let's look at dividing the Q1 value of 50.5 by the Q3 value of 4.625 to obtain a Q4 result.

```
Dividend: 50.5 (Q1, 0110010.1 binary)
Divisor: 4.625 (Q3, 00100.101 binary)
```

Since the result is to be Q4, we must add 4 to the divisor's Q factor, resulting in Q7. Now we must convert the Q1 dividend to Q7 by shifting the mantissa to the left by $7 - 1 = 6$. Since the result of the operation would result in a loss of the most significant bits, we must promote the variable to a 16 bit value. The result of this is 000110010.1000000 or 50.5 in Q7:

```
Dividend: 50.5 (Q7, 110010.1000000 binary)
```

Doing the integer divide results in the Q4 value 1010.1110 or 10.875:

```
Quotient: 10.875 (Q4, 1010.1110 binary)
```

Notice that 10.875 is different than the floating point division result of 10.918918.... This is due to the fact that .875 is as close as a Q4 number can get to .918918... without going over. If you require closer precision, you can use a larger Q factor that will result in a clos-er approximation, but you will need to take the resulting variable storage requirements into account as well.

The following example shows how to do fixed point division in code.

```
int16 q16val = (int16) ( 30.25 * (1<<16)); // 3.25 in Q16
int16 q14val = (int16) ( 1.25 * (1<<16));  // 1.25 in Q14
int32 q16result = (int32)((int64)q16val<<14) / q14val;
```

Note that q16val was promoted to an int64 because it had to be shifted to a Q30 value before it was divided by the Q14 value to end up as a Q16 value. Since q16val was 30.25, it took 35 bits to encode as a Q30 number (5 bits of integer plus 30 bits of fraction), hence the need for a 64 bit integer to avoid loss of bits during the calculation.

Square Root

Calculating the square root of a fixed point number is done by calculating the integer square root of the value with a Q factor of two times the desired output Q factor. In other words, if you need a Q6 output value of the square root of the Q1 value 2.5, convert the input Q value to 6×2 or Q12 and take the integer square root. If you don't have access to an integer square root function, a fixed point square root solution is included in the code examples below.

As an example of calculating the square root of a fixed point value, consider the Q1 value of 2.5 (0000010.1 in binary), with desired results in Q6.

First, convert the input Q factor to Q12, which requires shifting left by 11 (Q12 − Q1). This results in a binary value of 0010.100000000000 or an integer value of 10240.

The integer square root of this is 101 (in decimal) or 01.100101 in binary with a Q factor of 6. This is equivalent to 1.578125, which is as close to the floating point result of 1.581139 as a Q6 value can be without going over. Again, to get a more accurate result, choose a higher Q factor and adjust for the differences in variable storage requirements.

The following code provides a sample implementation of a fixed point square root routine.

```
#define sqrtStep(shift)                                     \
    if((0x400000001 >> shift) + sqrtVal <= val)             \
    {                                                       \
        val -= (0x400000001 >> shift) + sqrtVal;            \
        sqrtVal = (sqrtVal >> 1) | (0x400000001 >> shift);  \
    }                                                       \
    else                                                    \
    {                                                       \
        sqrtVal = sqrtVal >> 1;                             \
    }


/*=========================================
FUNCTION     sqrtQFx

DESCRIPTION
    This square root routine uses the fact that fixed point numbers are really
    integers. The integer square root of a fixed point number divided by the
```

square root of 2 to the F power where F is the number of bits of fraction
in the fixed point number is the square root of the original fixed point
number. If you have an even number of bits of fraction, you can convert the
integer square root to the fixed point square root with a shift.

The input value 'val' is in the input value 'QFactor' format.
The output value is in Q16.

DEPENDENCIES
  None

RETURN VALUE
  Returns the computed fixed point square root value.

SIDE EFFECTS
==*/
```c
int32 sqrtQFx(int32 val, int32 QFactor)
{
// Note: This fast square root function only works with an even Q_FACTOR
    int32 sqrtVal = 0;

    // Check for even QFactor
    if(QFactor & 0x1)
    {
        // QFactor not even
        // Correct values to even Q Factor
        QFactor -= 1;
        val >>= 1;
    }

    // Do the math for an integer square root
    sqrtStep(0);
    sqrtStep(2);
    sqrtStep(4);
    sqrtStep(6);
    sqrtStep(8);
    sqrtStep(10);
    sqrtStep(12);
    sqrtStep(14);
    sqrtStep(16);
    sqrtStep(18);
    sqrtStep(20);
```

```
        sqrtStep(22);
        sqrtStep(24);
        sqrtStep(26);
        sqrtStep(28);
        sqrtStep(30);

        if(sqrtVal < val)
        {
            ++sqrtVal;
        }

        sqrtVal <<= (QFactor)/2;   // This is the square root in QFactor format.

        // Convert the square root to Q16 format
        if(QFactor < 16)
          return(sqrtVal<<(16-QFactor));
        else
          return(sqrtVal>>(QFactor-16));
}
```

As an example of this, the following is an implementation of a common usage of the square root in graphics: normalizing a vector.

```
/*=======================================
FUNCTION      vec3NormFx

DESCRIPTION


DEPENDENCIES
    None

RETURN VALUE
    None

SIDE EFFECTS
=====================================*/
int vec3NormFx(V3Fx *a)
{
        int32 n;
        int64 sq;
        int   q;
```

```
a->X >>= 1;
a->Y >>= 1;
a->Z >>= 1;

// Compute the sum of the squares
sq = (int64)a->X*a->X+(int64)a->Y*a->Y+(int64)a->Z*a->Z;

// Normalize square by counting the number of leading zeros (unused precision)
// shifting the unused bits off and computing the square root.
// Note: sq is 64 bits wide, so we shift down 32 bits to examine the Most Significant
// bits.
q = CountLeadingZeros((int32)(sq>>32));
// q will contain the number of unused significant bits, so the larger the value
// of q, the less precision bits we have to shift off.
// sqrtQFx uses an adjustable Q factor for input. Q16 for output.
n = sqrtQFx((int32)(sq>>(32 - q)), q);
// n now contains the size (length) of the vector

// Zero length vectors are not allowed.
if (n==0)
{
    return 0;
}
// Normalize the vector by dividing each component by the length.
a->X = (int32)(((int64)a->X<<16)/n);
a->Y = (int32)(((int64)a->Y<<16)/n);
a->Z = (int32)(((int64)a->Z<<16)/n);

return n;

}
```

The preceding function calls CountLeadingZeros(), which is a useful utility function to have when doing fixed point math. The following is a sample implementation of this function. The function includes optimized ARM assembly code as well, which will be useful for most mobile platforms.

```
/*=======================================
FUNCTION     CountLeadingZeros

DESCRIPTION
    This function returns the number of leading binary zeros in
```

an unsigned int 32. This can be used for normalizing values.
It has been optimized to use the ARM CLZ (Count Leading Zeros)
Hardware instruction when available.

DEPENDENCIES
  None

RETURN VALUE
  None

SIDE EFFECTS
===*/

```
int CountLeadingZeros(uint32 value)
{
    int numZeros;
#if defined(T_ARM) && !defined(__thumb)
// Assembly Language Implementation using ARM instruction set.
    __asm
    {
        CLZ      numZeros, value
    }
#else
// C Language implementation
    for( numZeros = 0; numZeros < (sizeof(uint32)*8); numZeros++)
    {
        if(0x80000000 & (value<<numZeros))
            break;
    }

#endif
    return numZeros;
}
```

Trigonometric Functions

Sine and cosine are two functions used quite extensively in computer graphics, so their quick computation is essential to good performance. But sometimes speed and memory requirements are at odds in an embedded system, so I will give you two techniques to try to satisfy your needs for both.

Sine and Cosine Using Lookup Tables

A very quick method for calculating sine and cosine is to use a table of sine values and return the nearest entry for any given input value. Accuracy will depend on several factors, such as the number of table entries, whether interpolation is used for in-between values, and whether table space is optimized by computing the quadrant of the input angle, thereby only requiring table entries between 0 and $\pi/2$. The mapping of a 2π domain into a $\pi/2$ domain is as follows:

- If the input angle is in quadrant 1 (0 up to $\pi/2$), it is the lookup table value.
- If the input angle is in quadrant 2 ($\pi/2$ up to π), subtract the input angle from π and do the lookup.
- If the input angle is in quadrant 3 (π up to $(3\pi/2)$), subtract π from the input angle and do the lookup and reverse the sign.
- If the input angle is in quadrant 4 (($3\pi/2$) up to (2π)), subtract the input angle from 2π and do the lookup and reverse the sign.

Input and output Q factors are usually identified as part of the API (usually Q16), but internally you may use any Q factor that you require for your implementation. Just be sure to convert to the API specification before returning a value.

Since sine and cosine vary between 0.0 and 1.0 and Q16 is the usual required accuracy, table values are usually stored in unsigned integers and returned in signed 32 bit integers. The sign need not be stored in the table since it can be determined as a result of the calculated quadrant of the angle. A caveat is that since representing the value 1.0 in Q16 would require 17 bits (i.e. 1.0000 0000 0000 0000 in binary), the sine values need to be clamped at .9999847412109375 (i.e. .1111 1111 1111 1111 in binary). This is usually accurate enough for most purposes.

Since a cosine wave is just a sine wave with an offset of $\pi/2$, only one common table is required for both functions. Add $\pi/2$ to the input angle for a cosine and do the math for a sine lookup.

Calculating Trigonometric Functions Algorithmically

Lookup tables are a very quick and easy way to implement a method for calculating sine and cosine, but they do have a major drawback for many embedded systems: They require a significant amount of static memory, which may be at a premium in your application. They also require more tables if you need to implement additional trigonometric functions, such as tangent, arcsine, arccosine, and so on.

With these issues in mind, I researched other methods of computing fixed point sine and cosine and came across the method presented by Israel Koren in his book *Computer Arithmetic Algorithms* (ISBN 1-56881-160-8).

This book helped me immensely, and I highly recommend it. The one drawback is that it is pretty technical, and there is no source code provided in the book. Fortunately, after reading it over many times, I was able to translate his words into C code for your enjoyment. I have only developed the C code for the trigonometric functions, but with some tweaking of the basic techniques I use and reading his book very closely, you could modify them to provide many other mathematical functions. The benefits of using this technique are that all of the transcendental functions can be implemented using the same 17 16-bit table entries. I will not explain the mathematical basis behind the algorithm (buy the Koren book if you are interested in that), but I will walk you through the code and explain how the code itself works.

The table used by all of these algorithms is the ArcTan of the mantissa of 1 with increasing Q factors, shown in Table 4.3.

Table 4.3 ArcTan

Binary Value	Q Factor	ArcTan (decimal)	ArcTan in Q16
0000000000000001.	0	.785400390625	.1100100100010000
000000000000000.1	1	.463653564453125	.0111011010110010
0000000000000.01	2	.2449798583984375	.0011111010110111
0000000000000.001	3	.124359130859375	.0001111111010110
000000000000.0001	4	.0624237060546875	.0000111111111011
00000000000.00001	5	.0312347412109375	.0000011111111111
0000000000.000001	6	.015625	.0000010000000000
000000000.0000001	7	.0078125	.0000001000000000
00000000.00000001	8	.00390625	.0000000100000000
0000000.000000001	9	.001953125	.0000000010000000
000000.0000000001	10	.0009765625	.0000000001000000
00000.00000000001	11	.00048828125	.0000000000100000
0000.000000000001	12	.000244140625	.0000000000010000
000.0000000000001	13	.0001220703125	.0000000000001000
00.00000000000001	14	.00006103515625	.0000000000000100
0.000000000000001	15	.000030517578125	.0000000000000010
.0000000000000001	16	.0000152587890625	.0000000000000001

And here is the table represented in C:

```
// Arctan16 table is in Q16 for trig computations.
const uint16 arctanTable16[17] = {
    0xC910,
    0x76B2,
    0x3EB7,
    0x1FD6,
```

```
    0x0FFB,
    0x07FF,
    0x0400,
    0x0200,
    0x0100,
    0x0080,
    0x0040,
    0x0020,
    0x0010,
    0x0008,
    0x0004,
    0x0002,
    0x0001
};
```

The function sinCosFx() calculates sine and cosine simultaneously, which is more efficient since you usually need both together, and in calculating one, you get the other for free.

The input value is in Q16 radians, and the output sin and cosine values are in Q16 format.

See the comments for an explanation of the algorithm.

```
#define Q_FACTOR 16      // API is in Q16
#define SIN_Q_FACTOR 14 // Using Q14 internally to avoid having to
                        // promote values to 64 bit integers during computations


void sinCosFx(int32 val, int32 *sin, int32 *cos)
{
#define SIN_Q_FACTOR   14
#define ONEOVERK16   39796   // Constant 1/1.6468 in Q16 (See Koren Book for details)
// SIN_Q_DIFF is used to convert from API Q_FACTOR to Internal SIN_Q_FACTOR
#define SIN_Q_DIFF     (Q_FACTOR - SIN_Q_FACTOR)

#if (SIN_Q_FACTOR > Q_FACTOR)
#error Sin Q Factor greater than System Q Factor Not Allowed
#endif

#if (SIN_Q_FACTOR > 14)
    int64 x,s,r,w,z,newz;
#else
    int32 x,s,r,w,z,newz;
#endif

    int i, shift, quadrant;
```

```
    // Trivial 0 check
    // If the input value is zero, we know sine and cosine are 0 and 1 respectively
    if(val == 0) {
        *sin = 0;
        *cos = 1<<Q_FACTOR;
        return;
    }

    // Convert input value to internal Q format and store.
    x = (val>>SIN_Q_DIFF);
    s = 1;  // Initialize the sign value to positive.


    z = (ONEOVERK16>>SIN_Q_DIFF);  // Initialize z with constant 1/K in internal Q
format
    w = 0;



    /* First, modulo the input angle from 0 to 2 Pi, then
        compute which quadrant the angle is in.
    */
    // Compute Quadrant
    // Modulo to 2Pi
    x = x%(FIXED2PI>>SIN_Q_DIFF);

    // If the input angle is negative, invert the value and flag the fact for later.
    if(x < 0) {
        x = -x;
        r = -1;
    }
    else r = 1;

    if(x < (FIXEDPIOVER2>>SIN_Q_DIFF))
            quadrant = 0;
    else if(x < (FIXEDPI>>SIN_Q_DIFF))
    {
            quadrant = 1;
            x = (FIXEDPI>>SIN_Q_DIFF)-x;
    }
    else if(x < (FIXED3PIOVER2>>SIN_Q_DIFF))
    {
            quadrant = 2;
```

```
              x -= (FIXEDPI>>SIN_Q_DIFF);
    }
    else
    {

              quadrant = 3;
              x = (FIXED2PI>>SIN_Q_DIFF)-x;
    }



    // Compute sin and cos with domain 0 < x < Pi/2
    // Repeat this loop for the number of bits of precision required.
    // w will converge the sine of the angle while z will converge to
    // the cosine of the angle as x approaches 0.
    for(i = 0; i < (SIN_Q_FACTOR+1); i++)
    {
        // As the loop iterates, decrease the Q factor used in algorithm
        shift = (SIN_Q_FACTOR)-i;
        // If x goes negative, reverse the sign
        if(x < 0)
        {
            s = -1;
        }
        else s = 1;
        // Converge on cosine value using previous sine and cosine values
        newz = z - ((s*(1<<shift) * w)>>SIN_Q_FACTOR);
        // Converge on sine value using previous sine and cosine values
        w = w + ((s*(1<<shift) * z) >> SIN_Q_FACTOR);
        // Store new cosine value
        z = newz;
        // Converge x to 0 using sign bit and arctan table
        x = x - ((s*(arctanTable16[i]>>SIN_Q_DIFF)));
    }

    // Clamp Sin and Cos to between -1 and 1 (precision issues can cause small
overruns)
    if(w > (1 << (Q_FACTOR - SIN_Q_DIFF)))
    {
        w = (1 << (Q_FACTOR - SIN_Q_DIFF));
    }
    else if(w < -(1 << (Q_FACTOR - SIN_Q_DIFF)))
    {
        w = -(1 << (Q_FACTOR - SIN_Q_DIFF));
```

```
        }
        if(z > (1 << (Q_FACTOR - SIN_Q_DIFF)))
        {
            z = (1 << (Q_FACTOR - SIN_Q_DIFF));
        }
        else if(z < -(1 << (Q_FACTOR - SIN_Q_DIFF)))
        {
            z = -(1 << (Q_FACTOR - SIN_Q_DIFF));
        }

    // Now that we have sine and cosine for one quadrant, map back to
    // the proper quadrant.  r is used to compensate for negative input
    // values.  Cosine computes the same values for negative and positive angles
    // so it does not need the r value adjustment.
    switch(quadrant)
    {
        case 0:
            *sin =  (int32)(r*w<<SIN_Q_DIFF);
            *cos =  (int32)(z<<SIN_Q_DIFF);
            break;
        case 1:
            *sin =  (int32)(r*w<<SIN_Q_DIFF);
            *cos =  (int32)(-z<<SIN_Q_DIFF);
            break;
        case 2:
            *sin =  (int32)(r*-w<<SIN_Q_DIFF);
            *cos =  (int32)(-z<<SIN_Q_DIFF);
            break;
        case 3:
            *sin =  (int32)(r*-w<<SIN_Q_DIFF);
            *cos =  (int32)(z<<SIN_Q_DIFF);
            break;
    }
}
```

Finally, the following code provides a sample tangent function using the same method.

```
/*========================================
FUNCTION    tanFx

DESCRIPTION
  Computes the fixed point Tangent of the parameter val.
  Algorithm developed from the book:
```

```
   Title:   Computer Arithmetic Algorithms (2nd Edition)
   Author:  Israel Koren
   ISBN:    1-56881-160-8


DEPENDENCIES
  None

RETURN VALUE
  Returns the resulting Q16 tangent of val.

SIDE EFFECTS
===========================================*/
int32 tanFx(int32 val)
{

#define TAN_Q_FACTOR    14
#define TAN_Q_DIFF      (Q_FACTOR - TAN_Q_FACTOR)

#if (TAN_Q_FACTOR > Q_FACTOR)
#error Tangent Q Factor greater than System Q Factor not allowed.
#endif

#if(TAN_Q_FACTOR > 14)
    int64 x,s,w,z,newz;
#else
    int32 x,s,w,z,newz;
#endif

    int i, shift, quadrant;

    x = (val>>TAN_Q_DIFF);
    s = 1;

    z = (ONEOVERK16>>TAN_Q_DIFF);
    w = 0;

    if(x < 0)
    {
        x = -x;
        quadrant = -1;
    }
    else quadrant = 1;
```

```
// Compute Quadrant
// Modulo to Pi
x = x%(FIXEDPI>>TAN_Q_DIFF);

if(x > (FIXEDPIOVER2>>TAN_Q_DIFF))
{
    quadrant = -quadrant;
    x = (FIXEDPIOVER2>>TAN_Q_DIFF) -
        (x - (FIXEDPIOVER2>>TAN_Q_DIFF));
}

// Compute sin and cos with domain 0 < x < Pi/2
for(i = 0; i < (TAN_Q_FACTOR+1); i++)
{
    shift = TAN_Q_FACTOR-i;
    if(x < 0)
    {
        s = -1;
    }
    else s = 1;
    newz = z - ((s*(1<<shift) * w)>>TAN_Q_FACTOR);
    w = w + ((s*(1<<shift) * z) >> TAN_Q_FACTOR);
    z = newz;
    x = x - (s*(arctanTable16[i]>>TAN_Q_DIFF));
}

// Compute Tangent by dividing sin by cos (w by z) and adjusting the
// sign based on quadrant
return ((quadrant*(w<<TAN_Q_FACTOR)/z)<<TAN_Q_DIFF);
}
```

Summary

In this chapter, you learned the basic concepts of fixed point math. The most important thing to remember is to always know what Q factor you're working with. The Q factor you are using will determine your precision error when doing multiple operations. You've also been provided with some standard fixed point math routines that should give you a good start in writing your own math routines for mobile devices that require fixed point math. Even if you're an experienced game developer, we hope that the code in this chapter will give you some insight into optimizing your math code.

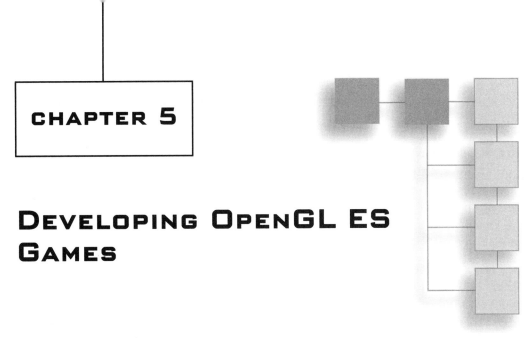

CHAPTER 5

DEVELOPING OPENGL ES GAMES

by Anders Granlund

In this chapter, you'll learn the details of developing a commercial OpenGL ES game. We will walk you through the process of porting a console game to OpenGL ES. With the limitations of the medium, we will focus on optimizing and performance tips for games using OpenGL ES. This chapter will give any professional or novice game developer the basic framework for getting started.

In this chapter, we'll cover the following information:

- The difference between consoles and mobile devices
- Optimizing your game code for mobile devices
- Helpful tips for handling constant frame rates and different screen resolutions
- An overview of geometry and texture animation
- Using OpenGL ES to render 2D content

Overview

Mobile platforms have come a long way since the likes of Snake and Tetris. Hardware specifications on these devices keep improving quite rapidly, probably thanks to the demand for playing bigger and better games. Higher phone specifications have allowed us to go from low resolution black-and-white games to fast-paced action games with many simultaneous sprites onscreen at once. Some phones with fast CPUs are even able to do 3D games using software 3D rendering engines. The big revolution is finally here—just as the first 3D accelerators for PC computers dramatically raised the bar for 3D graphics speed and quality, we are seeing the same thing happening for mobile devices. It looks as if 3D accelerators are here to stay!

Just as OpenGL is a standard API supported by almost all computer platforms, it is a safe bet to say that OpenGL ES will be supported by all current and future 3D accelerated mobile devices. This is a good thing because it gives developers a graphics API that many are already familiar with, and it allows them to quickly develop or port an existing game to a mobile device. Because it is similar to its desktop counterpart, developers can also port an already existing game engine to a mobile device, which is faster and less painful compared to working with a brand new custom API. OpenGL ES is already supported on major mobile platforms such as Windows CE, BREW, and Symbian OS, so games written for OpenGL ES can be deployed on all of these platforms with little or no changes to the rendering engine.

At Climax we successfully ported the Xbox version of *MotoGP2* to OpenGL ES as shown in Figure 5.1. The mobile version of *MotoGP2*: Ultimate Racing Technology runs on various mobile devices, all with different hardware specifications. Getting the game running on a wide variety of configurations was made easier by OpenGL ES, but it was still not without complications. The following sections will discuss scaling down a console game for a mobile device and provide some general tips and ideas for game development using OpenGL ES.

Figure 5.1 OpenGL ES version of MotoGP2: Ultimate Racing Technology.

From Console to Mobile

Before attempting to port from one of the current high-end consoles or the PC platform, it is important to identify the differences between them. These high-end machines are powerful beasts compared to mobile devices, and in the past, games ported to these devices had very little resemblance to the original version of the game. Hardware 3D graphics accelerators and the OpenGL ES API have dramatically closed the gap between the mobile devices and home consoles. Of course, gaming consoles will always have awesome graphics and better special effects, but games that are ported from a console to a mobile platform no longer means having a completely different 2D version of the original game (or a slow software rendered 3D game).

The main issues faced when porting a console game are:

- CPU speed
- GPU speed
- Lack of HW floating pt on the CPU

- Size and speed of system memory
- Storage capacity

As you are porting source code from a console to a much lower-end platform, it will become necessary to optimize that code in as many places as possible to get it running fast enough and in the memory space available. While the developers of the original game, be it yourself or someone else, have probably optimized the critical parts of the game, it can almost always be taken further. It all comes down to how much time you are willing to spend on it.

Porting a game doesn't necessarily mean porting *all* of the original source code. Some parts of the game might be better to rewrite from scratch. If getting the original code running and running fast enough is estimated to have a longer development cycle than to rewrite a simpler version from scratch with the specs of mobile devices in mind, then you should focus on parts of your game that could be rewritten to increase performance for a mobile platform. When porting *MotoGP2*, we ported some parts of the original source code and rewrote some other parts; for example. the physics engine was rewritten from scratch in a more simple fashion because the original physics model was too complex for the CPU on your standard mobile device.

A Few CPU Side Performance Tips

The single most important factor when it comes to getting good performance out of your application is to avoid using floating point data types anywhere in the code. While OpenGL ES supports both fixed point and floating point data types, almost none of the currently available mobile devices have support for native floating point operations on the CPU. Floating point operations emulated in software are extremely slow, and fixed point should always be used instead. When porting a console game, this can be a big issue because unless you are porting from the Playstation1, all original math operations will likely be using floating point, and it will be necessary to convert them. Some platforms might not have hardware divisions or other math operations; in these cases, it is recommended that you use lookup tables for these tasks. If the platform is unable to do divisions in hardware, then a lookup table will help boost performance compared to using a standard library function. A sine lookup table is very useful as well if the platform is unable to calculate the sine value in the hardware.

If the CPU is ARM-based, you have the choice of compiling code for Arm or Thumb mode. Choosing which one to use depends on the bandwidth of the memory and the bus from memory to CPU. Arm instructions are 32 bit instructions and will execute faster than the same code compiled to Thumb instructions on a full 32 bit platform. In addition, in Thumb mode integers are 16 bits instead of 32 bits, which can create major problems when running OpenGL ES games.

Memory and Storage Capacity

Keeping the application size down is important for mobile devices. Not only do you have very limited physical space on the storage medium, but also games are usually distributed as downloads over the Internet directly to the device and must be kept as small as possible for this reason. Not many people will bother buying your game if it takes hours to download it to their mobile phone. Game data resources such as graphics, music, and sound are the dominating factors that make up the total size of the application, so these are the ones to concentrate on when trying to keep the size down or shrink the size of a game being ported to a mobile device. Obviously, console titles do not suffer from any problems with storage capacity due to the CD and DVD format. Likewise, memory sizes on these platforms are quite generous when compared to mobile devices.

Out of all the graphics resources available, textures are often the ones taking up most of the space, so when porting a game. simply scaling down the textures will bring down the total size of the application quite a lot. Due to the small physical screen size on mobile devices, textures can quite easily be rescaled to a small size without sacrificing any noticeable visual quality. Because screens usually have a pixel resolution of 240×320 or smaller, having incredibly large textures will not improve the visual quality anyway. If the game is still too big even after reducing all the textures by a certain factor, then it is time to start looking at individual textures and downscaling some of them even further. You can also remove similar-looking textures and sometimes even remove textures entirely—perhaps an object can look equally good with only Gouraud shading.

Reducing the size of geometry data makes sense, as this is something that has to be done anyway for the sake of rendering performance. A lower polygon count and smaller data types for vertices will automatically reduce the size of the game data, which will be discussed in detail later on.

In general, most data can be compressed for storage and then decompressed in the game when a level loads into memory. Loading time will take a hit, but it is worth it if it means having better quality artwork or sound. Different algorithms can be applied for different types of data; for example, PNG is a great format for lossless image compression, and generic data such as geometry could be compressed with something like zip or lzw.

Both texture memory footprint and memory bandwidth are limited resources on a mobile device, so OpenGL ES implementations support native, compressed texture formats. Games can take advantage of this by compressing the texture data to appropriate compressed native formats.

Creating the Art Assets

Models and textures made for a PC or console game are more often than not too big and too detailed to bring straight across to a mobile device. Factors such as storage capacity, system memory, GPU speed, and video memory size and bandwidth will play a large role in how far art assets need to be scaled down to fit on the target device.

When scaling down or creating new artwork for a mobile device, it is important to keep in mind that different mobile devices can, just like home PCs, have different hardware configurations. A game running fine on one device might be struggling to keep a decent frame rate on another because the polygon count is too high. An easy way of making sure a game runs well on many devices is to develop with the lowest-spec device in mind and use that artwork across all other devices.

The obvious problem with this approach is that on a higher-spec device, the game will look sub-par when compared to a game that is optimized to take advantage of the higher specifications. Another approach—the one we took when developing *MotoGP2*—is to use different art assets for different spec devices. A device with a high GPU speed and memory footprint/bandwidth will use more detailed geometry than a device with a slower GPU. We did the same with textures by allowing devices that have large on-board video memory to load up high-resolution versions of the textures. The size and amount of textures allowed is determined by several factors, such as storage space, memory size, and the size of the on-board video memory of the 3D accelerator. Textures for PC and home consoles are usually big and not suitable to be directly put on a mobile device. Luckily, converting textures between different targets is not something terribly difficult or time consuming, so converting them down by hand might be an option unless the game has lots of different textures or you are planning to have many different builds that are all using different texture resolutions.

Another idea that might be better in the long run is to have the artist create all textures in the highest resolution and scale down with an offline tool as appropriate. This tool should be able to scale between different resolutions and pixel formats as necessary for the target platforms. When porting *MotoGP2*, we did a first pass by hand over the original Xbox textures. After that we created a custom tool as part of our build process, which took care of scaling the textures to fit the selected target device we were building for.

The speed of the GPU will be the biggest factor in determining how many polygons you are going to be able to render each frame. This will be a significantly lower number than what you are used to rendering on PC and home consoles, at least for the current generation of mobile devices. For this reason, effort must be taken to reduce the polygon count on the game geometry to a reasonable amount in order to have it running at a smooth frame rate. Maintaining different versions of geometry by hand can be a very time-consuming business and basically means that the artist will have to remodel all geometry for each level of detail.

At Climax, we model almost all source geometry in high-level curved surfaces. An offline tool takes care of tessellating the source artwork down to triangles, according to user-selectable parameters. Using high-level surfaces enables us to quickly output models of different levels of detail from one single source model. This method has proven to be very useful when doing multiplatform development for consoles, and we have applied the same technique when developing for mobile devices. Our geometry exporter can also ignore certain parts of the geometry, if needed, so for the lower-end devices we can easily skip details by simply not exporting some parts while keeping all the details enabled for higher-end devices. High-level surfaces will not magically make geometry work on all platforms, but they will certainly shorten the time that artists have to spend getting geometry ready for different spec targets. Converting highly-detailed PC and console geometry will still require a fair amount of work of scaling down the initial geometry, but after the base model is done, we can scale it automatically to suit all mobile devices. All major art packages have support for patch modeling, so if you are in the process of setting up your assets pipeline, I recommend you at least consider the possibility of using high-level surfaces.

Spend time to get it right because a well-constructed assets pipeline will save you a lot of time in the long run. Figures 5.2–5.6 show the different levels of detail for art assets.

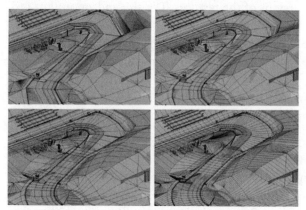

Figure 5.2 Race track at different detail levels.

Figure 5.3 Incredibly high level of detail, but not usable in game.

Figure 5.4 Very high level of detail for close-up views of bike.

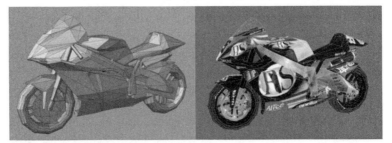

Figure 5.5 Medium level of detail.

Figure 5.6 Low level of detail for bikes farther in the distance.

Optimizing Your Game for the Graphics Pipeline

A well-optimized rendering pipeline can make the difference between a good-looking game and a great-looking game. The performance of your rendering engine will directly affect how many polygons you will be able to display on the screen while maintaining a decent frame rate.

While OpenGL ES is very efficient as it is, it is also very flexible in the sense that it allows the user to do many things differently, depending on the need of the application. This kind of flexibility is a great thing but requires a bit of thinking from the application programmer to get the most out of the device. Knowing what you want to accomplish and exactly what you need out of OpenGL ES is the key to getting the most performance out of it. While some of the following performance tips might be obvious to game developers already using OpenGL, they should prove to be very useful for developers new to the API.

Knowing Your Data Types

As already mentioned, you should avoid using floating point at all cost on CPUs that do not support them natively. Currently, this means not using it on most, if not all, mobile devices. Luckily, or rather because of good thinking, OpenGL ES supports a wide variety of data types. Unlike desktop OpenGL, you are now allowed to pass fixed point values to the API. Fixed point values can be 32 bit (s15.16 format), 16 bit, or 8 bit.

In general, using smaller data types usually means less vertex memory bandwidth, which should help the rendering performance if memory bandwidth is the bottleneck. The trade-off between precision and speed is a decision that has to be made, but in general, 16 bit fixed point precision will be perfectly fine for most geometry in a game, and for certain geometry, 8 bits might even be enough.

Besides increased performance, another positive effect of using smaller data types is that both the storage size and memory requirements for your geometry will decrease, so you should use as small data types as possible without sacrificing visual quality.

Consider the following case where you need vertices with the following information: coordinate, normal, uv, diffuse.

```
struct tVertex:
{
    GLfixed coord[3];
    GLfixed normal[3];
    GLfixed uv[2];
    GLuint diffuse;
};
```

This vertex uses $9 \times 4 = 36$ bytes per vertex.

Reducing some of the data to 16 bits:

```
struct tVertex
{
    GLshort coord[4];
    Glshort normal[4];
    GLshort uv[2];
    GLuint diffuse;
};
```

This vertex structure uses $10 \times 2 + 4 = 24$ bytes per vertex. A saving of 12 bytes per vertex might not sound like much at first, but it quickly adds up and gives a noticeable difference as you start pushing thousands of vertices every frame.

Note that in this case, the array size of the vertex coordinates and normals is one byte larger than it has to be. This is an optional speed optimization step as the GPU will in most cases be able to read the individual vertex elements faster if they are 32 bit aligned. The last byte in both the coordinate and normal array will simply be ignored.

Remember to use only larger vertex structures as needed. As an example, if dynamic lighting is not used on a certain object, it makes little sense to store normals in the vertex structure.

Organizing the Vertices

There is no equivalent of `glBegin()` and `glEnd()` that exist for OpenGL, so OpenGL ES assumes rendering will be done through vertex arrays only. While `glBegin()`/`glEnd()` is good for quick prototyping and testing, it is not something that is particularly useful because of performance reasons. So, not having these functions available is really no big deal.

OpenGL ES supports both nonindexed and indexed vertex arrays through the calls `glDrawArrays()` and `glDrawElements()`, respectively.

To get the best performance out of OpenGL ES, you want to minimize the number of duplicate vertices that are sent to the transformation stage of the graphics pipeline. Even if OpenGL ES transformation is fast (especially if supported in hardware), nothing can beat the speed of not transforming at all. In a standard nonindexed list of triangles, three vertices have to be stored for each triangle. For a quad made up of two triangles, you will need to store six vertices in which only four of those vertices are unique. In this particular case, you are letting OpenGL ES transform two unnecessary vertices. For big vertex arrays, the number of unnecessary vertices sent to the GPU for transformation can really add up. You want to avoid using nonindexed triangle lists for anything but very small vertex buffers, if at all.

So how do you avoid transforming unnecessary vertices? The answer is triangle strips or indexed triangle lists; both are very efficient, as all vertices in the array are unique. The method to choose is up to the application programmer, and there are advantages and disadvantages with both of them. The easiest one to use is indexed triangle lists. The only disadvantage is that you need to maintain an index list that describes the faces, but since the indices are normally only 16 bits each, it is not too much overhead and a good choice for organizing arbitrary geometry. Triangle strips do not need an index list, but they can be difficult to work with, as generating optimal strips from an arbitrary mesh tends to be difficult. In most cases, arbitrary objects need to be represented by many strips, resulting in more calls to `glDrawArrays()`.

Besides avoiding transforming duplicate vertices, it is equally important to avoid doing unnecessary calls to `glDrawArrays()` / `glDrawElements()`. Making fewer calls with many vertices at once is much faster than doing many calls with fewer vertices in each.

Vertex Buffer Objects for Even More Speed

Vertex arrays are great, but wouldn't it be better if you could avoid resending all your vertices from system RAM to the GPU each frame? Conveniently, there is an extension to OpenGL ES that allows you to do just this, and it is called `ARB_vertex_buffer_object`.

Tip

The vertex buffer object extension might not be available on all hardware, so it is important to query the OpenGL ES driver to find out if it is available before using it.

When creating vertex buffer objects, you tell the OpenGL ES driver how you intend to use it. These kinds of hints allow the driver to optimize the VBO, and it will store it wherever it thinks will best suit the application according to the hints provided. Static vertex buffer objects will most likely be stored in video memory and will therefore be very quick to render. If the vertices are never or very seldom going to be updated, then a static vertex buffer object is recommended. When vertices need to be updated frequently, a dynamic vertex buffer is the fastest one to use. Just make sure to update as many vertices sequentially as possible each time it is being updated. Vertex buffer objects are the best way of dealing with arrays of vertices on modern hardware. In *MotoGP2* for OpenGL ES 1.0, we saw a great performance increase from migrating most vertex arrays into vertex buffer objects. Since vertex buffer objects are not part of the standard OpenGL ES 1.0 specification and used through extensions, some devices might not support using them at all. When this happens, the game must provide a fallback code path that uses `glDrawArrays()` and `glDrawElements()` instead. Before using vertex buffer objects, your application should ask OpenGL ES if that extension is available on the device the application is running on. To find out what extensions the device has made available, you simply call the function `glGetString()` passing in `GL_EXTENSIONS` as an argument, which will return a pointer to a null terminated string that lists all the extensions available on the device. Each extension name is separated by a white space character. If no extensions are available at all, the function will return `NULL`. The following code example allows you to query OpenGL ES easily for a certain extension and will return true if the extension was available or false if it was not.

```
bool IsExtensionSupported( char *name)
{
    char *extensions;
    char *end;

    // Get string of extension names from OpenGL ES.
    // Return immediately if no extensions was found.
    extensions = (char*) glGetString( GL_EXTENSIONS);
    if(extensions == NULL)
        return false;
```

```
    // Find out if the name we are looking for is available
    end = extensions + strlen(extensions);
    while(extensions < end)
    {
        // Get the length of the current name in the
        // extensions string by looking for the next space.
        int length = strcspn(extensions, " ");

        // compare searched name against current name.
        if( strncmp( name, extensions, length) == 0)
        {
            // found the extensions so return true.
            return true;
        }

        // Prepare to compare the next name
        extensions += ( length + 1);
    }

    // Extension was not supported so return false
    return false;
}
```

Using the above function, it becomes very easy to find out if the device supports vertex buffer objects by having the following code in the initialization routing of the game:

```
bool haveVBO = IsExtensionSupported("GL_ARB_vertex_buffer_object");
```

Some examples of how to use vertex buffer objects will follow, and the structure and variables below will be shared for all the examples:

```
// Our example vertex structure
struct tVertex
{
    Glshort x,y,z
    Glshort padding;
    GLshort u,v;
    Gluint  color;
};
// Vertex and index buffer IDs
GLuint vertex_buffer;
GLuint index_buffer;

// Vertex and index data, these are assumed to be already
```

```
// filled with valid data before the example code snippets.
tVertex      *my_vertex_data;
GLsizei       my_vertex_count;
GLushort     *my_index_data;
GLsizei       my_index_count;
```

Before you can render using vertex buffer objects, you need to upload the vertices and indices to OpenGL ES. Doing this will copy the data you pass to it and put it inside video memory for extremely fast access by the graphics hardware.

```
void Init_Buffers()
{

  // Create and bind vertex buffer
  glGenBuffersARB( 1, &vertex_buffer);
  glBindBufferARB( GL_ARRAY_BUFFER_ARB, vertex_buffer);

  // Upload vertices to OpenGL ES buffer
  glBufferDataARB(
      GL_ARRAY_BUFFER_ARB,
      my_vertex_count * sizeof( tVertex),
      my_vertex_data,
      GL_STATIC_DRAW_ARB
    );

  // Create and bind index buffer
  glGenBuffersARB( 1, &index_buffer);
  glBindBufferARB( GL_ELEMENT_ARRAY_BUFFER_ARB, index_buffer);

  // Upload indices to OpenGL ES buffer
  glBufferDataARB(
      GL_ELEMENT_ARRAY_BUFFER_ARB,
      my_index_count * sizeof( GLushort),
      my_index_data,
      GL_STATIC_DRAW_ARB
    );
}
```

The code above creates a vertex buffer object from the data contained in my_vertex_data and stores the handle to the buffer in vertex_buffer.

glGenBuffersARB() generates one new vertex buffer object and writes the ID of the new buffer to vertex_buffer. glBindBufferARB() is used to bind the vertex buffer that was just created as the currently active one, and finally, glBufferDataARB() uploads the source data from my_vertex_data into the vertex buffer.

The `GL_STATIC_DRAW_ARB` flag specifies that no one is going to be modifying the data very often or at all. It then does the same thing again, but this time for the index buffer.

After something has been uploaded to an OpenGL ES buffer, OpenGL ES will always use its own local copy of that data so if the original data was dynamically allocated, it can safely be released after a call to `glBufferDataARB()`. Unless, of course, you want to modify the data and re-upload it during the game (for animations, perhaps), in which case you might want to hang on to it. Rendering the buffer is really quite simple as it is very similar to the way vertex arrays are rendered with just some minor changes.

Now let's look at the two methods for handling vertex data, one of which will use vertex buffer objects and one that will use the standard vertex arrays. Then we can compare them to find out what is different. First, let's start with how to render using vertex buffer objects:

```
void Draw_Buffers()
{
    // Bind vertex + index buffers
    glBindBufferARB( GL_ARRAY_BUFFER_ARB, vertex_buffer);
    glBindBufferARB( GL_ELEMENTS_ARRAY_BUFFER_ARB, index_buffer);

    // Enable client states needed for our vertex format
    glEnableClientState( GL_VERTEX_ARRAY);
    glEnableClientState( GL_TEXTURE_COORD_ARRAY);
    glEnableClientState( GL_COLOR_ARRAY);

    // Set up glPointers
    glVertexPointer( 3, GL_SHORT, sizeof(tVertex), 0);
    glTexCoordPointer( 2, GL_SHORT, sizeof(tVertex), 8);
    glColorPointer( 4, GL_UNSIGNED_BYTE, sizeof( tVertex), 12);

    // Draw the vertex buffer as an indexed triangle list
    glDrawElements(
        GL_TRIANGLES,
        my_index_count,
        GL_UNSIGNED_SHORT,
        0,
    );
}
```

A game should use vertex buffer objects if they are supported by the hardware but fall back to vertex arrays for hardware that doesn't support this extension. Implementing both of these paths is important to gain optimal performance on a wide range of platforms. The following code demonstrates how to render using vertex arrays.

```
void Draw_Arrays()
{
    // Enable client states needed for our vertex format
    glEnableClientState( GL_VERTEX_ARRAY);
    glEnableClientState( GL_TEXTURE_COORD_ARRAY);
    glEnableClientState( GL_COLOR_ARRAY);

    // Set up glPointers
    glVertexPointer( 3, GL_SHORT, sizeof( tVertex),
                        (void*) &my_vertex_data[0].x );

    glTexCoordPointer( 2, GL_SHORT, sizeof( tVertex),
                        (void*) &my_vertex_data[0].u );

    glColorPointer( 4, GL_UNSIGNED_BYTE, sizeof( tVertex),
                        (void*) &my_vertex_data[0].color );

    // Draw the vertex array as an indexed triangle list
    glDrawElements(
        GL_TRIANGLES,
        my_index_count,
        GL_UNSIGNED_SHORT,
        my_index_data
    );
}
```

Notice how similar both versions of the draw function are:

- Draw_Buffers() first needs to bind both the vertex buffer and index buffer that you are intending to use; this is something that is not done for vertex arrays.

- You enable the exact same client states for both versions of the draw function.

- The gl*Pointer() functions are almost identical except for one important difference. With vertex arrays, the last function argument is a *pointer to the start of the data,* while with vertex buffer objects, it is just the *offset in bytes to the start* of the data of the currently bound vertex buffer.

- Another slight difference is in glDrawElements(), where for vertex arrays you need to specify a *pointer to an array of indices* as a last argument to the function call. When using vertex buffer objects, this argument is the *start offset in bytes of the currently bound index buffer.*

One thing to keep in mind if you are using vertex buffer objects is that if you are going to mix rendering with vertex buffers and vertex arrays, then you will need to make sure that no vertex or index buffer is currently bound when you render vertex arrays. Unbinding a buffer is done by passing in an ID of 0. This example code unbinds the vertex and index buffers and allows the game to render by using vertex arrays:

```
glBindBufferARB( GL_ARRAY_BUFFER_ARB, 0);
glBindBufferARB( GL_ELEMENTS_ARRAY_BUFFER_ARB, 0);
```

After your application is done using a vertex buffer object, it has to be deleted and removed from video memory. Deleting the buffers in our example is easily done:

```
void Release_Buffers()
{
    glDeleteBuffersARB( 1, &vertex_buffer);
    glDeleteBuffersARB( 1, &index_buffer);
}
```

As you can see, using vertex buffer objects requires very little extra work to implement over vertex arrays. The minimal extra work involved supporting it and supplying fallback rendering through vertex arrays is well worth it, considering the big performance gain this extension provides.

While ARB functions are guaranteed to work on all hardware, provided that OpenGL ES exports the `"GL_ARB_vertex_buffer_object"` string to your application, some graphics hardware vendors might provide specialized functions that are vendor specific. Vendor-specific functions are usually faster and/or provide extra functionality over using ARB functions. Whether or not to support vendor-specific functions is a matter of how much time you want to spend on optimizing the rendering pipeline and how much performance gain it will give you by supporting it.

Here is the above example optimized for ATI. On devices that have ATI hardware, this will be much faster compared to using standard ARB vertex buffer objects.

After the code listings, we will go through and show how it is different from ARB vertex buffer objects.

```
void Init_Buffers_ATI()
{
  Glenum   idx_mode[1];
  Glenum   idx_type[1];
  Glsizei  idx_count[1];
  Glvoid*  idx_data[1];

  // Set up index buffer 0 of mesh-list.
  idx_mode[0]  = GL_TRIANGLES;
  idx_type[0]  = GL_UNSIGNED_SHORT;
  idx_count[0] = my_index_count;
  idx_data[0]  = (GLvoid*) my_index_data;
```

```
    // Create and bind vertex buffer
    glGenBuffersARB( 1, &vertex_buffer);
    glBindBufferARB( GL_ARRAY_BUFFER_ARB, vertex_buffer);

    // Upload vertices to graphics card
    glBufferDataATI(
        GL_ARRAY_BUFFER_ARB,
        my_vertex_count,
        sizeof( tVertex),
        my_vertex_count * sizeof( tVertex),
        GL_STATIC_DRAW_ARB
    );

    // Create and initialize index buffer(s)
    glMeshListATI( 1, idx_mode, idx_count, idx_type, idx_data);
}
```

Code-wise this is not hugely different from using ARB vertex buffer objects, but there are some differences that we should go through. `glBufferDataATI()` is almost identical to `glBufferDataARB()`, with the exception that you will now have to provide a more detailed description of how your vertices are structured. This allows the hardware to optimize how the data is going to be stored internally for better performance.

The biggest difference, however, is how index buffers work.

We are no longer creating a separate buffer for holding our indices, but instead we use the `glMeshListATI()` function call to embed the index information inside the same vertex buffer object as the vertices. A very neat thing about `glMeshListATI()` is that it allows you to specify multiple index buffers bound to the same vertex buffer object. In the example above, we are only creating one mesh-list with the `glMeshListATI()` function, but creating several is just a matter of passing in a number other than 1 as a first argument to the function.

Each mesh in the mesh-list is equivalent to a `glDrawElements()` call in terms of functionality, so this function effectively allows you to batch multiple `glDrawElements()` and index lists into one vertex buffer object (allowing the ATI hardware to optimize this in any way it sees fit before it comes to actually rendering it in the main loop).

```
void Draw_Buffers_ATI()
{
    // Bind vertex buffer object
    glBindBufferARB( GL_ARRAY_BUFFER_ARB, vertex_buffer);
```

```
    // Enable client states needed for our vertex format
    glEnableClientState( GL_VERTEX_ARRAY);
    glEnableClientState( GL_TEXTURE_COORD_ARRAY);
    glEnableClientState( GL_COLOR_ARRAY);

    // Set up glPointers
    glVertexPointer( 3, GL_SHORT, sizeof(tVertex), 0);
    glTexCoordPointer( 2, GL_SHORT, sizeof(tVertex), 8);
    glColorPointer( 4, GL_UNSIGNED_BYTE, sizeof( tVertex), 12);

    // Draw ATI mesh list
    glDrawVertexBufferObjectATI();
}
```

Again, very similar to our Draw_Buffers example that uses ARB functions, we no longer bind the index buffer since it is embedded in the vertex buffer object already through the glMeshListATI() function. And glDrawElements() has been replaced with the glDrawVertexBufferObjectATI() function. This function draws all mesh-lists for this vertex buffer object.

So, how can you recognize if the hardware supports vendor-specific functions? The most reliable way is to check if the functions you are going to call actually exist in the OpenGL ES driver. Functions might exist in the header file for OpenGL ES, but that does not necessarily mean that the functions exist in the driver. This is true for extensions and especially vendor-specific functions. Checking whether a function exists can be done through a call to eglGetProcAddress() passing in the name of the function. eglGetProcAddress() returns a function pointer that points to the function you are looking for, or if it doesn't exist, it will just return NULL.

The following code can be used to test if ATI-optimized vertex buffer objects are available on your platform:

```
bool IsVertexBufferATISupported()
{
    if( eglGetProcAddress("glBufferDataATI") == NULL)
        return false;
    if( eglGetProcAddress("glMeshListATI") == NULL)
        return false;
    if( eglGetProcAddress("glDrawVertexBufferObjectATI") == NULL)
        return false;
    return true;
}
```

You will need different code paths in the application, depending on what extensions are supported. This can be done using something as simple as an `if` or `switch` statement whenever something that depends on what method you are using is taking place or using class inheritance in C++ like this:

```
cRenderBase* CreateRenderer::CreateRenderer()
{
  cRenderBase* renderer;

  // First find out if vertex buffer objects exist at all.
  if( IsExtensionSupported("GL_ARB_vertex_buffer_object") )
  {
    // Test for vendor specific support
    if( IsVertexBufferATISupported() )
    {
      // Create a renderer for ATI VBO
      renderer = (cRenderBase*) new cRenderVBOATI();
    }
    else
    {
      // Create a renderer class for ARB VBO
      renderer = (cRenderBase*) new cRenderVBOARB();
    }
  }
  else
  {
    // Create a renderer class for vertex arrays
    renderer = (cRenderBase*) new cRenderVBONone();
  }
  return renderer;
}
```

This code checks for the best available way of rendering geometry for the particular device the application is running on. In this example, imagine a base rendering class and separate specific rendering classes that all inherit from the base class and overload the functions needed for rendering by using either vertex arrays, ARB vertex buffer objects, or ATI-optimized vertex buffer objects.

In C code you could achieve the same result by using function pointers and pointing them to different functions, depending on the hardware that the application is running on.

Only Draw What Can Be Seen

Only draw as many polygons as is absolutely necessary to ensure that you keep your frame rate up. It makes no sense to transform and rasterize a triangle if it is going to cover less than a pixel on the screen. Heavily detailed objects are good for close-up views, but as soon as those objects move further into the distance, a large number of triangles is not going to make any difference at all in visual quality because the triangles are too small to be seen. This is especially true on mobile devices that usually have very small screens compared to a TV set or a computer monitor. By assigning multiple versions of geometry at different polygon counts to each object, you can increase performance of a game by rendering the version that is most suitable, depending on how far away the object is.

How many different levels of detail to use depends on the amount of memory you can spare and how many different versions of the objects your artists (or tool) are able to produce. Usually, three levels are good—a high detail version of the object to use for close-up views, a normal detail version for objects a little bit further away, and finally a very low polygon version for objects that are far in the distance. By measuring the distance from the viewer to the center of the object, you can determine which version of the geometry to render for that object. Deciding when to switch between levels of detail totally depends on the size and polygon count of the geometry you have used and is subject to experimentation. You can also have the overall frame rate of the game affect the level of detail for your objects by switching the lower detail levels, just in case the frame rate is low in a particular scene.

More often than not, all objects in your scene graph will be spread out in the game world, some of them not in view, and some of them in view but at a different distance to the viewer. Those objects that are not visible at all should be recognized as early on as possible and simply ignored when your scene graph is rendered.

OpenGL ES clips all polygons for you, but this is on a per-triangle basis, and the process of submitting a whole lot of polygons to OpenGL ES isn't cheap. This is especially true if all polygons end up being thrown away in the end anyway due to them being offscreen. Not sending them to OpenGL ES at all would be faster indeed.

What you are going to want to do is to do a coarse test to see if any part of the whole object is inside the viewing frustum and only then render the object. A good and fast method is to test the bounding sphere of an object against the frustum and render the object only if it passes this test (see Figure 5.7).

Sphere against frustum tests are quick, so using this method will allow you to efficiently eliminate geometry that isn't visible anyway.

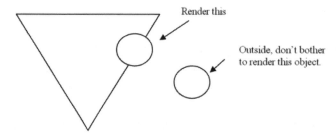

Figure 5.7 Frustum culling using bounding spheres.

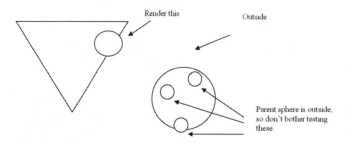

Figure 5.8 Faster frustum culling by grouping objects.

If you have a huge number of objects, you might even want to consider grouping those objects into a bounding sphere that covers them all (see Figure 5.8). This way you can test the big sphere that covers the whole group first and only if it is visible then go one level deeper and test the individual bounding spheres for each object. This big sphere might even be part of an even bigger sphere.

For static geometry, such as the game world, there exist many different algorithms for subdividing the world into smaller pieces. The main goal of all these algorithms is to provide a way to determine what is visible by culling away large chunks of geometry as quickly as possible. Each of the algorithms generally suits a different type of game. A game where your view is mostly blocked by corridors, such as indoor first-person shooters, will benefit from using a BSP tree algorithm. For outdoor environments, a quadtree or octree algorithm can help to subdivide the world effectively.

A quadtree surrounds the whole world with a single box; this box is then divided into four smaller boxes. Each of those smaller boxes is in turn divided into four smaller boxes and so on. The depth of this tree depends on your application; usually you are going to stop subdividing once the number of polygons in a box has reached a minimum value or the size of the box has reached a minimum size. You might also want to have a maximum depth value to stop from creating a tree that is too deep. Creating this tree is something that has to be done as a preprocessing step since it is too slow to be done at runtime; therefore, it is only really useful for static geometry, such as your game world. To render a quadtree, you simply traverse down the tree, starting with the root node that covers your whole world, and test each node for visibility. When a node is visible, continue down the tree checking the child nodes until you either come to a node that fails the frustum test or you reach the end of the tree, in which case you render all the polygons that have been assigned to that node. When a node is outside the viewing frustum, you stop traversing down that particular path, resulting in a quick cull of large chunks of geometry. There exist many different space subdivision algorithms, and the one to choose depends entirely on the application (and your preference).

An octree is very similar to a quadtree, except that it also splits the world in the Y axis, resulting in each node having eight child nodes instead of four. This is useful for games where you travel in the Y direction, as well as the X and Z, such as most platform games.

Space subdivision algorithms, no matter which one you use, can be used for any task that requires you to quickly find a small set of polygons from a mesh that originally contains a lot of polygons—not only for visibility testing. Another good use is for collision detection, where you want to minimize the number of per-triangle collision tests you have to perform when colliding with the world geometry. Subdividing the world gives you a quick and easy way to find a small set of polygons for performing your collision detection again instead of testing every polygon in the world, something that would be awfully slow.

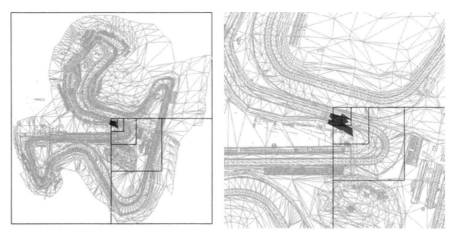

Figure 5.9 Quadtree algorithm used for collision detection.

Figure 5.9 shows a racetrack subdivided by using a quadtree algorithm. In this case, it is used for collision detection. For this particular point in the world, it took six bounding box to frustum tests to reach the end leaf of the tree, which narrowed down the list of potential collision polygons to 20 or so triangles from a world of several thousand triangles. Not bad, considering all it cost you was a couple of box collision tests, and it was definitely better than testing collisions against the whole world! The depth and width of the tree depend entirely on your application and what your world geometry looks like.

Minimize Render State Changes

When possible, you should always strive to reduce the number of render state changes you make during a frame. Render state changes are usually quite expensive, so if it is possible to sort the geometry by render state, a huge performance increase can be achieved. Setting texture ID is usually one of the more expensive render state changes, so sort by texture first and then the other render states.

So now let's talk about how we optimized rendering the motorbikes in the OpenGL ES version of *MotoGP2*. At first, we rendered all visible bikes one by one using `glDrawElements()`. Although this worked fine, it was clear that this area of the code could be heavily optimized. We ended up splitting the motorbike mesh up into one indexed triangle list per render state, which became body, front wheel, rear wheel, windscreen, and rider. On hardware that supports it, these triangle lists are stored in vertex buffer objects; otherwise vertex arrays are used.

When it comes to rendering the visible motorbikes, we rendered one bike part at a time, and we rendered this part for each visible bike before moving on to render the next bike part; the number of render state changes before and after optimizing can be seen here:

Before: with 4 bikes:

Vertex buffer object binds: $5 \times 4 = 20$

Texture binds: $4 \times 4 = 16$

After: with 4 bikes:

Vertex buffer object binds: 5

Texture binds: $3 + (1 \times 4) = 7$

Even when using only four bikes, you can already see a big difference in the number of render state changes we are performing, and once we start using more bikes, these numbers will show a huge difference. Now eight bikes would previously require 32 texture changes, but when our geometry is rendered sorted by texture, it requires only $3 + (1 \times 8)$ = 11 texture changes (assuming we use a unique texture for each rider).

The difference in frame rate is minimal when rendering eight bikes compared to just four on *MotoGP2* when running on hardware that supports vertex buffer objects.

A game usually makes use of many different textures, and let's face it, you don't really want to sacrifice the visual quality by removing lots of textures in order to save texture state changes.

A common and quite useful technique is to bunch lots of smaller textures into a single large texture. This texture, commonly called *texture page* (or *t-page*), will most likely be created by the artist while modeling the geometry or in some cases by a preprocessing tool. The main drawback with using texture pages is that it disables the ability to use repeating textures, so some textures still need to be unique. However, you are usually still left with a great number of textures that are suitable to be put into texture pages. The idea is to group textures that belong to vertices that can easily be batched into a single vertex array so that you can both reduce the number of texture state changes you are performing per frame and also reduce the number of vertex arrays you are submitting to OpenGL ES.

The OpenGL ES driver will generally do a bit of management every time a vertex array is being submitted to it, and because of this, sending fewer but larger vertex arrays is much better from a performance point of view than submitting many small vertex arrays. Deciding which textures to group and which texture pages to group them in will be different from case to case, and producing the optimal set of geometry + textures can be quite tricky. Sometimes, putting the same texture into different texture pages could improve the vertex list usage. A preprocessing tool could, in theory, be built to analyze your game geometry and texture usage, thereby outputting an optimal batch of texture pages and triangle arrays. At Climax Studios, we have a tool that does this, and it produces quite good results and saves us time trying to hand-optimize texture pages.

On-board video memory is another big factor to consider because this determines the number and size of textures you can use for rendering your scene. Best performance is achieved if all textures can reside on the on-board video memory and no textures are being swapped in and out between system memory and video memory. Once too much texture memory is being requested, textures will start to get swapped in and out from video memory as they are needed, and this can really hurt performance if it happens frequently inside the game loop.

If more texture space is needed for a level than what the device offers, then it makes good practice to try and spread out the textures in a way so that texture swapping happens seldom and only at controlled parts of the level. One part of the level might use one set of 2MB textures (if the machine has 2MB of video memory), and at another part of the level you start using other textures. This ensures that texture swapping will happen very seldom and in controlled points of the level but not all the time.

Running at a Constant Frame Rate

Mobile devices come in many different flavors. CPU speeds will vary across different devices and so will the speed of the graphics accelerator. In order to keep the game speed constant, independent of the device the game is running on, some care must be taken to avoid the game running too fast on powerful hardware and in slow motion on hardware that is underpowered.

To accomplish this task, you need a way to measure actual time, and the function to use depends on the operating system. For example, on Windows CE-based machines, this function is called GetTickCount() and will return the number of milliseconds since the operating system started. What time the function counts does not matter, as long as it counts time so that you can use it to count the time it took to execute one loop of the main game loop.

First, we are going to make sure the game does not run too fast on powerful devices by limiting the frame rate to 30 frames per seconds. Basically, 30 frames per seconds roughly equals 33 milliseconds per frame, so what we want to do is to detect if one full game loop took less than 33 milliseconds, and if so wait until we start the next frame. What frame rate to sync to is entirely up to you; 30fps is used in this example and is generally a good target frame rate to aim for on mobile games.

```
long time = GetTickCount();
while( game_running)
{
  // update physics
  Update_Physics();

  // render a frame
  Render_Frame();

  // Sync to 30fps
  while( (GetTickCount() - time) < 33 )
  {
    // wait here because we are running too fast.
  }

  // Reset time counter
  time = GetTickCount();
}
```

The example code above takes care of making sure that the game is never going to run too fast on powerful hardware. But what about hardware that is slower? In the current implementation, the game would go into slow-motion on a slower machine, which is less than ideal. The best solution is to skip frames when the machine is not keeping up to ensure that the game runs at a constant speed no matter what hardware the game runs on.

In order to achieve this, the physics code must be written to accept a scalar value telling it by how much to update the physics. If a character can normally move 1.2 meters per frame and the current physics scalar is 2.0, then the character should move 2.4 meters in that particular physics update.

Here is an example source code that does just this.

```
long time         = GetTickCount();
long time_elapsed = 33;
GLfixed frame_speed = (1 << 16);

while( game_running)
{
  // Update physics, take frame rate into consideration.
  Update_Physics( frame_speed);
```

```
  // Render a frame.
  Render_Frame();

  // Measure the time elapsed since last frame
  time_elapsed = GetTickCount() - time;

  // Sync to 30 fps.
  while( time_elapsed < 33 )
  {
    // Wait here because we are running too fast.
    time_elapsed = GetTickCount() - time;
  }

  // Calculate the frame speed to use in next frame
  // Value is in 16.16 fixed point format.
  frame_speed = (time_elapsed << 16) / 33;

  // Reset time counter.
  time = GetTickCount();
}
```

Using the methods described above, you will ensure that your game runs at a constant speed, no matter what the speed of the device is.

Handling Different Screen Resolutions

When making a game for mobile devices, chances are these devices will have different screen resolutions from each other. This is not as much of a problem since you are hardly ever working with absolute coordinates in your game. Different aspect ratios, however, can make your game look odd on devices that have a different screen aspect ratio than what the game was designed for. Most mobile devices have the screen laid out in portrait mode (such as 240×320), but some devices work in landscape mode (320×240).

Some of the most common screen resolutions on mobile phones and PDAs are:

- 320×240 (QVGA—Quarter VGA)
- 320×480 (HVGA—Half VGA)
- 640×480 (VGA)
- 176×144 (QCIF—Quarter CIF)
- 176×208 (Often found on Symbian phones, for example the Nokia N-Gage)

Running a game designed for one type of screen on a screen with a very different aspect ratio will make the game look squashed together and everything appear wider than it is supposed to. To avoid this kind of behavior, you must take the physical screen resolution into consideration when you create the projection matrix that you are going to use in the game.

The function for creating a projection matrix is called glFrustumx() and looks like this:

```
GLvoid glFrustumx( left, right, bottom, top, near, far);
```

This function is a bit tricky to master, and unfortunately the utility function gluPerspective() is not always available on OpenGL ES as it is on desktop OpenGL. The following code example gives you an easy-to-use function for setting up a projection matrix that works well on all screen resolutions. And note the code example is mostly in floating point math for clarity.

```
#define FIXED_SHIFT         ( 16 )
#define FIXED_ONE           ( 1 << FIXED_SHIFT )
#define FLOAT_TO_FIXED(x)   ( (x) * (FIXED_ONE) )
#define PI                  ( 3.14159 )

void SetProjectionMatrix(
        float screen_width, float screen_height,
        float FOV, float near_clip, float far_clip)
{
  float aspect = screen_width / screen_height;
  float top    = tan( (FOV * PI) / 360) * near_clip;
  float bottom = -top;
  float left   = aspect * top;
  float right  = -left;
  glMatrixMode( GL_PROJECTION);
  glFrustumx( FLOAT_TO_FIXED( left), FLOAT_TO_FIXED( right),
              FLOAT_TO_FIXED( top),  FLOAT_TO_FIXED( bottom),
              FLOAT_TO_FIXED( near_clip), FLOAT_TO_FIXED( far_clip) );
  glMatrixMode( GL_MODELVIEW);
}
```

The sample code above sets a projection matrix based on the screen dimensions of the device, the desired field-of-view, and the near and far clip planes your application wants to use.

The FOV variable determines the vertical field-of-view; horizontal field-of-view will vary depending on the aspect ratio of the device. A 90 degree field-of-view is a good base value that works quite well to start with. What near and far clip values to use is entirely up to each application and depends on the dimensions of your geometry. We will use near = 1 and far = 1000 for this example.

Using the previous example code, you can easily set up a working projection matrix for any screen dimension, and geometry will look like it should without being deformed by different screen aspect ratios, for example:

320 by 240 display: `SetProjectionMatrix( 320, 240, 90, 1, 1000 );`

240 by 320 display: `SetProjectionMatrix( 240, 320, 90, 1, 1000 );`

Now that you have a way to set the projection matrix, you are going to need to find out the screen dimensions of the device itself. The operating system is responsible for exporting the function to give you the screen resolution of the device.

As an example, you can get the screen resolution of a Windows CE-based device like this:

```
RECT winrect;
GetWindowRect( GetDesktopWindow(), &winrect);
int screen_width = (winrect.right - winrect.left);
int screen_height = (winrect.bottom - winrect.top);
```

And then finally, initialize the projection matrix:

```
SetProjectionMatrix( screen_width, screen_height, 90, 1, 1000);
```

Geometry and Texture Animation

The following sections touch on some details to consider when doing geometry and texture animation. While this is more of an overview, there are still some good points to keep in mind when doing geometry and texture animation with OpenGL ES.

Geometry Animation

Static geometry is nice, but in almost every game there are some objects that absolutely have to be animated. A platform game with sword fighting wouldn't be very fun to watch if the main character (and enemies!) were just static figures. The two most common methods of animating geometry are either through morphing meshes or using skeletal animation. Both have different pros and cons, and it is up to the developer to find out which method suits the project (and the platform) best.

Mesh Morphing

Each key frame of an animation sequence holds vertex coordinates and normals for all vertices of the mesh. Animation is done by interpolating each vertex linearly between two key frames in order to achieve smooth animation. This method is the easiest for the CPU because all that is needed is a linear interpolation for each vertex. The negative side is that key frame information has a very large memory footprint.

Vertex Skinning/Bone Blending

With this technique, there is no need to store the mesh multiple times, which gives it a much smaller memory footprint than mesh morphing, described previously. The mesh is stored in its bind pose only once. Each key frame of the animation holds a matrix for each bone in the skeleton (called a *matrix palette*). Each vertex in the actual mesh holds weighting information indicating how much each bone and matrix affects it. Because the animation data is stored per-bone rather than per-vertex, the key frame information has a very small memory footprint. Another neat thing is that it is easy to combine several animation sequences to form more complex animations. Rag-doll physics is another possibility in the future when mobile devices have grown a bit stronger. So you have much more control over the animations compared to morphing, but the added capability also means it can be more CPU intensive.

OpenGL ES 1.0 does not support doing any of the above methods, so it has to be done in software using the CPU. Depending on the platform, either choice might work well. If your target platform has lots of memory but a slow CPU, then definitely go for morphing. When the opposite is true, then skeletal animation might be the better choice. Unfortunately, mobile devices such as phones are usually relatively limited in both CPU and memory, although this is changing very rapidly, and more memory and faster CPUs are being put into mobile devices.

Tip

Support for vertex skinning has been added in OpenGL ES 1.1 via the `OES_matrix_palette` extension. See Chapter 9, "The Future," for details.

Skeletal animation is by far the most flexible way of animating geometry because it offers much more control than by just morphing a mesh from one stage to another. For example, you could quite easily combine several animations to form a more complex animation. In a platform game, you could combine the walk animation with the sword-slash animation to have the main character fight while walking. Doing this with mesh morphing would require a completely separate walk-and-slash animation (and remember that animation data for morphing has a large footprint!).

Even when using a separate animation sequence for walk-and-slash, you might get into sync problems between the different animations; just changing the current animation from walk to walk-and-slash could result in the animation skipping unnaturally. You can fix this by letting the walk animation finish a loop before changing sequence, but then the player might experience a lag between hitting the action button and seeing the animation onscreen. Combining animations when using skeletal animation is easy, since the only thing you need to do is to generate a new matrix palette by getting the current key frame for each of the sequences that you want to combine. Another cool thing is that it becomes incredibly easy to control individual parts of the body in code. For example, if you want a character to turn its head and look in a certain direction, this is easily done just by applying a rotation matrix on the bone used for the character's neck.

One problem that you will face until more direct support for animations is added into OpenGL ES is that you are going to have to resubmit all your vertices to OpenGL ES each time that you animate them. This takes away much of the benefit of using vertex buffer objects as discussed earlier. It is very likely that future versions of OpenGL ES and mobile 3D hardware will add more support for animation either by adding support for vertex shaders or by adding more specialized extensions, such as `ARB_matrix_palette` and `ARB_vertex_blend`, which both already exist on desktop OpenGL. Once this happens, then skeletal animation will be very feasible on mobile devices, as the GPU will do the hard work for you, and there will be little reason to use mesh morphing. Until then, mesh morphing is still a valid choice because of its ease of use on the CPU.

Figure 5.10 shows an example of vertex skinning and bone blending.

Texture Animation

An easy way of animating a texture is to bind a new texture to each frame when rendering a face. If you are going to use the same animated object multiple times, then unless the frames of the objects are synched, this would mean a texture change for each object.

Figure 5.10 The character Tal from the game *Sudeki* is being prepared for when OpenGL ES starts supporting accelerated vertex skinning/bone blending.

Consider the case where you have a smoke special effect using many animated billboards. Although animating the billboards by simply binding a texture before drawing each billboard works fine, it is not very efficient as you are going to be doing a lot of texture state changes. So how can you perform more efficient texture animation? The answer lies in using texture pages.

If you lay out all the frames of animations in a grid inside one large texture, you can simply activate this texture once and then draw all of your smoke billboards without wasting performance changing the texture each frame. In order to get the actual animations happening, you can use the texture matrix that is built into OpenGL ES. Before rendering a billboard, you simply create a translation matrix and bind it as the current texture matrix.

Example:

A texture page has been set up for holding four subtextures in a 2×2 grid, as shown in Figure 5.11.

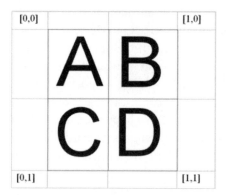

Figure 5.11 Texture page with four subtextures.

To activate the top right frame of the texture, you would simply do this:

```
#define FIXED_ONE (1 << 15)

GlMatrixMode( GL_TEXTURE);
glIdentity();
glTranslatex( (FIXED_ONE>>1), 0, 0);

// Now Render the geometry…
```

All texture UV coordinates processed after this code will be translated in the V direction by 0.5.

The billboard triangle strip shown in Figure 5.12 is set up for the example above and will be displaying the upper-left part of the texture (texture UV coordinates are shown):

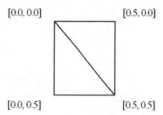

Figure 5.12 Billboard triangle strip (UV coordinates shown).

This technique can be useful for particle effects, such as smoke, where you are going to want to use many animated billboards. In such cases, you can simply bind the texture once and then render all the billboards instead of binding a new texture for each billboard as you render them.

In fact, the only thing that changes for each billboard is the texture matrix and the modelview matrix, so the geometry can be set up only once and then as you loop through all the billboards you want to render, you just have to change the matrices.

Skyboxes

Skyboxes are a good way to help players immerse themselves into the game world. Skyboxes help to enclose the game world and provide a way to draw things that are very far away, such as the sky and a mountain range far in the distance. Figure 5.13 shows an example of what a texture used for a skybox looks like.

Even though the name suggests a box, it does not have to take the shape of a box. Another nice way of drawing the sky can be achieved by using a half sphere, commonly called a *sky dome*, as shown in Figure 5.14.

No matter what shape the environment mesh takes, be it a sky box or a dome, the procedure of rendering it will be the same. To make it convincing and give the players the illusion that they are immersed inside the world, the sky mesh should be rendered so that its center is always at the position of the camera. The box will follow the player around, always surrounding him as he moves around the game world.

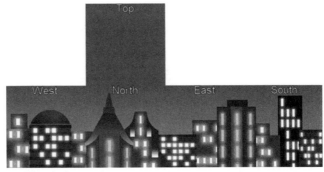

Figure 5.13 Sample texture page used to texture the inside of a skybox.

The procedure of rendering the box goes something like this:

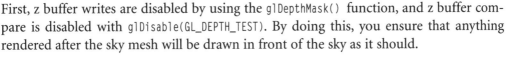

Figure 5.14 Sky dome mesh, shown in wireframe and textured on the inside.

```
glDepthMask( GL_FALSE);
glDisable( GL_DEPTH_TEST);

glMatrixMode( GL_MODELVIEW);
glLoadIdentity();
glRotatex ( player_yaw, 0, (1<<16), 0);

Render_Skybox_Mesh();

glDepthMask( GL_TRUE);
glEnable( GL_DEPTH_TEST);
```

First, z buffer writes are disabled by using the `glDepthMask()` function, and z buffer compare is disabled with `glDisable(GL_DEPTH_TEST)`. By doing this, you ensure that anything rendered after the sky mesh will be drawn in front of the sky as it should.

Tip

It's not actually necessary to disable z buffer writes if the depth test is disabled. By definition, the z buffer is never updated while depth testing is disabled.

After this, the modelview matrix is reset to identity, and then in this example it is rotated along the Y axis to match the direction the player is looking at.

Next, the skybox or dome geometry is rendered to the screen. The center coordinate of the box should be at (0, 0, 0) of the local coordinate system of the mesh.

After the sky mesh has been rendered, the z buffer is re-enabled again, as you are likely to want to use it when rendering the level geometry and objects.

What About 2D Games?

There will always be a market for 2D games, and the arrival of 3D accelerators for the mobile space does not necessarily spell doom for all 2D games. In fact, the arrival of graphics hardware accelerators can quite easily be taken advantage of to create very visually impressive 2D games with a graphics quality that it has not been possible to achieve before on mobile devices.

So how do you draw sprites with OpenGL ES 1.0? Easy, you just set up an orthogonal projection matrix and draw a sprite using two triangles.

Consider the example in Figure 5.15.

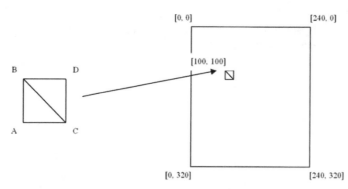

Figure 5.15 A 2D view with one sprite onscreen.

In order to render sprites in an ordinary 2D fashion, you must first set up an orthogonal projection matrix, which is done with a few simple OpenGL ES function calls. Unless your application needs to switch between different projection matrices, such as switching from 3D and 2D rendering modes, this can be done just once when your application starts.

```
// Set up a Orthogonal projection matrix for drawing 2D "sprites"
glSetMatrixMode( GL_PROJECTION);
glLoadIdentity();
glOrthox( 0, 0, 240, 320, 0, 1);
```

Now that the correct projection matrix has been set, you can simply draw two triangles to make a sprite.

Table 5.1 Sprite Coordinates

Texture	x	y	x	Description
A	100	110	0	bottom left
B	100	100	0	top left
C	110	110	0	bottom right
D	110	100	0	top right

Alternatively, instead of setting the actual world coordinates in the vertex data, you could represent the top left of the sprite with (0,0) and the bottom right of the sprite with (10,10) and use the modelview matrix to transform the sprite to the correct location on the screen like this:

```
// Translate sprite to the correct location on the screen
glSetMatrixMode( GL_MODELVIEW);
glLoadIdentity();
glTranslatex( 100, 100, 0);
```

The function declaration for glOrtho() is:

```
GLvoid glOrthox( GLfixed left, GLfixed right, GLfixed top, GLfixed bottom, GLfixed
znear, GLfixed zfar)
```

left and *top* are your upper left coordinates of the screen.

right and *bottom* are the bottom right coordinates of the screen.

znear and *zfar* are the near and far depth coordinates of the screen.

An important thing to keep in mind here is that the actual pixel resolution of the screen has no effect at all on what you set your projection matrix to. In our example above, the coordinate (240,320) will always represent the bottom-left point of the screen no matter what the actual pixel resolution of the device is.

Another interesting note about glOrtho() is that it allows you to set up the depth range of the screen. Unlike a normal projection matrix, drawing a sprite to different Z coordinates will not transform your vertices because you are working in a pure 2D projection matrix. It will, however, make sure that the triangles will be displayed in the correct depth order if the z buffer is enabled, which means you get depth-sorted sprites almost "for free" (unless you are drawing alpha-blended sprites, in which case you will need to depth-sort them manually before rendering them to the screen by drawing the sprite with highest Z coordinate first).

Special effects, such as alpha blending scaled sprites and rotated sprites, used to be very expensive, if not totally unfeasible to perform on past mobile devices. These effects now come almost for free with OpenGL ES accelerated hardware. All that is required to rotate and/or scale a sprite is to set up a different modelview matrix before rendering the sprite, and the graphics hardware will take care of the rest.

To increase the triangle throughput, you can batch the sprites together and try to render as many of them as possible between changing any render states. This is the reason why the previous example suggested using world coordinates directly in the vertex data. If you were to translate every sprite separately, you would need to set up the modelview matrix and render two triangles for each and every sprite.

A better solution performance-wise is to allocate a big vertex and index list and draw all or most of your sprites in one single `glDrawElements()` call. Just before it is time to render the sprites, you would loop through all your sprites and update your vertex and index list accordingly. Once this is done, you simply set up your `glVertexPointer()` and `glTexturePointer()` and call `glDrawElements()`, passing in the number of indices for the sprites you want to render, and all your sprites will get rendered through that single call.

```
struct tSpriteVertex
{
    GLshort x, y, z;
    GLshort u, v;
};


tSpriteVertex     my_sprite_vertices[ MAX_SPRITES * 4];
Glushort          my_sprite_indices[  MAX_SPRITES * 6];

while(1)
{
    // game logic
    // draw background layers
    // fill my_sprite_vertices with data according to
    // which sprites are visible on the screen
    int num_sprites = UpdateMySpriteData();

    // Set up pointers to for our sprite data
    glEnableClientState( GL_VERTEX_ARRAY);
    glEnableClientState( GL_TEXTURE_COORD_ARRAY);

    glVertexPointer
      (
        3,
```

```
          GL_SHORT,
          sizeof(tSpriteVertex),
          &my_sprite_vertices[0].x
       );

   glTexCoordPointer
       (
          2,
          GL_SHORT,
          sizeof(tSpriteVertex),
          &my_sprite_vertices[0].u
       );

   // Draw all of our sprites
   glDrawElements(  GL_TRIANGLES,        // Indexed triange list
                    (num_sprites * 6),   // number of indices
                    GL_UNSIGNED_SHORT,   // data type of indices
                    my_sprite_indices    // vertex array
                 );

}
```

This method assumes that all the sprites use the same texture page, which is not always going to be the case. Most likely, you will need to keep a couple of large vertex and index lists, one for each texture page, and render each list one after another. Any scaled or rotated sprites will need to be rendered individually since the modelview matrix has to change for each of those sprites. Drawing the sprites batched in this way will make sure you can draw a very impressive number of sprites to the screen.

Summary

Hopefully, you'll agree that finally having a proper 3D API, and especially such a well established one as OpenGL in the mobile space, is going to work wonders for mobile gaming. With the introduction of hardware accelerated 3D and the OpenGL ES API, it won't be long until you start seeing console-quality games on mobile phones! Properly optimized, these devices will be incredible, considering their small size and relatively low power.

We have covered the most important differences between console and mobile development and provided some good tips on how to optimize your game for mobile devices using OpenGL ES and hope this will help you, whether or not you are incorporating OpenGL ES into your existing game engine or writing your engine from scratch.

For further reading, we recommend the book *Real-Time Rendering* by Tomas Akenine-Möller and Eric Haines (ISBN: 1568811829). This book covers many game-related programming topics in great detail.

Obviously, the Internet is also a great resource to learn more about game programming topics. OpenGL ES is still a bit too new to be covered in much depth, but as it is very similar to its desktop counterpart, much can be learned from looking at OpenGL game programming Web sites, and source code examples can usually be ported to OpenGL ES with very little hassle.

Here are some good Web sites to get you started:

GameDev.net (General game development news and forums):

http://www.gamedev.net

NeHe Production (OpenGL tutorials):

http://nehe.gamedev.net

FlipCode (General game development news and forums):

http://www.flipcode.com

The Symbian OS Web site:

http://www.symbian.com

The BREW development environment:

http://www.brewdeveloper.com

The OpenGL ES Web site:

http://www.opengles.org

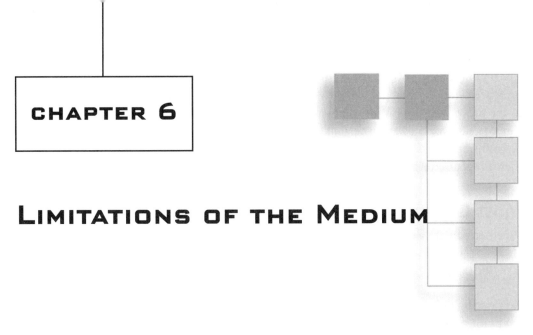

CHAPTER 6

LIMITATIONS OF THE MEDIUM

This chapter will cover some of the more common software and hardware limitations found in mobile devices. We will cover current OpenGL ES software implementations and commercial OpenGL ES graphics hardware. With new OpenGL ES platforms becoming available, it is important to learn how to optimize your game code for software and hardware. This chapter covers such optimizations and some performance tips and tricks to consider when developing your game.

In this chapter we'll cover the following information:

- An overview of current software and hardware limitations
- Graphics hardware acceleration for OpenGL ES
- How to optimize for OpenGL ES software implementations
- General performance tips and other platform limitations

Introduction

From low- to high-end cell phones, 3D gaming has been met with several software and hardware limitations. Most 3D games on the market today were developed using software-only rendering engines that contain a small set of highly tuned rendering APIs. Some of these 3D games look good and run well. So 3D gaming is a reality today with polygon counts of 15–30K triangles/sec and well over 100K pixel fill rates. Not too bad for software-only 3D game engines. With faster CPUs and increased memory on future phones, these engines will see a small increase in performance. Most current games run at relatively low resolutions (e.g., 220×176), using mostly smooth-shaded triangles and nearest texture filtering. These capabilities, while impressive for the devices in question, haven't been enough to excite commercial game developers about creating 3D games for these devices. That is about to change in a very big way.

The main problem with all these custom engines is that if vendors do start using 3D hardware acceleration, then game developers will have to port their engines from one device to the other each time. With the new OpenGL ES standard, both software and hardware vendors can work toward one goal of providing a common set of graphics APIs that will be common across all platforms. Even with a common standard set of APIs for graphics, there are still several limitations that you'll find on a mobile platform.

Most Common Limitations

Whether you are working on a low tier phone or a high-end mobile platform, there will always be limitations that will have to be considered when developing 3D games.

The following are the most common limitations found today on most mobile platforms:

No floating point processor: The main reason most mobile devices don't possess a floating point processor is because of power consumption. Nobody wants to play a game and have their battery die after a few minutes. Floating point data types can still be used, but they are extremely slow because they use a software-only implementation of real number data types. So avoid using them whenever possible. You should use fixed point data types and transformations instead for an increase in speed. The only disadvantage is that you may lose precision and accuracy when performing transformations and other fixed point math operations. Please refer to Chapter 4, "A Fixed Point Math Primer," for more information on fixed point arithmetic.

Limited CPU MIPS: Most handheld platforms run at slow clock speeds. For example, the ARM9 used in many commercial phones is clocked at 153–225MHz. In the next three years, mobile processors' speeds reaching 1GHz will appear. Until then there are limited MIPS available for your game, and you have to be very cautious not to burn extra CPU cycles, as that will directly affect your performance. Using software-only rendering engines, you lose a lot of MIPS to the graphics processing that could be used by the game itself.

Limited memory: Even today, memory is still at a premium for mobile phones. Most vendors will opt for the cheaper memory to save their bottom line. Memory bandwidth is also slower than you might expect with rates of 75MHz on average. Later in the chapter, you'll find a more detailed section on what to expect for memory configurations.

Low bus bandwidth: Slow system bus speeds will have a huge impact on vertex/polygon count and fill rates. Simply put, data sent from the CPU to the graphics engine either in software or hardware will be a bottleneck for the most part because of the bus bandwidth. Graphics vendors will optimize this as much as possible, but the developers should at least be aware of this limitation when performing certain operations, such as the data types used for vertex arrays. This will be covered in greater detail later in the chapter.

LCD screen size: Although the resolution on handheld devices is improving (with QVGA common now and HVGA appearing by next year), the screen sizes are still small. Even with a decent resolution, you, as a developer, should always be aware of different resolutions for different devices. If you want your game to run on several phones in the market, then you will almost certainly need to support multiple screen resolutions. You should design for a flexible aspect screen ratio and reduced color depth and color formats. A screen size of a few inches by a few inches also greatly limits the types of games that look good and are playable. There will be many things that might not even be worth adding to your game—such as very high-resolution textures—since they will add very little noticeable difference, at the cost of a large increase in your game's memory footprint.

Key pad and buttons: The controls and buttons available on most mobile devices are very limited. They are gradually improving, and we'll soon see devices with minijoysticks, better keypads, and additional game buttons, but for now, there should still be great consideration about what keys to use for your game. The controls should be mapped in a way that's consistent with other games and applications (e.g., using the exit key to leave the game). Care should also be taken not to map controls in such a way that playing the game will be uncomfortable due to hand and finger position on small devices.

Limited battery life: Battery life will always be a main concern. No one wants to play a game that drains his battery completely after only a few minutes. Great game play with high-quality visual effects and assets is always a constant trade-off when considering game play length. How long will people play your game before they have to close their phones and do something else? Always keep that in mind when considering game play length. All of the above limitations will affect battery life, some worse than others. It is always a balancing act when using CPU and memory cycles to create a game and trying not to kill your phone battery. Fortunately, batteries are continually improving, so this limitation will be reduced with time.

3D graphics hardware: 3D graphics hardware isn't a limitation but rather has an impact on the other limitations listed above. The more work that is done by dedicated graphics hardware, the more resources will be available for other things, such as AI, physics, special effects, and so on. However, 3D hardware also introduces its own share of issues that will have to be addressed. We will cover how to optimize and increase your performance using 3D graphics hardware in the next couple of sections of this chapter. There are always hardware limitations and features that are more optimized than others, so it's recommended that game developers read and understand the documentation provided by hardware vendors.

Getting To Know Your Platform

With so many new phones on the market that will be supporting 3D with software and hardware, the first thing you need to understand are the specifications of your platform. One thing to remember when designing your game is that not all platforms are created equal. The following information provides a general idea of what some current platform specifications look like with graphics hardware added to them.

Emerging high-end cell phones will likely support the following:

- ARM9 processor (400MHz)
- 32-bit SDRAM @ 100MHz
- 240×320 display
- 3D graphics hardware (e.g., ATI IMAGEON 2300 with 8MB of external frame-buffer, or some other 3D hardware)
- 30–60fps QVGA+ gaming
- Highly detailed 3D models (8K–10K polygons per frame)
- Texture footprint: 4–6MB
- Vertex buffer object footprint: 1–2MB

The following will be typical configurations for mainstream cell phones:

- ARM9 processor (100–200MHz)
- 16-bit/32-bit SDRAM @ 75MHz
- 176×220 to 240×320 display
- 3D graphics hardware (e.g., ATI IMAGEON 2302 with 2MB of framebuffer, QUALCOMM MSM6550 GRP, or some other 3D hardware)
- 30fps QVGA+ gaming
- Detailed 3D models (4K–5K polygons per frame)
- Texture footprint: Less than 1.5MB
- Vertex buffer object footprint: 200–300KB

One thing to note in viewing these specs is that many next-generation cell phones will have two CPUs—one for applications and one for the modem software. Vendors are already looking at 1GHz processors and even more memory with advanced 3D graphics features. In this chapter, we are only focusing on optimizations for current platforms supporting OpenGL ES and not what might be coming in the future.

For the most part, this chapter covers optimization and performance tips that can be applied to any mobile platform that has 3D graphics hardware. There are several 3D graphics cores and external chips that will start showing up in commercial phones very soon. The following 3D graphics hardware cores are worth mentioning because they already have or are working toward becoming OpenGL ES 1.0 compliant. Some of these handheld graphics chips include NVIDIA GSHARK PLUS and GoForce 3D, ARM MBX 3D graphics core, QUALCOMM's MSM6550 chipset supporting a 3D graphics core, and ATI IMAGEON™ 2300 series. We can't talk about every piece of mobile graphics hardware in detail, so we have focused on the ATI IMAGEON 2300 series and will briefly talk about the QUALCOMM MSM6550 series chipset that will be supporting OpenGL ES 1.0–compliant accelerated graphics hardware. The ATI W2300 and QUALCOMM's MSM6550 will be the first chips available in the mass market that will support OpenGL ES hardware. The ARM MBX core will also be available and should start showing up in phones early next year. There are other companies providing 3D graphics hardware that will be coming into the mobile market as well, so find out what graphics hardware is supported before you begin development. As you'll soon find out, every graphics hardware configuration will support different features and have different limitations than others.

For more information on NVIDIA GSHARK and GoForce 3D series and the ARM MBX core, visit the following Web sites:

http://www.gshark.com and http://www.nvidia.com

http://www.arm.com

For more information on other 3D graphics hardware supporting OpenGL ES visit the Khronos Group Web site: **http://www.opengles.org**.

The ATI IMAGEON™ 2300 Series 3D Graphics Processor

The IMAGEON 2300 is an OpenGL ES 1.0–compliant graphics processor that can render 1 million fully featured triangles per second while providing a fill rate of up to 100 million pixels per second (operating at 100MHz).

The IMAGEON 2300 delivers the following features:

1. Vertex Transform Engine

   - Vertex Transformation Performance: 1.5M vertices/sec
   - Accelerate both vertex and texture coordinate transforms
   - Support for "byte, short, fixed, and float" vertex and texture coordinate data formats. Byte and short data types are needed to keep the memory footprint down and also reduce the bus bandwidth required to send vertices to the graphics processor.

2. Triangle Setup Engine

   - Performance: 1M triangles/sec
   - Triangle setup with backface culling
   - Support for strips, fans, and triangle lists

3. Pixel Pipeline

   - 100M pixels/sec
   - 32 bit internal pixel pipeline

- Single Texture Pipeline with mipmapped bilinear and trilinear filtering, perspective correct texturing, OpenGL ES 1.0 texture combine modes
- Alpha blending, specular color, fog
- 16 bit z, 16 bit pixel buffers

4. 3D Engine

- Hardware 3D floating point pipeline
- Complete geometry process and pixel rendering pipeline
- OpenGL ES texture combine modes, mipmapping
- 8/16-bpp destination, 8/16/32-bpp texture, palletized texture
- Per-pixel perspective correction
- Bilinear and trilinear texture filtering
- Dithering, fog, alpha blending

5. Framebuffer

- Double-buffer support for up to QVGA (320×240) resolution
- 2MB–8MB of SDRAM, 384KB of SRAM

The IMAGEON 2300 handles the system limitations by implementing the following:

1. Native support for byte and short vertex and texture coordinates. For a majority of games the pretransformed vertex and texture coordinate data can be stored as shorts. For textures this means enabling an appropriate texture scale matrix. As an example, the OpenGL ES versions of both *GLQuake* and *MotoGP2* use GL_SHORT for the vertex and texture coordinate data. This also reduces CPU memory required to store the geometry and bus bandwidth.

2. Bus bandwidth requirements can be reduced significantly by caching the geometry. Caching geometry also requires a hardware transform engine. Extensions have been added to ATI's OpenGL ES 1.0 implementation to support this.

All of the above hardware improvements result in a high-performance gaming mobile device that is capable of real-time game play with excellent content quality and very low power consumption. In fact, if the features accelerated by the IMAGEON 2300 were implemented using only the ARM processor, the power consumption numbers for the ARM would be at least five times greater than the IMAGEON 2300.

IMAGEON 2300 Integrated Architecture offers a hardware floating point pipeline. This offloads the main CPU so games can support faster game loops with more advanced features like AI, physics, better character animations, and so on. With a fully-supported floating point pipeline, the precision errors with transforms and conversions are no longer a main concern.

The main graphics core has a 3D and 2D graphics engine plus JPEG and MPEG support, power management, primary and secondary display management, video capture, and a small 384KB embedded SRAM. On the substrate is also an optional low-power SDRAM, which is 2MB for the W2302 version of the chip. The W2300 supports up to 8MB of external memory. The W2300 has a CPU interface compatible with major manufacturers, notably for QUALCOMM's MSM6000 series chipsets.

The W2300 has been designed with low power consumption in mind. It implements several power-saving technologies that also found their way into the mainstream PC graphics solution. For example, the ATI RADEON X800 consumes a few watts less than the 9800 XT, based off some design changes that came from the W2300 development.

The IMAGEON 2300 series is a set of hardware 3D solutions dedicated to making console-like 3D games on mobile phone a reality. This new mobile 3D graphics processor will give the video game industry the ability to broaden its offerings into the mobile 3D gaming market.

The screenshots in Figure 6.1 are from *MotoGP2* ported to IMAGEON 2300 OpenGL ES and running on an ARM processor.

Figure 6.1 *MotoGP2*—240 x 320 x 16bpp screen resolution.

Optimizing Games for OpenGL ES Hardware

Now let's really talk about the hardware. We will walk through the 3D graphics pipeline and examine what features offer the best optimization opportunities. Then we will highlight the features and challenges of cell phone platforms and how the IMAGEON 2300 solution handles the most common limitations.

With accelerated graphics hardware, higher polygon counts for models and advance texturing are now possible. There are no more extra polygon reductions or additional texture-tweaking steps using graphics hardware. This means smoother control and more fluid animations with very high image quality in fully immersive environments.

With the advancement in electronics, 3D mobile graphics processors have very low power consumption with smaller die footprint (less silicon means cheaper parts as well).

The 3D Graphics Pipeline

In order to better understand how game specific features map to the way the OpenGL API works, you have to understand the hardware 3D graphics pipeline. Figure 6.2 is a simplified diagram of the OpenGL ES 3D pipeline. On the left, you'll see the vertex world where 3D geometry is processed, and on the right you'll see the pixel world where pixel fragments are analyzed and stored in the final framebuffer.

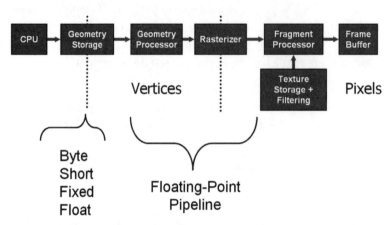

Figure 6.2 The OpenGL ES 3D pipeline.

The *CPU block* is where data is transferred in and out of the graphics pipeline.

The *Geometry Storage block* is where geometry is temporarily stored for processing. It lies partly in the device driver and partly in the graphics chip's internal storage. It can accept the following types: byte, short, fixed point, and floating point. The hardware does the conversion to floating point natively for all types. This saves a lot of system and graphics memory and ultimately bandwidth requirements for pushing the data down the pipeline.

The *Geometry Processor block* walks triangle arrays and transforms the vertices. It also converts the various formats into its internal floating point representation.

The *Rasterizer block* walks each triangle's edges and inner area, and it interpolates values on a pixel level.

The *Fragment Processor block* analyzes the resulting pixel fragments, shades and colors them, and then puts them in the framebuffer.

The *Texture block* performs texture lookup functions.

Finally, the *Framebuffer block* stores the resulting picture and makes it available for the LCD device.

The CPU

The CPU is the beginning of the 3D graphics pipeline and is responsible for transferring geometry data in and out of the graphics pipeline. Figure 6.3 highlights the CPU block in the 3D pipeline.

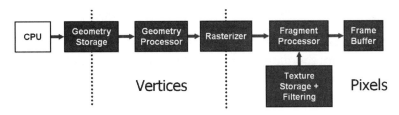

CPU to RAM Bandwidth: 600 MB/sec (32bits @ 150 MHz)

GPU-to-SDRAM bandwidth: 400 MB/sec (32 bits @ 100MHz)

CPU-to-GPU Bandwidth (discrete solution): ~10 MB/sec

-- PLATFORM-DEPENDENT ! --

Figure 6.3 The CPU block.

This is the chip's connection to the outside world. As discussed earlier, QUALCOMM and ATI plan to offer a discrete solution and an integrated solution. We show here the discrete solution's performance stats, but obviously those numbers will change with the introduction of the MSM7000 series; that solution will integrate the IMAGEON 2300 series. Performance data and availability of this part will be announced by QUALCOMM at a later date.

Geometry Storage

The geometry storage block straddles between the device driver memory and graphics memory. It is where geometry is stored in preparation for processing.

Figure 6.4 highlights the geometry storage block.

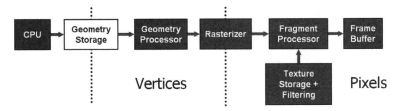

Figure 6.4 The geometry storage block.

The IMAGEON 2300 implements Vertex Buffer Objects (VBOs) in order to offset some of the costs associated with bandwidth limitations. The ATI VBO is basically a modified implementation of the ARB version of vertex buffer objects. Vertex buffer objects enable caching of geometry in graphics memory for vertex data and mesh lists.

Geometry Processing

Hardware vertex processing makes a *HUGE* difference. The geometry processor block is responsible for vertex and texture coordinate transformations as well as coordinate conversions to internal floating point representation. The triangle setup engine allows for performance numbers of 1M triangles/sec.

Figure 6.5 highlights the geometry processor block.

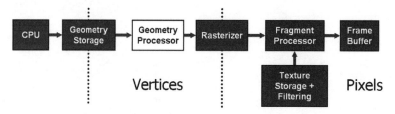

Figure 6.5 The geometry processor block.

The IMAGEON can transform both vertices and texture coordinates in parallel at a rate of 1 million vertices per second at a clock speed of 100MHz.

It can natively support byte, short, fixed, and floating point data formats. The cost of the internal conversion to floating point for processing is not significant enough to worry about. The vertex transform engine increases the vertex transform performance up to 1M vertices/sec. Both the vertex and texture coordinate transforms are accelerated with data formats of GL_BYTE, GL_SHORT, GL_FIXED, and GL_FLOAT.

Rasterizer

The rasterizer is responsible for interpolating pixel values across triangles' vertices and sends the resulting pixel fragments down the pipeline. The setup part can do 1 million triangles per second with the IMAGEON running at 100MHz. This performance is tuned with the earlier transform stage.

Figure 6.6 highlights the rasterizer block.

The rasterizer can do both flat and Gouraud interpolation, and it does per-pixel perspective correction (divide by W). (There is no significant difference between the two because the chip is hardwired to do Gouraud anyway.) The rasterizer block can do per-pixel perspective correction with no real cost to the performance of the platform.

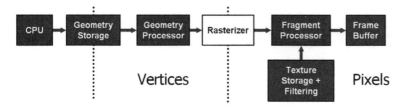

Figure 6.6   The rasterizer block.

The pixel pipeline can process 100 million pixel fragments per second when running at 100MHz.

Fragment Processor

The internal pipeline is RGBA, 8 bits per channel with a 32 bit internal pixel pipeline. This is a single texture pipeline chip (remember the size and power consumption requirements!). The cost of the texture lookup is one clock (10ns) per pixel.

Figure 6.7 highlights the fragment processor block.

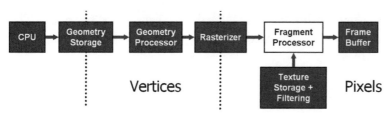

Figure 6.7   The fragment processor block.

It sports all the OpenGL ES texture combine modes.

It also has hardware-supported alpha blending, fogging, and dithering. Fogging is, in fact, piggybacked atop specular color interpolation in the rasterizer as vertex fog, so there is no cost in doing this except in the driver.

Texture Storage and Filtering

The chip allows LOD-driven filtering. You can use both GL_NEAREST and GL_LINEAR on the magnification and minification filters. The chip also supports mipmapping, so you can have GL_NEAREST_MIPMAP_NEAREST, GL_NEAREST_MIPMAP_LINEAR, GL_LINEAR_MIPMAP_NEAREST, and GL_LINEAR_MIPMAP_LINEAR filtering modes.

Figure 6.8 highlights the texture storage and filtering block.

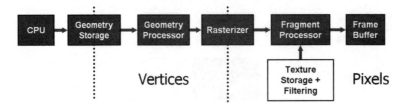

Figure 6.8 The texture storage and filtering block.

The texture picture data can have different formats (see below if you have questions), and the traditional organizations like 8, 16, and 32 bits per pixel are supported. The texture engine converts texels into an 8888 RGBA format before applying the texture combine function. The filtering component supports both bilinear and trilinear filtering modes. Mipmapping has a very big impact in reducing memory bandwidth and power consumption, along with improving image quality (i.e., reducing aliasing), and it is supported in hardware.

Filter modes:

- Magnification filter (nearest, linear)
- Minification filter (nearest, linear, NMN, LMN, NML, LML)

Supported texture formats:

- 8 bit palette (palette is 8888 RGBA)
- 88 AI (luminance + alpha)
- 8A (alpha)
- 8I (luminance)
- 565 RGB
- 1555 RGBA (1 bit alpha, 15 bits RGB)
- 4444 RGBA
- 8888 RGBA

When using hardware, mipmapping ensures that the best texture cache is used to improve bandwidth usage. As mentioned before, the GL_LINEAR_MIPMAP_NEAREST gives you the best performance while limiting the decrease in quality. For software versions you should avoid mipmapping because it will be a lot slower.

Framebuffer

This chip supports up to 8MB of external storage, and that storage is used for the framebuffer, VBOs, and texture data. The driver is optimized to allow the best allocation of memory among the three.

Figure 6.9 highlights the framebuffer block.

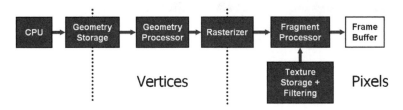

Figure 6.9 The framebuffer bloc.k

The hardware supports up to QVGA size (320×240) in double-buffered mode, and it stores the pixels in a 16 bit format (5-6-5); the z buffer is 16 bits. The hardware has 384KB SRAM, which is used to store z, pixel, and command buffers. The external SDRAM (2–8MB) is used to store texture data.

The Optimization Process and Limitations

Understanding and implementing an optimization process for all your mobile games is a must if you want to get a decent frame rate and be competitive in the mobile gaming market. With new 3D graphics hardware becoming available and faster software implementations now running on better hardware, you must still really take the time to optimize your games for the platform and always do your best to understand your platform limitations. Every game will have a bottleneck somewhere. Your role in optimizing a game title is to identify those bottlenecks and try to solve them so that the overall level of performance is maximized. By really understanding your platform, you should be able to avoid most bottlenecks as you design and develop your game.

Where To Begin?

The three most common things to consider when starting the optimization process for your game is determining if your game is bandwidth-limited, transform-limited, or fill-rate-limited. The most common metric used to measure performance is the frame rate or FPS (frames per second). Using the FPS measurement, start by walking the 3D pipeline, tweaking a few parameters at a time until you see improvements. Then move on to a more systematic optimization once you find the block in the 3D pipeline that is the main cause of your bottleneck. After that, just repeat the process over and over until you reach a frame rate that provides the highest quality and game play.

Figure 6.10 shows a simple overview of places to start your optimization process.

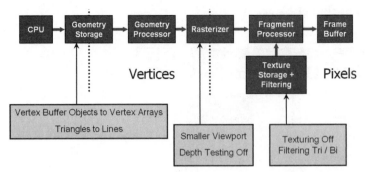

Figure 6.10 Simple overview of optimizations to consider.

First and foremost, you always want to know which side of the rasterizer stage is involved in the bottleneck under investigation. This will determine how to proceed. If the bottleneck is after the rasterizer stage, then there might be actual physical limits on the hardware itself that will not allow you to optimize your game any further. Texture size is always a consideration because it has an impact not only on the memory bandwidth, but also on the bus bandwidth in case all texture for a given level cannot be stored in graphics memory. We will cover all the stages of the 3D graphics pipeline, how to optimize them, and what limitations usually exist for each stage. These hints on how the 3D pipeline is affected when having game data feed through it will in general apply to most 3D graphics hardware on handheld devices.

CPU and Memory Transfer Limitations

The bus bandwidth will vary from one platform to another. Either way, you want to avoid the more obvious mistakes of unnecessary state changes or sending small vertex lists several times instead of one larger triangle array. Also, presorting the triangle data before sending the data down the pipeline will reduce the overhead of several memory access reads. Memory can be accessed in pages or blocks for each array instead of page faulting or recaching triangle data over and over because the data wasn't well organized or managed properly. By maximizing your triangle batch size, you can reduce the number of calls to transfer triangle data to the hardware. In terms of textures at the beginning of the pipeline, the higher the resolution of the texture, the higher the likelihood that not all of your textures for a particular level will fit in graphics memory. What this means is that the OpenGL ES driver may have to recycle textures from graphics memory and download the textures that were not in graphics memory. All of this data movement will go across the system bus, which will affect the game play and frame rate.

If after tweaking the pipeline and after optimizing all the other parts of the pipeline you conclude that bandwidth is your main limitation (which should be the case), then you might want to tweak the texture sizes and reduce the polygon count.

Geometry Storage Limitations

Graphics storage can run out of memory or be affected by memory-hungry applications. Try to use smaller data types and organize the models' topology in order to use triangle strips. Batch as much geometry as you can in a single call; the more triangles you send in a single lump, the better. By using triangle strips you can save memory and bandwidth.

The following are the more common things to consider for the geometry storage state:

Data type and size: These can affect the overall memory footprint on both the driver and chip sides. To lower the memory footprint, use smaller data types (i.e., byte or short) whenever possible.

Data sequencing: The driver is very efficient in handling the graphics memory on both the host and the GPU, but moving memory a lot can lead to heap fragmentation. On the host side, this behavior can differ from platform to platform. It's best to organize in advance how graphics memory is going to be used and load static scene elements first (those textures and models used in every camera shot are a good example).

Overloading VBOs: It makes no sense to reconstruct a VBO at every frame, and those models that are heavily animated are better stored as vertex arrays. Remember that VBOs, textures, and the framebuffer all share the same graphics memory; a VBO will revert to a vertex array if the GPU memory cannot be used, and that causes a performance penalty that's sometimes difficult to track down.

Geometry Processing Limits

In order to minimize the number of vertices being transformed, you should do some scene-level culling prior to sending the graphics data down the pipeline. Techniques such as PVS (potentially visible set) are good optimization candidates, although you should always try to do broad occlusion testing before potentially visible set data. You should also avoid redundant or intermediate state changes and only load matrices when actually used.

In the general case, CPU-to-GPU bus bandwidth is going to be your limiting factor, so you should not be hitting the geometry processing limit. If you do store a lot of geometry as VBOs and instance them frequently (like trying to show swarming bees), you may want to perform frustum occlusion testing on the CPU side.

Remember that transforms also need to be pushed to the chip, so the fewer mangles you do with transforms the better. Use a single lump of triangles for static objects; avoid deep scene DAGs (directed acyclic graphs) in those cases. (Animated characters are obviously exempt from this constraint.)

Rasterizer/Pixel Fill Limitations

The rasterizer's performance has been tuned to the geometry processor. It's rarely if ever the bottleneck for hardware-accelerated platforms. It is affected by the triangles' size onscreen in terms of pixels. Changing the viewport size obviously changes the fill rate performance.

Fragment Processing Limitation

Most graphics hardware pipelines have been tuned so that the fragment processor's performance is in line with that of the rasterizer, so this is rarely, if ever, a bottleneck. In general, too many fragments or too much processing per fragment is the typical culprit; that's a nonissue with most 3D mobile graphics hardware, especially the W2300.

Texture Limitations

Texture-related limitations are memory, fetching, and filtering related. Make sure you balance the texture size and filtering mode with the model; also, use memory saving features such as smaller texture formats and mipmapping. The W2300 has been designed for 3D gaming, so texturing is a well-oiled and performance-tuned feature. Specifically, mipmapping provides you with the best performance improvements. The linear-mip-nearest mode has the best visual quality for the FPS cost. Most mobile 3D graphics hardware becoming available will start supporting mipmapping and different filtering modes.

Depending on your platform's memory constraints for texture sizes, the texture cache size available (if any), and memory bus speed, you should always focus on tuning your textures to handle your known device limitations. Even if hardware supports all these features, if the memory bandwidth is too low, you'll lose out on the accelerated features. One thing to remember also is that you can use texture transforms in order to normalize the texture indices in the [0,1] range so that you can use small data types for texture coordinates, resulting in savings in both memory and bandwidth.

 The potential problems to consider are the following:

- Not enough texture memory
- Excessive texture filtering
- Unbalanced texture resolution
- Memory-hungry internal formats
- No mipmapping

Pixel Ops Limitations

The most common limitation is reading and writing pixels directly. This is true for all 3D graphics hardware. If you are used to reading and blitting pixels from developing 2D games, you should reconsider ever doing this or at least avoid doing this at all costs. Pixel operations in general are always heavy performance hits, and while these operations can provide some great effects, you have to balance and tune for even just one operation. Good luck with this stage; it is a common source of bottlenecks for some people who run on the PC and then find out just how limited a handheld platform can really be.

ATI OpenGL ES Extensions

Now that we've talked about optimization for mobile 3D graphics platforms, one last thing to consider is the hardware API extensions that allow you to take advantage of the hardware's optimized features. The ATI driver implements a modified version of the `ARB_vertex_buffer_object` function set in order to load geometry onto the chip's graphics memory. This offsets the inherent cost of CPU-to-GPU bandwidth. This extension also allows mesh lists to be specified through a simple call, which simplifies the handling of a set of VBOs. By using these ATI extensions, you can increase considerably the overall performance of your game. The OpenGL ES driver reverts to vertex arrays whenever graphics memory cannot be allocated.

The following is a list of ATI extensions that are available on the IMAGEON 2300 series.

- Modified `GL_ARB_vertex_buffer_object`
- `glBindBufferARB( … );`
- `glDeleteBuffersARB( … );`
- `glBufferDataARB( … );`
- `glBufferDataATI( … );`
- `glBufferSubDataARB( … );`
- `glDrawVertexBufferObjectATI( … );`
- `glMeshListATI( … );`

As a game developer, you should be aware of these types of extensions and use them whenever possible. However, there will be several OpenGL ES hardware-accelerated platforms that will *not* support this type of performance improvement directly. Please refer to Chapter 5 on how to use these extensions in your game and how to detect if these extensions exist on your platform.

A Quick Hardware Case Study: *MotoGP2* Demo

Having a good idea of the likely handset configuration is nice to know, but nothing compares with an actual case. Here we present *MotoGP2* (shown in Figure 6.11) that was developed by the Climax Group under a license from THQ. The game's original code base came from the Xbox and was adapted to the IMAGEON platform.

MotoGP is an example of a game that ATI qualifies as "Fully Optimized for the IMAGEON."

Microsoft XBOX

ATI IMAGEON™ 2300

Figure 6.11 Optimized *MotoGP2* for the IMAGEON.

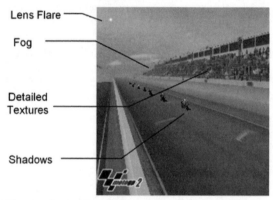

Lens Flare

Fog

Detailed
Textures

Shadows

Figure 6.12 Visual effects fully enabled doing normal game play.

Figure 6.12 shows some of the visual effects of the game. With all these features enabled, the following data was collected on the overall performance of the game.

Platform:

- ARM9-based @ 168MHz, 64Mb
- W2300 @ 80MHz
- 8MB framebuffer

Performance:

- 3808Kb of texture
- 7826 triangles/frame avg
- 11862 vertices/frame avg
- Frame Rate: 25 fps avg
- Throughput (avg): (~200,000 triangles/sec, ~300,000 vertices/sec)

Scene Data:

- 8 bikes: 700 triangles each
- Track: ~ 14,000 triangles

OpenGL ES Features Used:

- Mipmapping
- Gouraud shading
- Alpha blending
- Single textures
- Fog
- Alpha textures

Optimizations Used:

- VBO/mesh lists
- Mipmapping
- Frustrum culling (CPU)

Climax did a fantastic job of optimizing their OpenGL ES game code for the W2300 graphics hardware. If you would like to know more details of how to port and scale your games down to a more limited 3D graphics hardware device, then look at Chapter 5, which goes into great detail on the optimization and performance tuning that was done by Climax for *MotoGP2*.

OpenGL ES Development Platforms

Aside from obtaining a precommercial handset from an OEM or carrier, there are a couple of very useful OpenGL ES development platforms available for the professional game developer. Even if you are not a professional game developer, you could still have access to these devices.

The ATI Development Platform

The ATI PCI bridge card shown in Figure 6.13 allows you to use your existing PC development environment without incurring a major retooling. This card currently has the ATI IMAGEON 2300 series chipset on it with 8M of SDRAM and a QVGA screen. You can leverage your existing custom tools and even use third-party libraries (Win32 or BREW) so that you can get the game's visuals up and running quickly. The PCI card combined with the steps we described earlier allows you to have a fast development cycle without losing control over how the game is transformed. The ATI dev kit has all the available Win32 drivers and BREW OpenGL ES examples. Developers interested in obtaining an ATI dev kit should contact ATI Developer Relations.

The QUALCOMM Development Platform

Figure 6.14 should give you an idea of what the next generation of phones will look like. The phone shown here is a fully loaded multimedia QUALCOMM enhanced and convergence series prototype device. This phone is actually a development platform for game developers wanting to port their games to a hardware-accelerated OpenGL ES platform and to gain early access to the next generation 3D hardware.

Figure 6.13 ATI PCI bridge card.

Figure 6.14 QUALCOMM enhanced series platform.

The following are some of the performance characteristics of the enhanced series:

- 100K triangles/sec
- 7M pixels/sec
- Target depth complexity of 1–3 for QVGA screen at 30fps
- OpenGL ES 1.0 compliant

The following are some of the performance characteristics of the convergence series:

- 4M shaded triangles/sec
- 3.5M textured triangles/sec
- 133M textured pixels/sec
- 65M multitextured pixels/sec
- Target depth complexity > 10 on VGA screen at 30fps
- Will be OpenGL ES 1.0 compliant

A Software View of 3D Graphics

Figure 6.15 shows a software view of a 3D graphics implementation on a mobile device using the ARM processor with DSP acceleration. This is basically the QUALCOMM multimedia platform software configuration. The performance tips below will work for most software implementations of OpenGL ES. We provide this overview as a reference for this section.

The following lists show typical multimedia platform performance characteristics for software-only versions of OpenGL ES platforms:

Fixed point pipeline:

- Reduced power consumption
- Precision optimized for ARM/QDSP performance

Performance specifications:

- 50K lighted triangles/sec
- 400K textured, z buffered pixels/sec
- 1M shaded, z buffered pixels/sec
- 8M flat shaded 2D pixels/sec

Some performance characteristics:

- Optimized for vertex lighting and shaded triangles
- Transformations offloaded from ARM
- Fast clears have been optimized
- Target depth complexity of 1–2 for QCIF screen at 15fps

With software and DSP-accelerated platforms (no 3D graphics hardware), you have the following limitations that should be considered when designing your games:

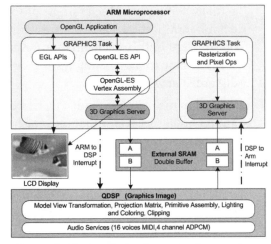

Figure 6.15 A typical software implementation view of OpenGL ES.

- Limited MIPS, graphics processing is shared between the CPU and DSP, which will burn more cycles and kill your AI and physics budgets.
- With a software-only version and no DSP, you have vertex transformation/rasterization all being done on the CPU.
- Limited system memory size and bandwidth will directly affect your game performance and will force you to limit the amount of geometry you can push. Smaller memory-hungry data types for vertices and texture coordinates help a lot in controlling this limitation.

Performance Suggestions for OpenGL ES Software Implementations

The following are some of the most common suggestions for improving your game performance when developing on software-only OpenGL ES platforms.

- Use the OpenGL ES Common Lite profile and be careful with matrix/vertex precision.
- The ARM processor is a fixed point processor (no floating point support), so you should use fixed point math for your game.
- Consider the software architecture and how it is really implemented. For example, with QUALCOMM's software implementation, the transform and lighting are fast and run on the DSP, not the main CPU, and are thus rarely a bottleneck. However, you should probably focus on optimizing the rasterization stage.
- The default OpenGL ES states are really designed for hardware acceleration. You should be aware of these default states and change them to less expensive settings if you don't need them. You should also be sure to disable any features that aren't

actually being used. One example of this would be texture filtering, where the default minification state is nearest-mipmap-linear, which will be slow inevitably on software-only implementations. Another example would be setting your shading state to flat if using texture replace, since the results of shading are discarded anyway.

- Related to the previous points, there are a number of features that can be enabled but set up in such a way that the rendering results are equivalent to having the feature disabled. In many cases, the default settings for these features produce exactly this effect. For example, alpha blending by default is set to use GL_ONE as the source blending factor and GL_ZERO as the destination blending factor, which is exactly what happens when blending is disabled. As a result of this, it's possible to have features enabled that you're paying a price for that produce no visible results in your game. You should be aware of what these features are and be sure to have them disabled when you're not using them. Examples of these features include blending, logic ops, depth test, alpha test, and scissoring.

- Most of the time using only one light source will have no performance degradation if lighting is being done by the co-processor (DSP). This includes ambient, specular, and diffuse components. Use OpenGL ES vertex lighting to offload lighting from the ARM. Again, be careful; you have to know your platform and how the features are supported.

- glDrawElements() will almost always be faster than glDrawArrays(). Software-only implementations will probably not support VBOs, so you have to work with what you have. You should also try to send large batches of triangles with a single call.

- The rasterization and fragment operations will be done on the main CPU. This is usually the largest bottleneck with most software implementations.

- Check to see if the software supports early z test (before textures if state allows). When possible, draw large occluders first.

- Check to see if glClear() is accelerated. Use glClear() instead of drawing triangles. Use the scissor test to clear a portion of the screen and do not clear it if it is not necessary. When using textures for background images, use native 2D calls and not the 3D pipeline, using EGL functions for synchronization. Use glClear(GL_DEPTH_BUFFER_BIT) if clearing only the z buffer is sufficient.

- Keep in mind that glFinish() can really kill performance. It should really only be used for profiling. eglSwapBuffers() automatically performs necessary synchronization, so there is no need for your game to flush or finish at the end of a frame. In addition, EGL provides several functions for synchronization purposes (eglWaitGL(), eglWaitNative()), so these should be used instead of calling glFlush() or glFinish().

- Be especially careful with textures. Use smooth- or flat-shaded polygons if textured pixels are not required. The following are more suggestions for increasing your performance when using textures: Turn off perspective correction when possible by using glHint(); this could provide a significant performance increase. Use nearest instead of bilinear filtering when possible. Avoid using mipmapping, since it is considerably more expensive in software than bilinear filtering.

- While all OpenGL ES texture formats have to be supported to be compliant, they will more than likely be converted to one of three internal formats during texture loading: RGB565, RGBA5551, or RGBA4444. So you should try and match the texture format as closely to the internal format as possible.

Standard Memory Layouts

With a variety of phones on the market, there are a variety of memory configurations. Memory can change drastically from one device to the next, depending on whether it is a low- or high-tier platform. OEMs have several trade-offs they have to consider when determining what type of memory to use and what memory densities make the most sense for features on their phones, while still trying to hit the price margin set for the market they are targeting.

The most common memory configurations will be a combination of NOR, PSRAM, NAND, and SDRAM. What type of memory you have is very important and will affect what you can include in your game. It will also directly affect the overall code size both for storage and heap space. The file size is typically on a NOR/NAND flash configuration. Before we get into some of the details of memory, keep in mind that most mobile devices have a boot loader that copies the phone code from one memory component (typically flash) to another memory unit (typically SDRAM). This is mainly for a speed increase of the phone software, and if running on SDRAM, you can usually get a larger heap space and in some cases lower power consumption. These types of memory components are just briefly discussed as follows.

NOR FLASH

This type of flash memory is usually used for both code storage and executable code. The OEM boot code and phone software can run directly from NOR flash and don't need to be copied. NOR flash always has high-speed random access abilities, but the erase speed and moving around large blocks of data with this memory can be very slow (up to hundreds of milliseconds!). And that is the main reason that running games from NOR flash just doesn't seem like a good idea.

NAND FLASH

This type of flash memory is usually used just for code storage. NAND flash can be less expensive than NOR and even have higher densities (more memory). With the increase of memory sizes, NAND is great for phone software and application storage. When reading and writing data in blocks, NAND will outperform NOR flash. So, overall, NAND seems like a good solution for both cost and speed.

PSRAM

This is pseudo-SRAM memory that is on the low end of cost and has lower bandwidths. PSRAM supports page mode and burst mode, which gives this memory fast random access times for both read and writes. This memory is attractive to a lot of OEMs for its low power consumptions as well. But again it all comes down to cost.

SDRAM

This is synchronous DRAM that can run at high bus speeds of 75 to 133MHz or even higher. The SDRAM memory can be built as a low-power component. The only disadvantage of SDRAM is price. Since OEMs aren't always willing to pay for the extra high speed memory, a lot of mobile devices will be limited in what games can run on them.

Low- to Mid-Range Multimedia Phones

The OEM code will be executed directly from NOR flash. This is slower memory, and thus any 3D software rendering engines will run more slowly. Regardless of how optimized your game code will be if you are running on phones that have this memory configuration, you may be able to do a 3D screen saver, but a 3D game won't work. These phones are really designed for the low-end market for folks who want the basic cell phone to make calls and do text messaging. With the OEM code running directly from NOR flash, this really limits the overall speed of the device and thus makes this configuration not really usable for 3D gaming. Also, the overall heap space and the file system storage space are just too low to store a full 3D game, let alone many of them.

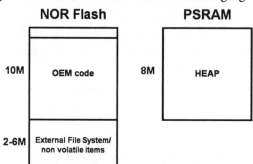

Figure 6.16 Low-range memory layout.

Figure 6.16 shows the standard memory layout for low- to some mid-range multimedia phones.

Mid-Range Multimedia Phones

The OEM code is executed from SDRAM, which is a better platform for running your games at a decent speed. However, there are memory size limitations for mid-range phones. The SDRAM could be 16MB to 32MB. Again, OEMs will decide what memory configuration makes the most sense to hit their market price. But with phones that have

SDRAM for heap and OEM code execution, you'll start to see a platform that is capable of supporting real 3D games. One major constraint here is the file size. If you want to be able to have several games on your phone, you'll have to have some pretty short-playing 3D games. Overall, this is a start for a simple 3D game platform, but again very limited in what you can do with this platform in terms of 3D gaming.

Figure 6.17 shows the standard memory layout for mid-range multimedia phones.

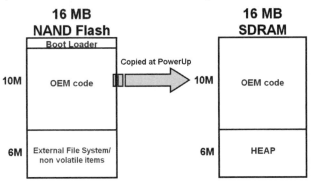

Figure 6.17   Mid-range memory layout.

High-End Multimedia Phones

The OEM code is executed from SDRAM. This is the best case for running your games at a decent speed and getting the best quality. For example, you get the speed of SDRAM, and with the higher end memory densities you also get a larger file system and larger heap space, all of which are critical for 3D gaming. This memory configuration is available today on some commercial phones. With phones that have a 3D graphics core or a 3D graphics accelerator external chip attached to them, you'll need to run from SDRAM to get bus speeds and bandwidth to a level that will work with 3D hardware. A larger heap size will allow more levels, art assets, audio, textures, game data, and so on to be loaded into memory for faster and smoother game play.

Figure 6.18 shows the standard memory layout for high-end multimedia phones.

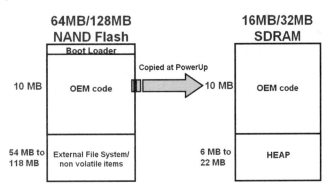

Figure 6.18   High-end memory layout.

Network Data Rates

While this chapter's main focus is how to use and optimize your games for OpenGL ES software and hardware, we want to highlight other limitations of the medium that developers should be aware of. For developing network games, you should be aware of the type of data networks available and their typical data rates. Network and data rates will vary on different devices in the market. The following sections will give you a general idea of some of the average download and network data rates available on phones today.

These data rates are based on numbers collected in the San Diego area on Verizon's network. While these are just estimates and average data rates, they will vary from carrier to carrier and in general depend on your cell coverage areas. The other things to consider are multiple phones in a sector that could decrease your available network rates. So, these numbers are just averages, and until you test your phone on your local network, at least you can use these numbers for initial tuning of your games. With the idea of multiplayer network games moving into the mobile space, the following data has been provided to give developers a general idea of what to expect in terms of average network data rates that are available today.

1X Phones

QUALCOMM defines 1X as the following: "CDMA2000 1X is an International Telecommunications Union (ITU) approved 3G wireless communications standard that provides voice and data capabilities within a standard 1.25 MHz CDMA channel for outstanding spectral efficiency and flexibility." CDMA2000 builds on earlier CDMA technology (known as *cdmaOne*) to provide a natural evolution to 3G services. It nearly doubles voice capacity over second-generation (2G) cdmaOne networks and supports high-speed data services, offering a peak data rate of 153Kbps.

CDMA2000 was first commercialized in October 2000 in South Korea. Since then, more than 70 operators on six continents have launched CDMA2000 services. Networks and devices supporting these services are backward compatible with those based on 2G cdmaOne, preserving operator spectrum and equipment investments, while providing best-in-class voice capacity and effective data capability. For more information on CDMA2000, you can go directly to the source: **www.qualcomm.com**.

For 1X phones, the average data rate can be 60–120Kbps.

UMTS/WCDMA Phones

QUALCOMM defines WCDMA as the following: "Wideband CDMA (WCDMA) is an approved 3G standard that uses 5MHz channels for both voice and data, offering excellent voice capacity and a peak data rate of 384Kbps." NTT DoCoMo launched the first WCDMA service in 2001 and now has millions of 3G subscribers.

WCDMA (UMTS) is also the 3G technology of choice for many GSM/GPRS operators, with dozens currently trialing the technology and more than 100 having licensed new spectrum with the intent to launch services in the next few years. For more information on WCDMA, you can go directly to the source: **www.qualcomm.com**.

For UMTS/WCDMA phones the average data rate can be:

- 250Kbps in the forward link (up to 384Kbps on a clear channel)
- 125Kbps in reverse link

DO (Data Only) Phones

QUALCOMM defines DO as the following: "CDMA2000 1xEV-DO is an evolution of CDMA2000 and an approved 3G standard for fixed, portable, and mobile applications." CDMA2000 1xEV-DO is "data optimized," providing a peak data rate of 2.4Mbps.

The first 1xEV-DO commercial service began in January 2002. There are already more than 7 million 1xEV-DO users today, with many more networks expected to launch this year and next. For more information on 1xEV-DO, you can go directly to the source: **www.qualcomm.com**.

For DO phones the average data rate can be:

- 400–600Kbps in the forward link (up to 2Mbps on a clear channel)
- 75–100Kbps in the reverse link

Bluetooth®

Bluetooth technology enables transfers of wireless data and audio between multiple devices.

This is the most common case for Bluetooth today. The n-gage allows you to connect up to eight devices through Bluetooth, so they are ahead of the game. However, you can always network multiple masters together that could be used as routers to your slaves.

For Bluetooth the average data rate can be:

Localized peer-to-peer connection (up to 10 meters): 400+ Kbps

With 1 master and 3 slaves (4 devices networked, for example): 65Kbps

Summary

In this chapter, you learned about some of the most common limitations for OpenGL ES platforms. From a software-only implementation to a highly-optimized hardware solution, there are still limitations and performance recommendations that should be considered when designing your game. The best way to control both the memory footprint and bandwidth is to use the graphics hardware transform engine to its full extent. Remember that you can input byte, short, and fixed point data into the engine with little or no conversion cost. The scene data can also be adjusted by tweaking the transforms instead.

You also learned about some important things to remember about vertex data:

- To radically improve your triangle rate, use vertex buffer objects for reduced bus traffic. If VBOs are not available, then group vertex data into strips or presort them to avoid additional function calls and state changes.
- Use hardware API extensions whenever possible (for example, the modified version of `ARB_vertex_buffer_object` enables caching of geometry in graphics memory).
- Try to keep all vertex data in fixed point, short, or byte format.
- Texture coordinates can also be in short or byte format and normalized to [0,1] via the texture matrix.

We also briefly covered standard memory layouts and data rates that you should be aware of when porting your games to mobile platforms. The most important thing to remember from reading this chapter is to *know your platform* by understanding its limitations and features that have been optimized. The best approach for optimizing and tuning your game is to start with the 3D graphics pipeline and identify your bottlenecks. Start by identifying if the problem is on the vertices side or the pixel side of the pipeline. Once you find your bottlenecks, break them down one by one and make it an iterative process of grinding down your code until you get the quality and frame rate you desire.

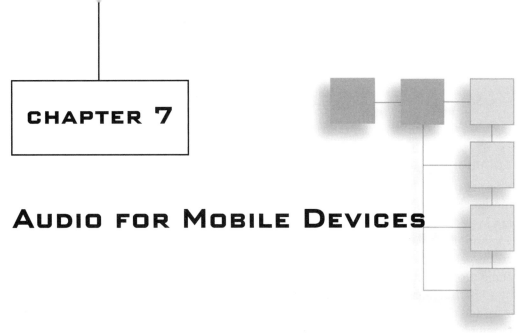

CHAPTER 7

AUDIO FOR MOBILE DEVICES

by Devin Maxwell with Matt Wagner and Quentin Tolimieri

This chapter focuses on audio production for mobile phones. We hope to provide a common ground for producers, audio content creators, and programmers of mobile applications. Currently, the audio capabilities of handsets on the market vary widely in terms of both functionality and quality, which makes developing audio content for mobile devices difficult and time consuming. While an in-depth explanation of every tool and every file format used for mobile audio production is beyond the scope of this chapter, we will cover the following information:

- An in-depth look at mobile audio production
- Production methods for commercial mobile game audio
- Creation of audio in the BREW environment
- Additional resources and tools for mobile audio

Introduction to Mobile Audio

Content and application development for mobile devices is fairly time consuming and complicated. The wide range of formats and their different versions, all with different capabilities, quickly turns the realm of mobile audio into a nearly incomprehensible sea of letters and numbers. This chapter will clear up some of this confusion by defining concepts, working procedure, terminology, formats, and tools common within the realm of mobile audio production. This information should allow producers, programmers, and content creators to have a shared understanding of the basic concepts of mobile audio and also allow them to make intelligent decisions about what is appropriate for their application. We will explore three high-level concepts before getting into the details.

153

- Communication
- Selection of an Audio Producer
- Quality Control

Communication

Effective production of quality audio content for mobile devices relies on strong communication between the producer, programmer, and content creator. If they're not all speaking to each other about the right things in a highly efficient manner, audio quality and application quality are sunk. All three parties—programmer, producer, and content creator—must have a common understanding of the concepts and terminology used in audio production. The production process must also be clearly understood and planned by all parties. Memorization and understanding of all the file formats is a good place to start, and the glossary provided at the end of this chapter should help clear up any foreign terminology, but proper management is the key here. The programmer and the content creator must work together implementing the audio on every phone. It seems like a simple idea, but it's really a radical concept because it requires budgeting time and money before the project begins. If you don't plan to work together on the audio for every phone from the beginning, you will probably have to pay more money later in the process to fix audio, which could have been done right the first time.

Selection of an Audio Producer

Since this whole chapter is about raising the quality of audio, we would like to present a working model for the roles of the following positions: producer, programmer, and content creator.

Producer

The producer of the project needs to have an understanding of the audio capabilities of the handsets targeted for development. He also needs to have the creative management skills to enable content creators to provide quality content that is appropriate for the mood of the application. The better the producer is at enabling the content provider through placeholder music, screenshots, keywords, and comparisons, the better the audio will be. The producer should also work with the content creator and the programmer to facilitate technical discussions regarding file size, formats, and other capabilities.

Programmer

The programmer should provide the technical expertise to implement the audio into the game, application, or animation. Essentially, the programmer is the facilitator of the producer's ideas.

Content Creator

The content creator is responsible for the creation, formatting, and revising of the content to fit each handset or build group. He is also responsible for testing the content in the application on the handsets. The content creator should work closely with the programmer while testing. Once the application is working properly, the programmer and content creator should bring the build to the producer **on the phone**. Then revisions should be made, if necessary.

While we're talking about who does what, let's talk about who you should choose to produce audio. The following are the skills I would personally look for in a mobile audio developer:

- Experience writing music for hire and scoring to picture (hitting deadlines, taking criticisms, and revisions, etc.).
- Extensive knowledge of MIDI programming.
- Extensive knowledge of audio engineering.
- Extensive knowledge of digital audio formats, including file compression.
- File/asset management skills.
- Advanced computer knowledge (a little programming preferred).
- Capability to troubleshoot, learn technology (including new software), and solve problems quickly.
- Access to mobile phones or a phone-testing lab.

Here are people I don't hire:

- Some guy who plays music in a band (and believe me, I know a lot of them. Some of them are quite good).
- A graphic designer who has a bunch of expensive equipment and a fantastic demo who has never composed music for a living.
- My girlfriend's friend who is teaching music and playing some gigs who could use the extra income.
- A programmer who really likes music.

I'm being a bit facetious here, but what I'm saying is that if you're going to buy audio (whether it is music, SFX, or dialogue), there are people in this world who create and sell audio for a living. **Find them. Use them.** Your kids will thank you, your boss will love you, and your application will be better. Trust me on this. I've seen a lot of projects waste time and money having the wrong person do the wrong job when it comes to audio. Currently, the most experienced content creators for mobile audio work will be musicians or sound designers with experience in the video game industry. Any experience in programming for Game Boy Advance or other handheld consoles is a major plus. These content creators usually have all the technical audio qualifications needed for this kind of work and the patience and cunning to hack into and test the devices. I've also found that certain kinds of compressed audio formatting for certain devices can be done quite well by experienced recording engineers. A good recording engineer will take it as a personal challenge to make the small speaker on the phone sound excellent.

Because it can be hard to find good people, here are some links to get you started in your search for the right audio person:

Games 411

www.games411.com

Gamasutra (under audio contractors)

www.gamasutra.com

Game Audio Network Guild (G.A.N.G.)

www.audogang.org

GameDev.net jobs

www.gamedev.net

Quality Control

The following is not a hint; it is a commandment:

TEST ON THE PHONES

Tip

If you're not going to allow the content creator to test on the *actual phones*, then don't bother putting audio into your application.

I know that's a bold statement, but I've yet to run into a device that actually adhered to its specifications. Often, the audio capabilities are overstated and understated at the same time. Certain files that *should* work (as indicated by the spec of the phone) don't work, and certain files that should *not* work actually play back on the phone. I might get the Wireless Understatement of the Year Award, but I'm going to say it anyway: **There is not necessarily a correlation between what the device emulator will do and what the actual device will do.**

Sound functionality on emulators can be deceiving for two reasons. First, the speaker on which you're playing back the audio is usually going to sound much, much fuller than the device speaker, so the sound on the emulator is not going to be representative of what is really happening. Phone speakers—and speakers on mobile devices generally—are too small to reproduce low frequencies, so if you want to have audio sound excellent on a phone, you have to test it on the speaker of the phone. Secondly, sound support is usually added to device emulators as an afterthought and more often than not has many bugs or other technical problems. With bogus specifications and buggy emulators, the only way to truly know what your audio is going to sound like is to throw the actual content on the actual phone in the actual application.

So, once again… if you want audio in your application, communicate, coordinate, have the right person do the right job, and **TEST ON THE PHONES.**

Mobile Audio Production

For phones or other mobile devices, we're basically dealing with two kinds of production: digital audio and MIDI. Digital audio production involves the recording and manipulation of actual sounds, while MIDI production involves the programming of musical information to produce real-time performances from synthesizers embedded on the devices. Digital audio files tend to be larger and tax more of the phone's resources, while MIDI files are smaller and less processor intensive. Many devices currently on the market support MIDI; only a fraction will support digital audio. However, the field is evolving, and before long all devices will support digital audio. That said, MIDI will be an effective tool in games for years to come. The increased capabilities of future devices are most certainly not going to be devoted entirely to audio, so I expect that it will be quite some time before we hear a full game score with full digital audio soundtrack.

MIDI Production versus Digital Audio Production

Essentially, a digital audio file is the recording of an actual sound that has been converted into digital data. That sound can be any sound imaginable: a person's voice, a symphony orchestra, etc. Because the data is stored digitally, many different resolutions and file compression techniques can be applied to digital audio in order to reduce the file size or increase the resolution of the approximated curves (more on curves later). Each of these techniques results in its own file format or codec, such as WAV, MP3, AIFF, QCP, and AMR. Each compression is a different file format that changes the sound to a degree; however, when played back on multiple devices, files using the same compression level should sound very similar to one another. For example, a WAV file compressed to 8kHz (kilohertz) 8 bit mono (monophonic) will sound similar on all devices. However, an 8kHz, 8 bit mono file will sound different from a 16 bit, 44.1kHz stereo file. While digital audio files sound very similar on all devices, they are rather large files. A standard 5-minute song takes up approximately 50 megabytes of disk space.

Tip

16 bit, 44.1kHz stereo is called CD-quality audio because it is the standard compression level for audio CDs.

MIDI, on the other hand, is only a record of the performance data related to a musical event, rather than the event itself. So if you play a note on a MIDI-enabled keyboard, it stores data about what note you played, how fast you pressed down the key, how long you held it down, and what you did to it while you held it down. Standard MIDI files (SMFs) store all of this performance data in the same way that a player piano roll captured performance data at the turn of the last century. SMFs also store data about the MIDI channel to which the note is assigned and which instrument (also called a "patch") is to be triggered. When you want a MIDI file to play back, the performance data held in the SMF is sent to a synthesizer, which re-performs the piece in real time.

Every phone that has MIDI capabilities has a synthesizer built into it. Each synthesizer has a limited number of voices. (There are between 4 and 72 voices available on phones currently in the market. I'll go into detail about voices a little later, as it can be a bit confusing.) Because MIDI files are only storing small bits of performance data (note on, note off, velocity, instrument, etc.), they are much smaller than digital audio files. Unfortunately, the reduced file size comes with a trade-off. Every synthesizer will play back the MIDI data differently. Digital audio files will basically play back the same way on every device, but MIDI files vary greatly from device to device. For example, AudioExample1.mp3 on the included CD is a MIDI file played back on a Nokia 3650. AudioExample2.mp3 is the exact same MIDI file played back by a Motorola V300. AudioExample3.mp3 is the same MIDI file played back by a SoundBlaster Live synthesizer, and AudioExample4.mp3 is that same MIDI file played on a Korg Triton Synthesizer. Remember that all four of these are recordings of the *exact* same MIDI file.

Tip

There is a *very, very* wide range of performance of MIDI files from one phone model to another. Phone-specific testing is essential for quality content.

MIDI (Musical Instrument Digital Interface)

- Performance instructions sent to synthesizer
- Very few different subformats
- File size can be in the range of 5K to 10K for 5 minutes of music
- Wide variance of sound on handsets
- Limited by number of voices

MIDI is a record of the performance data for a musical event. The data stored consists of what MIDI note was pressed (pitch), how fast it was pressed (velocity), the channel on which it was played, the instrument ("patch") with which it should be played, and when the note should stop. This data is stored in SMFs (extension .mid).

SMFs organize the stored performance data in one of two ways: Format 1 or Format 0. Format 1 files have information stored on multiple tracks, while Format 0 files have the information stored on one track. Most development done for mobile phones is Format 0. On that one track, you can assign up to 16 independent channels, each playing a different patch. The channels are marked with numbers 1–16; channel 10 is reserved for drum set.

Most audio programs have three basic graphic representations of MIDI data: Event List view, Piano Roll view, and Musical Notation view. Event List view, shown in Figure 7.1, is best used for low-level editing of MIDI data. Piano Roll View, shown in Figure 7.2, is best used for editing note lengths and inserting certain kinds of graphically represented performance data (such as volume swells or modulation wheel data), and Musical Notation view, shown in Figure 7.3, is best used for correcting notes and understanding the musical logic of a piece.

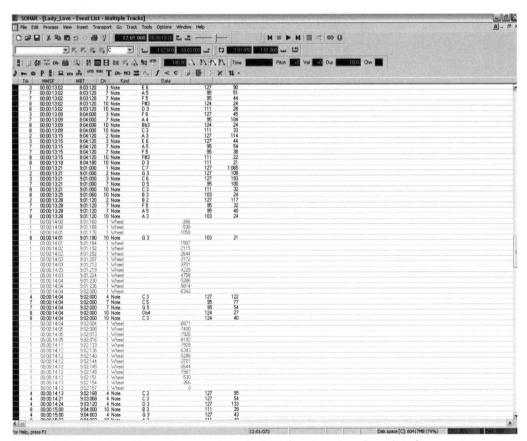

Figure 7.1 Event View: The performance data of a MIDI file when viewed as a list of consecutive events.

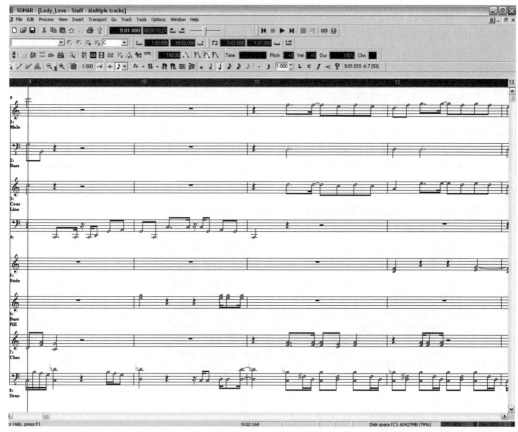

Figure 7.2 Musical Notation View: The performance data of the same MIDI file when viewed as standard musical notation.

Voices versus Instruments versus Channels

OK, it's going to get a little confusing now. The voice count of synthesizers is becoming fairly important for the marketing of certain phones. Manufacturer X has a 32-voice synthesizer in its phone, so Manufacturer Y needs to build a 48-voice synthesizer, and now the general public is making their purchasing decisions based on the number of voices that their phones can play. But do they really understand what they're buying? No! Voices are confusing! Let's start by figuring out what voices are *not*.

Voices are *not*:

- The number of instruments available on the phone.
- The number of instruments that can play at the same time on the phone.
- The number of separate MIDI channels on the phone.
- The number of MIDI files that can be triggered at the same time.

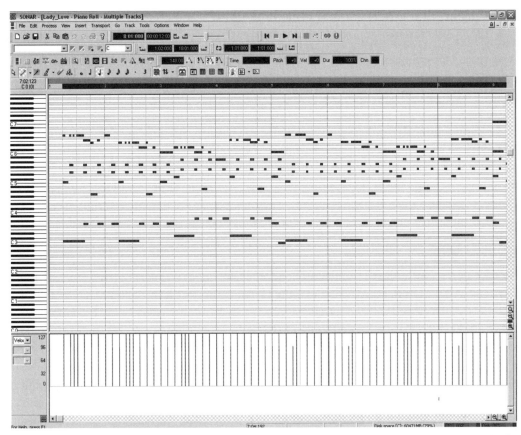

Figure 7.3 Piano Roll View: The performance data of the same MIDI file when viewed as a piano roll. All three of these graphics are simply graphic representations of the performance data stored in an SMF.

Voices *are*:

■ The number of simultaneous sounds that a synthesizer can produce at any one point in time. Each note triggered by MIDI data counts for one voice.

Instruments *are*:

■ The number of unique timbres available to the phone. For most phones, the instrument list will consist of the General MIDI instrument list included with this chapter, i.e., one drum set instrument and 127 other instruments. Therefore, most phones are 128-instrument devices.

Channels *are*:

■ A fixed number (16) of playback slots stored within an SMF. Each MIDI channel can have (among other things) individual volume and instrument assignment.

Channel 10 is used for drums, while all the other channels can be assigned to any other instruments.

A 64-voice synthesizer can have up to 64 sounds playing at any given moment. It will always have 128 instruments and 16 MIDI channels. A 4-voice phone will also have 128 instruments and 16 MIDI channels. However, a 64-voice synthesizer can't have 64 separate instruments playing at once, but that is a limitation of using MIDI, rather than a limitation of the synthesizer. MIDI files can only handle 16 channels at a time, so you can only have 16 unique instruments playing at one time. However, within those 16 tracks you can trigger multiple voices. So, if you have a 4-voice synthesizer, you can still have 16 channels playing unique instruments as long as they never play more than four pitches simultaneously. Conversely, if you play 24 pitches at the same time on channel 1 and you only have a 24-voice synthesizer, you will have used up all of your voices using just one channel.

General MIDI

Because every synthesizer manufacturer adhered to the MIDI specification in different ways, the MIDI Manufacturer's Association, in association with the Japan MIDI Standards Committee, developed a basic set of standards to which all General MIDI devices must adhere. This standard was called *General MIDI* and was developed in 1991. Before General MIDI, there were no standard instruments, and even worse, there were no standard drum maps, so the same note played on different synthesizers would result in different drum sounds. You would think you were triggering a snare drum and instead play a triangle. There were also no standards for what kind of controlling data (e.g., panning or pitch bending) could be received by the devices. For instance, AudioExample5.mp3 is a drum beat played on a general MIDI synthesizer, while AudioExample6.mp3 is that same MIDI file played on a nongeneral MIDI synthesizer. Believe it or not, that is the same file. In light of these problems, a specification was created, and devices branded with the General MIDI logo must adhere to that specification. For the most part, mobile devices have the following instruments and capabilities, as defined by the General MIDI standard:

GENERAL REQUIREMENTS for MIDI:

MIDI Channels: 16

- Simultaneous Melodic Instruments = up to 15
- Simultaneous Percussion Kits = 1 (Channel 10)

SUPPORTED CONTROL CHANGE MESSAGES

- Modulation Depth (cc#1)
- Channel Volume (cc#7)
- Pan (cc#10)
- Expression (cc#11)

- Data Entry (cc#6/38)
- Hold1 (Damper) (cc#64)
- RPN LSB/MSB (cc#100/101)
- Pitch Bend
- All Sound Off, All Notes Off, Reset All Controllers

SUPPORTED RPNs (Registered Parameter Numbers)

- Pitch Bend Sensitivity

SUPPORTED UNIVERSAL SYSTEM EXCLUSIVE MESSAGES

- GM1 System On

Table 7.1 shows the general MIDI Instrument ("Patch") Map. These instruments are available in one form or another on all of the phones on the market. You can assign one instrument to each MIDI channel other than Channel 10, which is used for the drum set.

Table 7.1 General MIDI Level 1 Instrument Patch

PC#	Instrument	PC#	Instrument
1	Acoustic Grand Piano	65	Soprano Sax
2	Bright Acoustic Piano	66	Alto Sax
3	Electric Grand Piano	67	Tenor Sax
4	Honky-tonk Piano	68	Baritone Sax
5	Electric Piano 1	69	Oboe
6	Electric Piano 2	70	English Horn
7	Harpsichord	71	Bassoon
8	Clavi	72	Clarinet
9	Celesta	73	Piccolo
10	Glockenspiel	74	Flute
11	Music Box	75	Recorder
12	Vibraphone	76	Pan Flute
13	Marimba	77	Blown Bottle
14	Xylophone	78	Shakuhachi
15	Tubular Bells	79	Whistle
16	Dulcimer	80	Ocarina
17	Drawbar Organ	81	Lead 1 (square)
18	Percussive Organ	82	Lead 2 (sawtooth)
19	Rock Organ	83	Lead 3 (calliope)
20	Church Organ	84	Lead 4 (chiff)
21	Reed Organ	85	Lead 5 (charang)
22	Accordion	86	Lead 6 (voice)

continued

23	Harmonica	87	Lead 7 (fifths)
24	Tango Accordion	88	Lead 8 (bass + lead)
25	Acoustic Guitar (nylon)	89	Pad 1 (new age)
26	Acoustic Guitar (steel)	90	Pad 2 (warm)
27	Electric Guitar (jazz)	91	Pad 3 (polysynth)
28	Electric Guitar (clean)	92	Pad 4 (choir)
29	Electric Guitar (muted)	93	Pad 5 (bowed)
30	Overdriven Guitar	94	Pad 6 (metallic)
31	Distortion Guitar	95	Pad 7 (halo)
32	Guitar harmonics	96	Pad 8 (sweep)
33	Acoustic Bass	97	FX 1 (rain)
34	Electric Bass (finger)	98	FX 2 (soundtrack)
35	Electric Bass (pick)	99	FX 3 (crystal)
36	Fretless Bass	100	FX 4 (atmosphere)
37	Slap Bass 1	101	FX 5 (brightness)
38	Slap Bass 2	102	FX 6 (goblins)
39	Synth Bass 1	103	FX 7 (echoes)
40	Synth Bass 2	104	FX 8 (sci-fi)
41	Violin	105	Sitar
42	Viola	106	Banjo
43	Cello	107	Shamisen
44	Contrabass	108	Koto
45	Tremolo Strings	109	Kalimba
46	Pizzicato Strings	110	Bag pipe
47	Orchestral Harp	111	Fiddle
48	Timpani	112	Shanai
49	String Ensemble 1	113	Tinkle Bell
50	String Ensemble 2	114	Agogo
51	SynthStrings 1	115	Steel Drums
52	SynthStrings 2	116	Woodblock
53	Choir Aahs	117	Taiko Drum
54	Voice Oohs	118	Melodic Tom
55	Synth Voice	119	Synth Drum
56	Orchestra Hit	120	Reverse Cymbal
57	Trumpet	121	Guitar Fret Noise
58	Trombone	122	Breath Noise
59	Tuba	123	Seashore
60	Muted Trumpet	124	Bird Tweet
61	French Horn	125	Telephone Ring
62	Brass Section	126	Helicopter
63	SynthBrass 1	127	Applause
64	SynthBrass 2	128	Gunshot

Table 7.2 shows the general MIDI Level 1 Percussion Key Map. These are the MIDI note assignments for triggering separate percussion instruments when using MIDI Channel 10. MIDI Channel 10 is always used for percussion and is the only single patch that supports multiple timbres.

Table 7.2 General MIDI Level 1 Percussion Key Map

Key#	Drum Sound	Key#	Drum Sound
35	Acoustic Bass Drum	59	Ride Cymbal 2
36	Bass Drum 1	60	Hi Bongo
37	Side Stick	61	Low Bongo
38	Acoustic Snare	62	Mute Hi Conga
39	Hand Clap	63	Open Hi Conga
40	Electric Snare	64	Low Conga
41	Low Floor Tom	65	High Timbale
42	Closed Hi-Hat	66	Low Timbale
43	High Floor Tom	67	High Agogo
44	Pedal Hi-Hat	68	Low Agogo
45	Low Tom	69	Cabasa
46	Open Hi-Hat	70	Maracas
47	Low-Mid Tom	71	Short Whistle
48	Hi Mid Tom	72	Long Whistle
49	Crash Cymbal	74	Long Guiro
51	Ride Cymbal 1	75	Claves
52	Chinese Cymbal	76	Hi Wood Block
53	Ride Bell	77	Low Wood Block
54	Tambourine	78	Mute Cuica
55	Splash Cymbal	79	Open Cuica
56	Cowbell	80	Mute Triangle
57	Crash Cymbal 2	81	Open Triangle
58	Vibraslap		

Voice Management Using SP-MIDI Files

SP-MIDI is a standard that was developed by Nokia and Beatnik in association with the MIDI Manufacturer's Association and the Association of Musical Electronics Industry (AMEI). SP stands for *scalable polyphony*. The idea behind SP-MIDI is that you can create one file that will work on both a 4-voice and a 24-voice phone. Currently, a 4-voice MIDI file will play on both a 24-voice phone and a 4-voice phone, but it won't really take advantage of the 24 voices. A 24-voice MIDI file playing back on a 4-voice phone will have problems because it exceeds the capabilities of the synthesizer. Using the SP-MIDI format (which still has the extension .mid), you can add logic to the MIDI file to mute or unmute channels based on the capability of the synthesizer. SP-MIDI is going to become a big part of music for mobile games as soon as multiple MIDI files can be triggered by the devices. For instance, if your sound engine can handle 16 voices, but only 8 when a QCP file is playing, you'll need that MIDI file to scale itself down to 8 voices and back up to 16 when the sound effect is over. If you want to see an excellent SP-MIDI tutorial on creating SP-MIDI files, try the following link: **http://sonify.org/tutorials/links/pages/mobile_audio/authoring/sp-midi/**

Tip

Voice usage varies from phone to phone. A 16-voice file on one phone may use up to double that number of voices on another phone because the decay of the patch might be longer. Remember that if you have a voice playing and it has a 5-second decay, any note triggered before that note finishes its decay uses up another voice. Every phone manufacturer uses a different instrument set with a different set of decays, so the only way to know for sure if your voice management is good is to listen on all the target devices.

Digital Audio

The history of recorded sound is too large a topic to really cover here, but I will try to give a general overview. Understanding basic concepts of recording technology is important for understanding mobile audio production. The first concept that needs to be defined is the idea of a sound wave. Sound is the result of compression (and therefore rarefaction) of airwaves. Because sound is nothing more than the transfer of energy, that energy can be converted to another form (i.e., electrical energy), and certain characteristics of that sound can be captured and archived for later reproduction. These characteristics are pitch (the frequency of the sound wave), volume (the amplitude of the sound wave), and duration (the length of the sound wave). The digital terms for storing that data are sampling rate, bit-depth, and time length. Pitch is the relative highness or lowness of a sound, while volume is the relative loudness. A bass drum has a very low pitch, while a flute has a high pitch; a whisper is quite soft, while a rock concert is rather loud. In addition to those physical characteristics, digital files can also store the number of channels that will be used in reproduction of the sound. The standard number of channels stored is two: one left channel and one right channel. This is called *stereophonic* or *stereo sound. Monophonic (mono) sound* stores only one channel of data.

The original media used to archive sound were analog, which stored continuous data. Examples of analog media are magnetic tape and vinyl records. Records and tapes capture the original waveform and store (and thereby reproduce) pitch, volume, and length in a continuous fashion rather than an intervallic fashion. These media capture the waveform more accurately than digital media because analog techniques can reproduce a curve;

however, they are difficult to edit and very fragile compared to digital media. Some people prefer the sound and process of recording analog media, but the ease of use of digital media has taken over in most professional and consumer markets.

Digital media like DATs, CDs, and DVDs can only approximate the idea of a curve because they store the data in a series of samples. They don't capture the actual waveform, but approximate it by saving small slices of the wave and reproducing them so quickly that we hear them as continuous sound. To get an idea of what a digital audio waveform looks like, refer to Figure 7.4. If you want to increase the quality of a digital file, all you can do is increase the sample rate, which determines the resolution of your approximation of a curve; however, the more you increase the resolution of the file, the more you increase the size of that file. While analog media have a different and sometimes more desirable sound than digital media, because analog relies on a physical medium (the actual tape) and cannot really be transferred from that medium as analog data, digital media have taken over for most practical storage and distribution of music. Digital dominance is both a blessing and a curse, because digital copies of music all have exactly the same audio quality, which allows for potentially unlimited illegal copying. So the protection and security of digital music are comparatively weak, but at the same time editing, manipulation, and distribution are much easier.

The following list highlights some key points about digital audio:

- Actual recording of musical performance
- Many subformats (WAV, MP3, AAC, AIFF, QCP, AMR-WB)

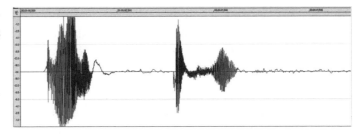

Figure 7.4 A graphical representation of a digital audio waveform. Notice the striking difference between this graphical representation and the MIDI data.

- File size can be up to 50 megabytes for 5 minutes of music
- Little variance of sound quality between similar formats (i.e., all 16 bit, 44.1 kHz stereo files basically sound the same)

Because mobile devices require such small file sizes, we're almost always going to be downgrading the quality of a digital audio signal, so in the next few sections we'll explore some common ways to reduce the size of a digital audio file.

Bit-Depth

The technical definition of bit-depth is the resolution at which the amplitude of a waveform can be stored. For our purposes, just understand bit depth to be a means of controlling file size by reducing quality. There are two options for bit-depth: 16 bit and 8 bit.

You'll find an example of a 16 bit WAV file on the CD, as well as an example of an 8 bit WAV file. Reduction from 16 bits to 8 bits halves the file size. One technique for mitigating the loss of quality when converting the bit-depth from 16 bits to 8 bits is called *dithering*. This is the process of intentionally adding a bit of noise to the recording.

Sampling Rate

Sampling rate is the number of samples of data that are taken per second. The Nyquist theorem states that if you want to hear a pitch whose frequency is x, you must sample the wave at a rate of at least 2x. Since the upper limit of human hearing is about 20,000 hertz, the sampling rate for CD quality audio is 44,100 hertz (44.1 kilohertz). You can set the sampling rate to any number, but standard sample rates are 22,500, 11,250, and 8,000 hertz. These reduce the file size to $1/2$, $1/4$, and approximately $1/5$ the original file size, but result in a corresponding loss of sound quality. There are examples of files at each of the sampling rates included on the CD accompanying this book.

Data Compression

Once you've got the basic information about a waveform, you might want to compress the data rather than simply cutting out information that is stored. The WAV and AIIFF are two forms of uncompressed audio data, while MP3, QCP, AAC, AMR, and IMA ADPCM WAV files are all forms of compressed audio. Each compression format has different settings at which you can compress the data. The harsher (more degrading to the original sound) the setting of the compression, the smaller the file size will be. In addition to that, most files must be uncompressed before playing back, which can be taxing on a mobile device's processor.

The following are the most common audio compression formats used in mobile audio production:

- QCP
- AMR/AMR-WB
- AAC
- IMA ADPCM WAV
- MP3

Mobile-Specific Formats (A Real Bloody Mess)

Audio on mobile phones has had a rough and troubled history. In a very short period of time, the audio capabilities of handsets have grown exponentially, which has contributed to the turbulence of their coming of age. The first sets of phones were only capable of playing back simple tones, because they were used only as phones. As the mobile phone took on different roles in people's lives, such as being their personal organizer, pocket MP3 player, pocket computer, or handheld game system, the audio needs and capabilities grew. The first phones were only able to play single lines of monophonic music as *ring-tones* and reproduce the caller's voice through the near-field speaker. These phones had proprietary formats for their ringtones and network-specific codecs that were used for the compression/decompression of the voice data transmitted across the network. These proprietary formats sort of coalesced into the first wave of formats for phones. Two of the monophonic ringtone formats that emerged from this period were RTTL and iMelody. These formats allowed for the programming of musical data into the phones and thus began the development and sale of monophonic ringtones. Subsequently, digital audio codecs and formats like QCP, AMR, and AMR-WB emerged as standards for transferring the voice data over wireless networks. These codecs were excellent for capturing the frequency range of the human voice and for leveling out any volume fluctuations in speech, but they were terrible for reproducing any kind of music.

Once the ringtone industry started taking off and the need for multimedia content on phones grew, third-party companies who had already developed audio playback and synthesis technology started licensing their technology to phone manufacturers. QUAL-COMM developed the CMX (Compact Media Extension) format for synchronizing graphics and audio, Yamaha developed the SMAF (Synthetic Mobile Application Format), Beatnik developed the SP-MIDI specification and introduced RMF and XMF, Sseyo developed and licensed the Intent Sound System (which includes the Advanced Polyphonic Ringtone Engine), and quite a few other formats have been developed as well. Each of these solutions is non-exclusive, although a lot of them have overlapping ideas. For instance, CMX and Beatnik have both announced that their audio systems will have the capability to play back files that adhere to the SMAF standard. Most of these formats or audio engines are based on the same principle, which is the ability to play MIDI and digital audio simultaneously. The basic idea is that you can use MIDI for certain applications and digital audio for others.

Monophonic Tones

Monophonic tones are still useful in wireless applications because they are very small and very useful for working with a wide range of handsets. While other formats exist, two basic standards have emerged for creating monophonic rings: RTTL and iMelody. On the CD is an example of an RTTL monophonic ring. Content creation and testing for these rings can be a bit of a hassle because there are no real authoring tools for them, but these formats are used even in the high-end devices because they are small enough to be sent over SMS. Monophonic tones may have uses in both game and nongame applications where alert sounds are needed.

SMAF (Synthetic Mobile Application Format)

SMAF is a multimedia data format that has been developed by the Yamaha Corporation. It is a hardware-dependent format, meaning that to take advantage of all its capabilities, the mobile device must have a special chip inside of it. Using the tools and converters available on the Yamaha Web site, a professional electronic musician can get started creating SMAF content rather quickly.

SMAF has three levels, each of which has different audio capabilities:

SMAF MA-2

- FM sound generator
- Polyphony: 16-note (16 independent sounds can be generated simultaneously)
- ADPCM playback function: single-channel 4 bit ADPCM decoder
- Sampling rates: 4kHz, 8kHz

The MA-2 specifications are the most limited within SMAF. All SMAF levels incorporate an FM synthesizer rather than a wavetable synthesizer. Without getting into a fairly technical discussion, this means three things: You can customize your instrument sounds, each phone will play back your MIDI files the same, and your files will have a very "electronic" sound to them. The MA-2 specification also allows for playback of digital audio files using ADPCM compression. Figure 7.5 shows a screenshot of the SMAF MA-2 authoring tool.

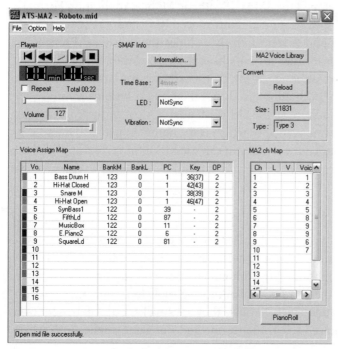

Figure 7.5 Screenshot of the SMAF MA-2 authoring tool.

SMAF MA-3

- Stereo hybrid synthesizer system
- Improved fundamental FM waveforms and algorithms
- Default tones for FM and waveform table synthesizers stored in ROM; tones can be downloaded to RAM
- Polyphony: 40-note (40 independent sounds can be generated simultaneously; 32 FM tones + 8 waveform table tones)
- Sampling rates for PCM/ADPCM playback: 4kHz–48 kHz

The MA-3 specification is one level above the MA-2 specification in terms of its capabilities. It is still, for the most part, an FM synthesis-based MIDI playback system, which provides the same advantages as MA-2. The MA-3 specification also allows for more sophisticated use of digital audio simultaneously with MIDI files.

SMAF MA-5

MA-5 is a versatile hybrid sound chip incorporating various different synthesizers. It incorporates FM synthesis, wavetable synthesis, PCM (WAV) streaming, and analog synthesis. The exact specs are not available yet, but the MA-5 authoring tool is shown in Figure 7.6.

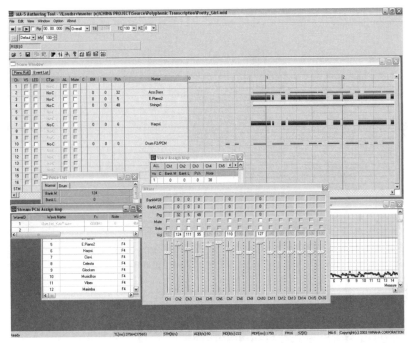

Figure 7.6 The SMAF MA-5 authoring tool. As the capabilities of the devices grow, so does the complexity of the authoring tools.

Currently, there are only MA-2 and MA-3 phones on the market. SMAF is backward-compatible, which means that MA-2 files will play on MA-3 phones, but not the other way around. I'm not going to go into great detail about how to use SMAF or what it can do because it's really beyond the scope of this chapter. However, it's good to know that SMAF phones have a very powerful audio engine that handles both MIDI and digital audio files very well.

Compact Media Extension (Extension .pmd)

CMX is a hardware-accelerated multimedia format developed by QUALCOMM that allows for the synchronization of images, animation, digital audio, and MIDI files. The three current versions of CMX are:

- Version 2.0
- Version 3.0
- Version 4.0

All versions can play back MIDI files and QCP files at varying degrees of quality. Versions 3.0 and higher can play back IMA ADPCM files. QUALCOMM has also announced that future versions of CMX will be able to play back SMAF files. Figure 7.7 shows the CMX Studio Authoring tool.

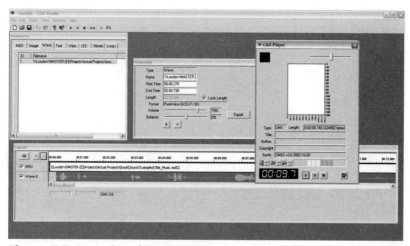

Figure 7.7 Screenshot of the CMX Studio Authoring tool. Notice that it has a similar interface to most digital movie editing software.

Mobile Audio Production Tools

There are a number of tools available that are useful for developing audio for mobile devices. The following sections provide an overview of the most useful of these tools.

Beatnik

The Beatnik audio engine is currently used in a lot of Nokia and a couple of Sony Ericsson phones. Originally developed as a solution for Web audio, Beatnik never really caught on, so the technology was licensed as a software solution for audio playback by mobile devices. There are two main formats that are native to Beatnik: RMF and XMF. In addition to these formats, all Beatnik phones can play SP-MIDI, MIDIe, RTTL, iMelody, and certain kinds of WAV files. RMF content can be created using the Beatnik Editor; XMF content is created using the Beatnik Mobile Sound Builder. The audio capabilities of the Beatnik engine vary from device to device, so it's always best to check the Beatnik Web site for the most up-to-date information. Figure 7.8 shows the Beatnik Editor, and Figure 7.9 is a screenshot of the Beatnik Mobile Sound Builder.

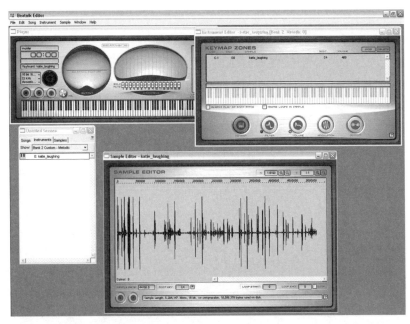

Figure 7.8 The Beatnik Editor, used to create RMF content for mobile devices. Essentially, it works like a sampler.

Sonar

SONAR is a music production program that can process MIDI files as well as WAV and other forms of digital audio. The MIDI programming capabilities are extensive, and the multitrack audio capabilities are adequate for most production. Figure 7.10 shows the SONAR audio production tool.

ProTools

ProTools is hardware-accelerated digital audio production software emphasizing the recording and manipulation of digital audio. ProTools is not recommended for MIDI work in the mobile realm. Figure 7.11 shows the ProTools Edit view.

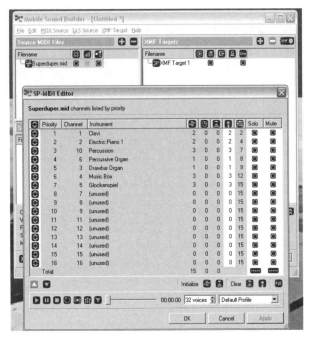

Figure 7.9 Beatnik Mobile Sound Builder, used to create SP-MIDI files and XMF content.

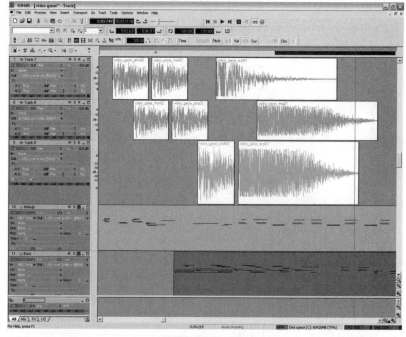

Figure 7.10 The main view of the SONAR audio production tool, used to create MIDI files as well as all kinds of digital audio files.

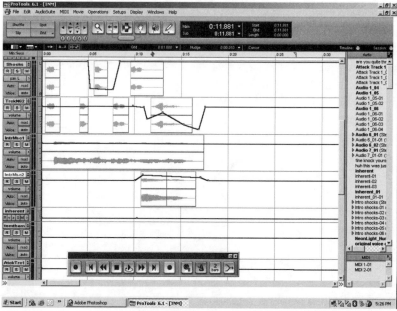

Figure 7.11 Edit view of ProTools. ProTools should only be used for digital audio editing in the realm of audio for mobile devices.

Sound Forge

Sound Forge is a two-track WAV editor that is very useful for the dithering, compression, downsampling, and manipulation of digital audio. Sound Forge has no MIDI editing capabilities. It is useful for the mastering of digital audio files and conversion to most final formats. Anyone serious about mobile audio is going to have a special relationship with Sound Forge. Figure 7.12 shows the Sound Forge authoring tool.

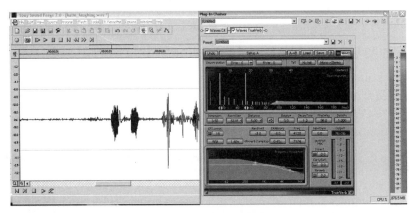

Figure 7.12 The Sound Forge authoring tool filtering a monophonic waveform.

Production Methods

In order to produce quality audio content, we've got to come up with a method. Here's my rough outline for production of content (audio or otherwise) for mobile audio:

- Preproduction
- Production
- Testing
- Porting
- Testing

The steps above are slightly different for games and applications compared to animation/sync and picture content. With that said, we will only focus on the production methods for games and applications.

Preproduction

Preproduction is when the bulk of the creative work and technical research is done. Assuming that the basic research has been done and the basic audio design has been completed, an audio design document must be created. This document has a separate page for each build group or target handset that lists the audio capabilities of the device. For example, let's say we're producing a Western-themed target shooting game in which the player shoots a revolver at tin cans. For the title screen, we'll want some Western-themed music; for the game itself, a sound effect for when you shoot the gun, a sound effect for when you hit a can, another sound effect when you hit ten cans in a row, and some short music for when you win or lose. We're making two different file size builds: 64K and 128K. For the 64K, 8K (compressed) will go to audio. For the 128K, 20K (compressed) will go to audio. There are going to be two builds: one JAVA build for Device A, and one BREW 2.1 build for Device B.

Step 1) Research devices and capabilities

We know that Device A is capable of playing MIDI files. We also know that it has a 24-voice synthesizer. Because we're limited to a 5K file size, we're going to use MIDI files for Device A. For Device B, we know that the device can play MIDI files and QCP files, so we'll try to use some QCP files for the sound effects.

Step 2) Produce audio design document with capabilities and build lists

We started to list earlier the features needed for the game, but let's be a little more disciplined about it now. We need title screen music, win music, and lose music. As far as sound effects go, we need a gunshot sound, a can hit sound, and a ten-in-a-row can hit bonus sound. Let's start making our audio design document now:

Table 7.3 shows our audio design.

Table 7.3 Audio Design Layout

Master Assets Needed	Description
Title music	15–30 second title music Western-themed
Lose game music	Very short music cue for when the game is lost (<200 points)
Win game music	Very short music cue for when the game is won (>200 points)
Gunshot sound	A gunshot sound
Can hit sound	Sound when a can is struck by a bullet
Bonus can hit sound	Sound when 10 cans are struck in a row without missing

Production

We now can begin production of the assets. We know that we're going to use MIDI music for both builds and that we're going to need QCP files for the BREW build. QCP files are a compressed digital audio format, so we're going to need to create some WAV files in order to make the QCP files. So let's start making our production list.

Table 7.4 shows our audio design table with formats to use.

Table 7.4 Audio Design Format Layout

Master Assets Needed	MIDI	WAV	QCP
Title music	YES	NO	NO
Lose game music	YES	NO	NO
Win game music	YES	NO	NO
Gunshot sound	YES	YES	YES
Can hit sound	YES	YES	YES
Bonus can hit sound	YES	NO	NO

I usually start with MIDI stuff, but one can go in either direction. The focus for the MIDI work is to create a great piece of music and fairly rough sound effects. The testing on the phones will affect the sound effects very much, so you shouldn't spend much time on that now. The only limitations to take into account for the music are the standards set by the General MIDI standard. We'll deal with the rest when it comes to porting the assets. To do this kind of work, I recommend a General MIDI soundcard or a low-quality General MIDI synthesizer and SONAR. It doesn't make sense to do this work on expensive synthesizers or high-end samplers, because it really won't sound that way on the phone at all. Figure 7.13 is a graphic of the MIDI file for the title music. `AudioExample7.mp3` is a recording of that MIDI file at this point.

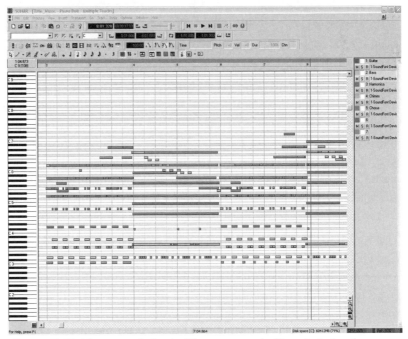

Figure 7.13 Theme music for the Western game in Piano Roll view for SONAR.

At this point, we create the MIDI sound effects. MIDI sound effects require a LOT of testing on the specific phones, so at this point just sketch out the very basic idea of what is going to happen. AudioExample8.mp3 is the MIDI gunshot sound at this point. Figure 7.14 shows the MIDI gunshot sound effect in the SONAR tool.

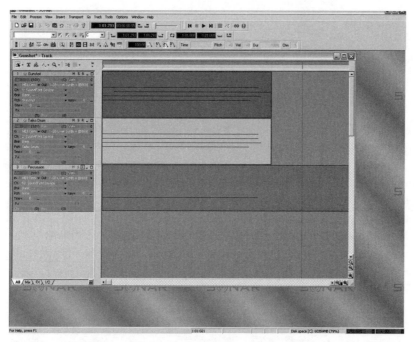

Figure 7.14 MIDI gunshot sound effect when viewed in the main view of SONAR.

Then it's on to digital audio sound effects. Much time is going to be spent making the sound effects really good at this stage, because with digital audio, you're only as good as your original source. The first step is to use multitrack digital audio software like Pro-Tools or SONAR to create the asset. We pick and choose from the gunshot sounds and layer them together to create an entirely new gunshot sound. Because SONAR can handle digital audio as well, we can use that for the creation of the sound effect, or we can use other programs like ProTools. Figure 7.15 is a picture of the multitrack production used for the gunshot sound for this project.

That multitrack production is then bounced down to a single 16 bit, 44.1 kHz stereo .WAV file, which becomes our source asset when it comes to porting. AudioExample9.mp3 is the source gunshot that we just created. After the sound effects are created, we used Sound Forge to properly prepare the audio for conversion to QCP. QCP files sound best when converted into QCP from 16 bit, 8kHz mono files. Here are step-by-step instructions for creating a 16 bit, 8kHz file from a 16 bit, 44.1kHz file: If you want to do this conversion yourself, use the file Gunshot.wav that is included on the CD.

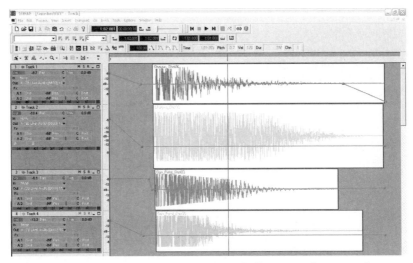

Figure 7.15 The digital audio gunshot sound effect in production. We're using four gunshot sounds to make one sound for the game.

Step 1) Open the source file in Sound Forge, shown in Figure 7.16 and Figure 7.17.

Step 2) Convert the stereo file to mono, as shown in Figure 7.18, Figure 7.19, and Figure 7.20. Use Process, Channel Converter. One of the presets is called *Stereo to Mono*. Use both channels at 50%. Generally, you can use this preset.

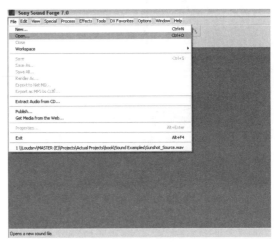

Figure 7.16 To open a file in Sound Forge, go to File, Open.

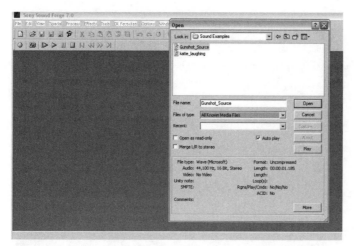

Figure 7.17 Locate the source file you want to open and open it.

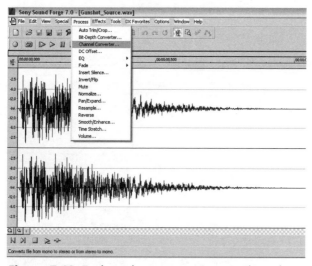

Figure 7.18 To channel convert, use Process, Channel Converter

Step 3) Resample the file to 8kHz as shown in Figure 7.21 and Figure 7.22. Use Process, Resample. Set the interpolation accuracy to high (4), make sure to apply the anti-alias filter (which will help preserve the original sound), and set the sample rate to 8,000. Make sure you do not check the Set the Sample Rate Only box.

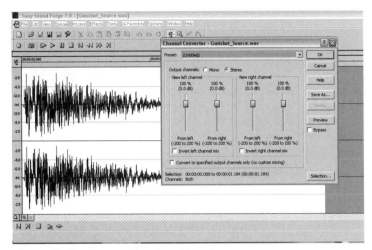

Figure 7.19 Now you need to select a preset.

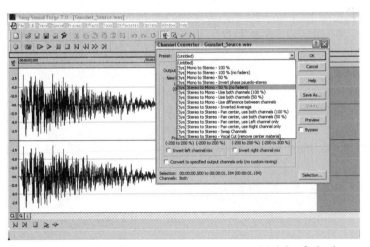

Figure 7.20 Select the preset Stereo to Mono—50% (no faders).

Step 4) Save your asset as this new file shown in Figure 7.23 and Figure 7.24. Make sure the description in the Save As box says "Render 8,000 Hz, 16 Bit, Mono PCM wave file." Also make sure you have the box Save Metadata with File unchecked.

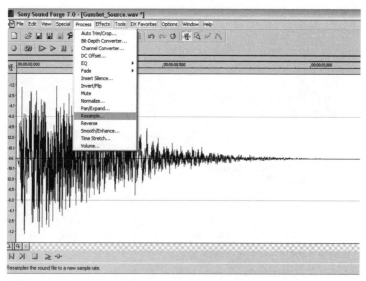

Figure 7.21 To resample, go to Process, Resample.

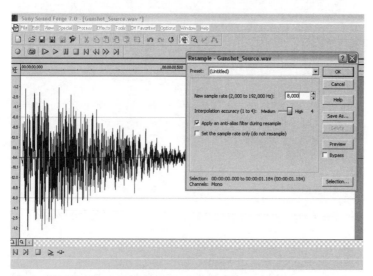

Figure 7.22 Insert 8000 for New Sample Rate, make sure to check the Apply an Anti-Alias Filter During Resample, set the quality to high, and make sure that Set the Sample Tate only (Do Not Resample) is unchecked.

At this point, you've properly prepared your WAV file for QCP conversion. All of that was only half of the work!

You need to use a new tool, CMX Studio, to successfully create a QCP file. The following are step-by-step instructions for exporting a QCP file from CMX Studio.

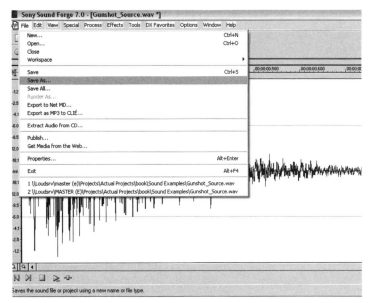

Figure 7.23 Now you need to save the preconverted file. Don't save over your original source, so go to File, Save As.

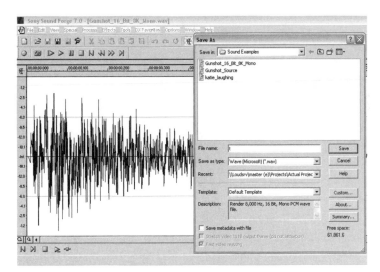

Figure 7.24 Now, save your file with a new name.

Step 1) Open CMX Studio and select the Wave tab, shown in Figure 7.25.

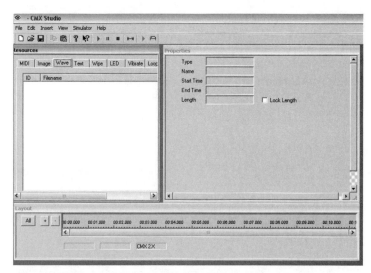

Figure 7.25 Open CMX Studio using CMX version 2.0 and select the Wave tab.

Step 2) Right-click on the window below the Wave tab and select Insert WAV, shown in Figure 7.26.

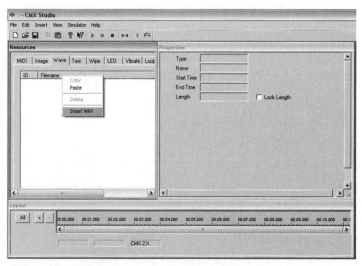

Figure 7.26 Right-click in the window below the Wave tab and select Insert WAV.

Step 3) Select the WAV file you want to import, shown in Figure 7.27.

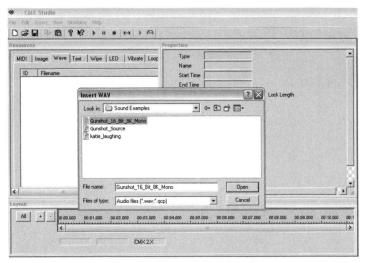

Figure 7.27 Select the WAV file you want to import.

Step 4) In the Properties window, click on Export, shown in Figure 7.28.

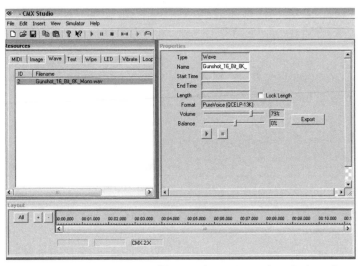

Figure 7.28 Now your WAV file is in the project. Take a look at the Properties window. Click on Export.

Step 5) Save your new QCP file, shown in Figure 7.29.

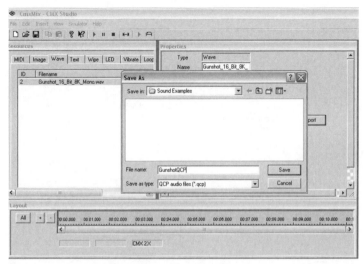

Figure 7.29 Once you click on Export, you'll be able to save your
WAV file as a QCP file.

Congratulations! If you followed those instructions, you successfully converted a WAV file
to a QCP file. AudioExample10.mp3 is a recording of the QCP gunshot sound.

Testing

At this point, we'll test and revise the MIDI files on Device A.

Table 7.5 shows our asset list for this device:

Table 7.5 Audio Asset List for Build A

Build A	Format	File size
Title music	MIDI	<3K
Lose game music	MIDI	<1K
Win game music	MIDI	<1K
Gunshot sound	MIDI	<1K
Can hit sound	MIDI	<1K
Bonus can hit sound	MIDI	<1K

From this point on, all the work should be done in tandem with the programmer. Ideally,
the content provider should be able to insert and test the newest version of his sounds and
make his own build, but that's not always the case, so there has to be clear programmer
support.

Porting

Once Device A is complete, we can take the MIDI asset we're going to use over to build B and replace the sounds for which we want a digital effect with QCP files.

Table 7.6 shows our asset list for this device:

Table 7.6 Audio Asset List for Build B

Build B	Format	File size
Title music	MIDI	<5K
Lose game music	MIDI	<1K
Win game music	MIDI	<1K
Gunshot sound	QCP	<5K
Can hit sound	QCP	<5K
Bonus can hit sound	MIDI	<1K

Testing Again

All that's left to do is test assets for the devices in the application. Keep revising until it sounds good. Table 7.7 and Table 7.8 show our audio asset list for our builds.

Table 7.7 Audio Asset List for Build A

Build A	Format	File size
Title music	MIDI	AudioExample9a.mp3
Lose game music	MIDI	AudioExample10a.mp3
Win game music	MIDI	AudioExample11a.mp3
Gunshot sound	MIDI	AudioExample12a.mp3
Can hit sound	MIDI	AudioExample13a.mp3
Bonus can hit sound	MIDI	AudioExample14a.mp3

Table 7.8 Audio Asset List for Build B

Build B	Format	File Name
Title music	MIDI	AudioExample9a.mp3
Lose game music	MIDI	AudioExample10a.mp3
Win game music	MIDI	AudioExample11a.mp3
Gunshot sound	QCP	AudioExample12a.mp3
Can hit sound	QCP	AudioExample13a.mp3
Bonus can hit sound	MIDI	AudioExample14a.mp3

A Brief Overview of Audio in BREW

Each version of BREW has more sophisticated audio capabilities than the last. However, even in BREW, you still have to do the research for each specific device. For instance, if you want to use the CMX functionality of a phone, you have to make sure that the phone supports CMX; if you want to use a 16-voice MIDI file, you have to ensure that the device synthesizer supports 16 voices; and so on and so forth. Keep that in mind as you look over this summary of audio functionality for each BREW version. We're not going to get into the nitty-gritty of coding audio here, as there is a good resource already out there if you're looking for that: *Wireless Game Development in C/C++ with Brew* by Ralph Barbagallo.

There are basically three different kinds of audio in BREW:

- Tones/rings/beeps/vibration
- MIDI
- Compressed digital audio

Tones, Beeps, Rings, Vibration

Tones, beeps, rings, and vibration are very difficult to control and use, but require little to no resources. A beep is simply a beep generated by the phone and played through the ringer speaker. A tone is a tone generated by the phone, but you have more control over the frequency, length, and volume than you do with a simple beep. You can also load tone lists, which are sequences of tones that are to be played back by using one command. Rings can also be triggered as alerts if you have an application that needs to alert the handset owner as a ring.

MIDI Files

MIDI files are usually played back as MIDI files. If needed, you can play back a MIDI file in a PMD wrapper (discussed earlier in this chapter), which is often done on CMX-enabled devices in BREW 2.1 or higher. Using the ISOUNDPLAYER interface, you can control the pitch and tempo of a MIDI file. Tempo is the speed of music (see example 1), and pitch is the frequency of sounds. A thunderclap has a very low pitch, while the clink of silverware has a very high one. By changing the pitch and tempo of a piece of music, you can change its mood. For instance, AudioExample15.mp3 is a piece of music at its appropriate pitch and tempo. AudioExample16.mp3 is that piece at half the pitch. AudioExample17 is the same piece at twice the tempo. BREW gives you this kind of control in the code, so with a limited number of audio assets, you can have a richer audio experience. One way to use this in a game is to increase the tempo and/or pitch of the music as the levels increase. Or, if there is a time-slow effect in your game, you can play the music back at half the speed and half the pitch to get the effect of time slowing down.

Compressed Audio Files

Compressed audio files come in all shapes and sizes. QCP is currently the most common, and it is very useful for sound effects. Using BREW 2.1 or higher, you can send MIDI data to trigger QCP files in order to play back more than one sound at a time. QUALCOMM MSM5100-based devices can have a MIDI or QCP file playing in the background and up to 4 QCP files (in this case extension .qcf) playing on top of that file. This allows for background music and up to four simultaneous sound effects. And, of course, another common format for compressed audio is MP3. Playback of MP3 is supported in all versions of BREW. MP4, AAC, and ADPCM WAV files can all be played on BREW 2.1 or higher handsets. In addition to all of that, there are some hardware-accelerated phones that support CMX and SMAF playback, but be sure to check the phone first.

Brew Audio Formats and Capabilities

Table 7.9 shows the BREW audio formats per version.

Table 7.9 Audio Formats in BREW

BREW VERSION	Tones/ Rings/ Beeps/ Vibration	MIDI	MP3	QCP	QCF	SPF	MP4	AAC
1.0.1	Y	Y	Y	N	N	N	N	N
1.1	Y	Y	Y	Y	N	N	N	N
2.0.1	Y	Y	Y	Y	N	N	N	N
2.1	Y	Y	Y	Y	Y	Y	Y	Y
3.0.1	Y	Y	Y	Y	Y	Y	Y	Y

Table 7.10 shows the BREW audio capabilities per version.

Table 7.10 Audio Capabilities in BREW

BREW VERSION	MMF	ADPCM/ WAV	PMD	Streaming Audio	Multiple Sounds at Once
1.0.1	N	N	N	N	N
1.1	N	N	N	N	N
2.0.1	N	N	N	N	N
2.1	Y	Y	Y	Y	Y
3.0.1	Y	Y	Y	Y	Y

A Simple BREW Audio Example

In the interactive BREW 2.0 demo on the QUALCOMM Web site, you will find the game *Yao Ming Basketball* developed by Sorrent. This game has some pretty sophisticated use of audio and can serve as a demonstration of some of the audio capabilities of BREW. Audio is still very much in its infancy in the mobile game space, but let's walk through it and take a look at the audio implementation and design. For the splash screen before the main menu, a short piece of compressed audio is played back. This could be an MMF, a QCP, an ADPCM WAV, or an MP3, depending on the handset. It could also be a PMD with a QCP or an ADPCM WAV synced to the graphic. Once the game starts, QCP sound effects are used for the basketball dribble sound, the ball hitting the rim, the squeak of the shoes, and the crashing down of the basketball basket for a slam dunk. These could also be QCF files, which are simply QCP files triggered by MIDI messages and played through the MIDI out. If your shot is blocked by the defender, a beep or tone is played. An animation plays between the two halves, accompanied by MIDI music. Or it could be an example of a PMD file that contains both the MIDI and animation data. *Yao Ming Basketball* takes good advantage of all the capabilities of the BREW audio specifications.

The Future of Mobile Audio

The mobile market is certainly going to grow, and audio quality is going to become more and more of an issue. The more quality becomes an issue, the greater the need for qualified people who do good work, which means that the budgets for applications and content are going to grow, and for sure the capabilities of the phones are going to grow. Here are some of the things I see coming soon to mobile devices.

- XMF content with customizable sound banks.
- SMAF MA-5 FM, wavetable, and analog synthesis.
- Digital effects processing for speaker versus headphones.
- Stereo and 3D positional audio.
- Streaming CD-quality music.
- Mobile phone-specific sound effects libraries to speed up development.
- Tighter integration and control over vibration and LED content.

All in all, the future for mobile devices is very, very exciting. I only hope that some industry-wide standards come out of all of this, and that the manufacturers and carriers will make it easier to develop content for phones. Right now, certain carriers make it very difficult to develop and test content on their devices, and unless they allow mobile applications to turn into a real market (by allowing publishers to effectively market their products), mobile production will never be a big enough business for development budgets to overcome the cost of device testing.

Resources

http://emusician.com/ar/emusic_phone/

http://www.cdmatech.com/solutions/products/cmx.jsp

http://smaf-yamaha.com/

http://www.beatnik.com/

http://www.gamasutra.com/resource_guide/20030528/wilde_01.shtml

http://www.sonify.org/

http://withintent.biz/aux-files/issfactsheet.pdf

http://withintent.biz/aux-files/apre.pdf

http://www.ummu.umich.edu/facilities/groundworks/docsystem/whatis/docs/digitalaudio/page1.html

http://hem.passagen.se/tkolb/art/synth/intro_e.htm

Key Terms Used in Mobile Audio Production

Bit-Depth: In the digital domain, resolution of the amplitude of a wave form. There are two bit-depths used: 8 bit and 16 bit. A file converted from 16 bit to 8 bit will be exactly half the file size of the 16 bit file.

Codec: Any technology used for compressing/decompressing data. MP3, AMR, QCP, and AAC are examples of audio codecs.

Digital Audio: The representation of an analog waveform via digital means. The wave is represented by a collection of discrete points, which serve to approximate the original continuous waveform.

Dither: The process of adding certain kinds of noise to an audio file in order to lessen the effects of reducing the bit-depth.

Downsampling: The process of reducing the sample rate of a digital recording. For instance, reducing the file from 44.1kHz to 8kHz will reduce both its file size and its quality.

Frequency: The speed at which any given audio signal oscillates. Generally given in terms of oscillations per second (for example, a sine wave with a 400Hz frequency is oscillating 400 times per second). The frequency of a wave determines that wave's pitch: the higher the frequency, the more oscillations per second, and the higher that wave's pitch.

FM-Synthesis: A form of synthesis (frequency modulation) that involves modulating one wave's frequency with another. The mobile audio format developed by Yamaha (SMAF) utilizes a form of FM-synthesis for its synthesizers. This kind of synthesis tends to sound very "electronic."

Hertz: The unit of measurement used for representing frequency. A kiloHertz is 1,000 Hertz.

IMA ADPCM: A form of compressed digital audio that certain phones can play natively and other phones can play back as RMF files.

MIDI Files: A MIDI file is, essentially, a collection of performance data. It will contain, among other things, information regarding which notes should be played, when, and at what volume. A MIDI file is used to "play" a synthesizer. In and of itself a MIDI file contains no audio data, only a collection of instructions for a synthesizer to realize.

Monophonic (Digital Audio Term): A digital audio file that has only one channel. A stereophonic (stereo) file has two channels of audio, for the left and right speakers. A monophonic (mono) file has only one channel of audio, for one speaker. A stereo file is exactly twice as large as a mono file.

Monophonic (MIDI Term): A MIDI file containing one line of music with no triggering of simultaneous sounds.

Polyphonic: A MIDI file containing multiple voices sounding at the same time.

Polyphony: The number of voices that a synthesizer can play at once. A 4-voice synthesizer can have up to 4 voices playing at once. A 64-voice synthesizer can have up to 64 voices playing at once. The only way to accurately test polyphony is to listen to the file on the device, as the same MIDI file can have a different voice count on a different synthesizer.

QCP: A form of audio compression developed by QUALCOMM in order to transfer voice files over telecommunication networks.

Sample Rate: In the digital domain, the rate at which the positions of an audio signal's waveform are recorded. At a sample rate of 44,100, a waveform's position is recorded 44,100 times per second. During playback, these samples of the audio signal's position are used to redraw or approximate the original waveform. The higher the sample rate, the more samples per second, the more accurately the original waveform can be approximated, and thus, the higher the sound quality. To hear any given frequency, you must sample at double frequency. Therefore if the upper limit of human hearing is 20,000Hz, you must sample at twice that frequency, or more, to hear the pitch.

SP-MIDI: A way of assigning a hierarchy to the various voices within MIDI files so as to deal with scalable levels of polyphony. For example, if a 16-voice SP-MIDI file is played on a 4-voice synthesizer, that SP-MIDI file will contain information concerning which 4 of its voices should be played and which 12 should be discarded, while still maintaining the musical integrity of the file.

Synthesizer: An electronic music instrument. In this context, each phone has its own synthesizer, which is a device capable of performing standard MIDI files.

WAV Files: A common digital audio format that stores audio waveform data. It stores four kinds of data about recorded audio: bit-depth, sampling rate, length, and number of channels (stereo or mono).

Wavetable Synthesis: A form of synthesis that uses very small recordings of instruments to generate sound. The Beatnik audio engine has a wavetable synthesizer.

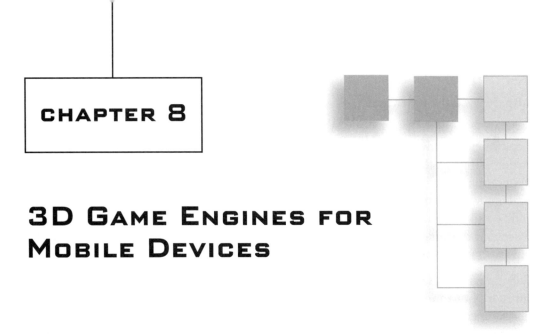

CHAPTER 8

3D GAME ENGINES FOR MOBILE DEVICES

This chapter focuses on commercially available 3D game engines for mobile phones. Each mobile 3D game engine offers something unique in terms of features or capabilities. Support for these engines will vary, depending on the carrier and device manufacturer, but it's likely that at least one of them will be supported on the devices for which you're developing. These engines may be available as an extension (such as those offered by the BREW platform), or they may be built into the phone software.

The three game engines mentioned in this chapter all have great capabilities and quality to offer any commercial game developer. They also either already support OpenGL ES or have announced future support for OpenGL ES. The following sections have been provided by the companies involved in developing and releasing these commercial 3D mobile game engines, and the authors of this book have worked with them to provide as objective a view as possible. We suggest going to each of the vendors' Web sites for more information.

All three of these game engines have been optimized on various platforms and have been tuned to deal with the limited resources for those devices. While you might still opt to develop your own game engine, we would recommend that you still consider these engines as a cost-effective solution.

In this chapter, we will cover three of the most popular mobile 3D game engines:

- The Fathammer X-Forge engine
- The Superscape Swerve engine
- The HI Corp Mascot Capsule V4 engine

X-Forge®

http://www.fathammer.com

X-Forge is a comprehensive set of technologies and tools, which enable the creation and deployment of advanced console-quality 3D games and other rich 3D content on all major mobile platforms. X-Forge has been developed to enable the most demanding 3D application there is: hardcore 3D games. X-Forge is also designed to support advanced and innovative game play, including cross-device multiplayer, pervasive gaming, as well as online and community features. It is also a natural fit for multichannel publishing, where essentially the same game is released into multiple format categories, such as consoles, PC, advanced mobile and—in the future—set-top-boxes.

X-Forge has been targeted to advanced mobile devices. The device can include wireless features or phone functionality, but it is not required. Typically, these devices have an open development environment and operating system. Because the device market is fragmented, the preferred development model with X-Forge is a true multiplatform development from the beginning, as opposed to single platform development and sequential porting.

X-Forge has already been used in more than 15 commercially released titles. It has also been used in numerous demos and internally developed titles. This experience has allowed Fathammer to redesign the second generation of X-Forge to demanding real-world game projects. Internal game development is the driving force behind X-Forge development. It means that most features have been added and most problems solved before the system sees its first customer.

X-Forge 2

The primary goals in X-Forge 2—the second generation of X-Forge—have been the ease of development, additional emphasis on the artist tool chain, and clearly improved performance under real-world gaming conditions. An important performance goal was also the native use of 3D acceleration where available. Also, various server-side and networking features have been added. X-Forge still retains the previous flexibility with distribution and billing options to enable the business model that developers select for the game they create.

X-Forge is licensed to game developers and publishers who want to create cutting-edge, advanced mobile games with high performance and stunning visual quality. X-Forge can be used to develop many kinds of 3D games. However, to facilitate a quicker development cycle and to achieve optimal performance, X-Forge has been specially optimized for the most popular game genres, such as racing, first-person shooters, and action/adventure games.

X-Forge has been designed from the ground up for mobile devices, taking into account limited memory, performance, and control interfaces. The X-Forge game engine completely abstracts the underlying operating system and device hardware, allowing game developers to develop once on Windows and then deploy to multiple mobile platforms.

Fathammer provides professional developer support to give expert advice on advanced mobile game development issues. Developers get access to updates and new versions of X-Forge, a direct e-mail channel to the X-Forge engineering team, and access to the X-Forge Developer Forum.

X-Forge provides a solid foundation for game developers to build their games. Using a tried and proven game engine, development risk, schedules, and budgets can be drastically reduced. Game developers can focus on what really counts: game play, rather than technology development.

Capabilities

X-Forge is geared toward the development of advanced mobile games, the high end of the range. The main capabilities to support this are performance, flexibility, and development process orientation. Supporting capabilities include easy multiplatform development and porting, support for scalable content creation to cover the range of mobile platforms, and support for deployment of games for the range of platforms. Naturally, top quality developer support is included in the total package.

X-Forge has been optimized for complex worlds and games. There are no arbitrary limitations on world sizes, number of objects or actors, or other elements in the game. X-Forge has several advanced performance enhancement features for these situations, and it also natively uses several device capabilities.

The architecture of X-Forge has been designed to be completely modular. Any component can be replaced, from the rendering pipeline to the physics models. For example, the physics behaviors can be easily tailored to be different for different objects in the game. This means that different objects can use separate models, either provided by Fathammer or programmed by the developer. In this way, no processing is wasted in unnecessary models, and no development time is wasted in trying to fit the wrong or too general model for the problem. The developer's existing code-base can usually be integrated easily into an X-Forge-based game.

X-Forge also provides support for many different packaging and distribution models. Additional downloadable items, as well as content packs, can be produced easily. Content negotiation in multiplayer games can be done at desired granularity. Different business models and billing methods can also be accommodated easily.

X-Forge architecture and tool set has been designed for easy applicability to common game development processes. For X-Forge, this includes the whole life cycle up to game tuning, building, verification, and deployment. The tedious and repetitive tasks have been reduced, which allows the developer to concentrate on playability and game quality. One way that X-Forge provides high-level support is Genre Packs, an X-Forge original concept that has been adapted also to other engines. Genre Packs provide the concepts and solutions that are standard and useful in a specific genre—e.g., a shooter or racing game—and reduce development time considerably.

Figure 8.1 shows how the X-Forge development system scales on multiple platforms.

Figure 8.1 Same X-Forge game on multiple platforms.

The X-Forge development system supports simultaneous development for multiple platforms with minimal additional effort. *Stuntcar Extreme* was developed for a wide range of devices and runs on all of those essentially unchanged. For the actual in-game, the only variation is the size reduction of larger textures on lower resolution displays. The largest change was in the menu graphics and the user interface, which is now easier in X-Forge 2 as it supports vector-based graphics formats in menus.

Device events are the final problem the developer encounters. X-Forge makes sure all events from a low battery to an incoming call are handled correctly. X-Forge also enables testing of all events of all platforms on the development PC. This speeds up the development and test cycle tremendously. The other debugging and testing facilities of X-Forge are also extensive.

Recent X-Forge Game Titles

The following sections highlight a few games that have been developed using X-Forge.

Stuntcar Extreme™

Genre: Driving

Players: 1–2

Release Date: Q3/2003

Stuntcar Extreme is a fast-paced stunt driving game. This is the most extreme form of racing, and only the best of the best or the craziest of the crazy participate in the ruthless duels on the dangerous tracks. Advanced car physics, fearsome opponents, and insane jumps guarantee that the experience will be hair-raising!

Screenshots from *Stuntcare Extreme* are shown in Figure 8.2.

Figure 8.2 *Stuntcar Extreme* in OpenGL ES.

Spy Hunter®

Genre: Action Driving

Players: 1–2

Release Date: Q4/2003

Spy Hunter, shown in Figure 8.3, thrusts gamers through seven high-adrenaline missions around the globe in exotic locations in a quest to save the world. The ultimate counterintelligence prototype vehicle with morphing abilities, the G-6155 Interceptor, has offensive and defensive weapons including machine guns and heat-seeking missiles. The Interceptor morphs on-the-fly into a deadly speedboat, a turbo jet watercraft, or a supercharged motorcycle.

Figure 8.3 *Spy Hunter.*

Geopod®

Genre: Racing

Players: 1–2

Release Date: Q4/2002

Geopod brings a sense of speed into mobile gaming. It is a fast and furious racing game where your task is to take the helm of a hovercraft and compete against opponents on futuristic rollercoaster-like race tracks. In the career mode, you engage in a quest to become the *Geopod* champion. With the multiplayer mode, you can challenge your friends for some intense *Geopod* action (see Figure 8.4).

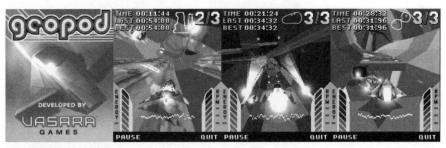

Figure 8.4 *Geopod.*

SGS—SpeedGun Stadium

Genre: First-Person Shooter

Players: 1–2

Release Date: Q4/2004

Hungry for action? Do you feel comfortable with firepower? Then take your chances in *SpeedGun Stadium*, the most popular TV sport in the solar system! Hear the audience cheer you on as you defeat your enemies in spectacular fashion, or face a torrent of booing if you fail their expectations. Fame and glory are within your grasp, but you have to get there with style. Some concept screenshots from the game are shown in Figure 8.5.

Figure 8.5 *SpeedGun Stadium.*

Hockey Rage 2004

Genre: Sports

Players: 1–2

Release Date: Q2/2005

Fast and furious *Hockey Rage 2004* brings ice hockey in its full roughness to your mobile game console. Tackle, cross-check, or hook the members of the opposing team on your way to deck their goalie. Play with any of the 16 best national hockey league teams in the world. *Hockey Rage 2004* is the one and only advanced mobile hockey game you ever want to play!

Figure 8.6   *Hockey Rage 2004.*

Additional Games

Figure 8.7 shows screenshots from the game *Red Faction*® on the Nokia N-Gage, published by THQ, and Figure 8.8 shows a screenshot from *Galactic Realms* on the Tapwave Zodiac.

Figure 8.7   *Red Faction.*

Figure 8.8   *Galactic Realms.*

X-Forge Unveiled

The main component of X-Forge is the game engine. It uses a two-layer architecture where the lower layer provides hardware abstraction and a standard set of functionality on all supported platforms, and the upper layer provides a full-featured 3D game engine and game graph object model through which the world in a game application can be manipulated. Figure 8.9 shows the arrangement of the layers.

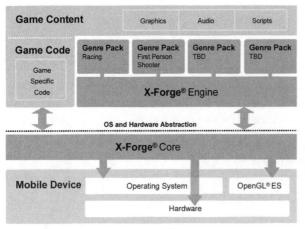

Figure 8.9 The X-Forge architecture.

The X-Forge core is the low-level layer of the X-Forge game engine and includes all the fundamental components and services used by the high-level engine layer. For game developers, the core layer provides a consistent platform on which they can build their game application without worrying about the specifics of the underlying operating system or hardware. The game application framework solves this by unifying the way the application communicates with the surrounding hardware and operating system. The framework defines standard ways of receiving and mapping control, rendering, and device events.

The X-Forge Engine layer sits on top of the core and provides game developers with a high performance, extensible, and flexible 3D scene graph, called a *game graph*. The game graph uses the low-level services provided by the core layer, but hides most of the complexity and lets the game developer deal with higher-level concepts like objects, object hierarchies, portals, meshes, cameras, lights, etc.

The X-Forge engine has a highly modular architecture, enabling expert game developers to write their own extensions and game-specific optimizations. Considerable attention has been paid to ensure that the engine is easy to use, without compromising performance and flexibility. High-rendering performance is achieved even with very complex scenes, thanks to the built-in support for portals, world subdivision, and spatial databases that decide quickly and efficiently which areas of the game world are relevant for the frame that is about to be rendered. Collision checking and the process of controlling dynamic game object activities enjoy similar benefits, all without any need for game developers to concern themselves with the complexities of how the high performance is achieved. This frees up developers to focus on making the game fun and playable.

X-Forge Game Graph

X-Forge extends the traditional scene graph to a powerful game graph, which is the most essential and central part of the X-Forge engine from the game developer's point of view. The central philosophy is that the game graph is the game world (game level) itself. When developing a game using X-Forge, the major component of X-Forge is the game engine.

It uses a two-layer architecture, where the lower layer provides hardware abstraction and a standard set of functionality on all supported platforms and the upper layer provides a full-featured 3D game engine and game graph object model through which the world in a game application can be manipulated. The previous Figure 8.9 shows the arrangement of the layers.

The game code deals with the game graph in one way or another. The game graph is a tree structure, divided into a set of subtrees that are connected to the game graph root. There are two types of subtrees: actors and zones. Actors represent the dynamic objects in the game world, such as cars, characters, monsters, weapons, and so on. Zones represent the static, unchanging world.

Below each subtree is a hierarchy of nodes that describe that subtree. These include things like meshes, sprites, particle systems, cameras, lights, sounds, microphones, etc. Some nodes are concrete and visual in nature, while others are more abstract. Hierarchy is important for achieving good performance, because it allows X-Forge to prune out large parts of the game graph and only concentrate on the relevant parts.

Division of the game world into zones is important for two reasons: Zones represent the first level of hierarchy for the static world and the existense of portals, and zones are separated from each other by portals, which are used to speed up both rendering and collision. Actors are always considered to be in at least one zone, and they move into other zones by passing through the portals that separate the zones. This allows X-Forge to optimize collision-checking by only considering the zones that an actor is in, as well as other actors that are in those zones.

Figure 8.10 illustrates what a game graph looks like.

Actor nodes are central to all X-Forge-based games, since all the dynamic entities in a game level are represented by actor nodes. An actor node—on its own—does nothing. What makes an actor come alive is the controllers assigned to it. An actor can have any number of controllers, and the controllers can be in a freely defined hierarchy. Artists can create complex behavior for the actors by creating parameterized controllers under the groups in 3ds max and the game code to take advantage of them in whatever manner the programmer has intended, be it AI or physics.

Game graph nodes typically use a large number of resources of various types, such as textures, vertex buffers, and so on. These are commonly shared between nodes in complex ways that are nearly impossible to track manually. X-Forge handles these shared resources with a resource manager that tracks the usage of the resources and frees the resources that are no longer in use.

For each rendered frame, the game graph goes through two phases: the control phase and the rendering phase. During the control phase, the controllers are ticked and the clock advanced. After the control phase, the current game world state is rendered in the rendering phase.

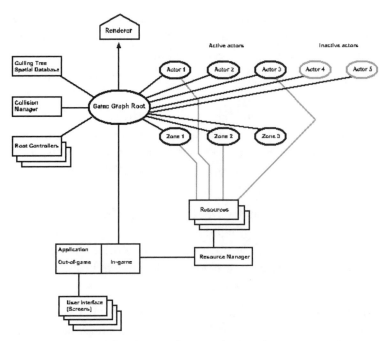

Figure 8.10 Simplified outline of a game built with an X-Forge engine.

The game graph renderer uses culling trees to figure out which renderable nodes are potentially visible and then asks these renderable nodes to render themselves. The actual rendering of an object is always up to that object itself, which enables developers to define their own custom renderable objects. Culling trees and the renderer are both pluggable components.

The 3D sound system in X-Forge mirrors the graphics rendering system in most ways. For example, there are a sound renderer, sound culling trees, and sound nodes. Instead of having a camera that defines the view similar to graphics rendering, there is a microphone that defines the point from which 3D sound is rendered.

The visual appearance of an entity in X-Forge is represented in the game graph by a renderable node. In the same way, the physical appearance used for collision detection is represented by collider nodes. X-Forge implements a number of different types of colliders that are suitable in a wide range of different situations: box and the sphere colliders are usually very good in use with player objects such as cars, human characters, etc. Heightfield colliders are designed especially for complex terrain that can be simplified into a heightmap representation of the surface, for example a race track. For indoor scenes with rooms of various shapes, X-Forge has CSG (constructive solid geometry) colliders. CSG colliders are useful in first-person shooter games to create collider walls for your rooms and tunnels. In addition to these, there are also other collider types, such as line segment and sprite colliders, and game developers can develop their own fairly easily. Artists may create these different collider types in 3ds max.

X-Forge Core Feature List
The following are the major features offered by the X-Forge core.

3D GL
3D GL is the X-Forge 3D graphics library with both software and hardware rendering. The 3D GL library has a switchable rendering pipeline between software renderer and hardware renderer at compile time.

Table 8.1 shows the features of the 3D GL library.

Table 8.1 3D GL Features

Feature	Description
Hardware renderers	OpenGL ES, architecturally ready for OpenGL, Direct3D 7+, Direct3D Mobile
Primitive types	Triangle list, strip, fan, indexed triangle list, strip, fan, polygon list
Polygons	Convex and planar polygons with unlimited number of vertices
Blending modes	Solid, additive, multiplicative, weighted average
Shading modes	Matte, flat, Gouraud, grayscale Gouraud
Texturing modes	Linear, perspective correct, alpha-masked
Camera modes	Perspective, orthogonal
Dynamic lighting	Point, directional and spot lights, maximum of eight simultaneous lights
Texture formats	16 bit solid, 16 bit with 1 bit alpha, 8 bit paletted
Depth buffer format	Fathammer proprietary CZ-buffer
Other	Mip-mapping, render target switching, GL toolkit including environment mapping, billboards

2D GL
2D GL is the X-Forge 2D graphics library with both bitmap and vector graphics. Table 8.2 shows the features of the 2D GL library.

Application Framework
The application framework consists of a multiplatform main loop with application start-up and memory reservation. It includes the following:

- **Device event handling:** Incoming/outgoing phone calls, SMS, audio lost, focus lost/gain, etc.
- **Memory handling:** Consistent memory allocation across all platforms
- **Other:** Unicode support, threads, and mutexes

Table 8.2 2D GL Features

Feature	Description
Framebuffer modes	Pixel doubling, FSAA, rotation in 90 degree with control mapping changing accordingly
2D acceleration	Common interface for accessing 2D operations, regardless of available hardware acceleration
2D transformations	Rotation, stretching, transformation
Blending modes	Solid, additive, multiplicative, weighted average, alpha mask, color-key
High quality filters	Resampling, dithering, skewing, rotation, transforming
Line operations	Line and anti-aliased line drawing and rectangle filling
2D vector support	Comprehensive 2D vector rendering pipeline capable of full SVG rendering support
SVG profiles	SVG tiny + selected SVG 1.1 properties (filters, gradients, patterns, line properties)
SVG file formats	Fathammer proprietary custom SVG binary format, standard SVG format
Fonts and sprites	Bitmaps, RLE compressed sprites, and SVG fonts
Image loader formats	Plug-in interface with PNG, JPG, TGA, and PCX plug-ins available

Audio

X-Forge core audio support includes sound effects mixing and streaming with music support, including the following:

- **Sample formats:** 8 and 16 bit WAV, mono, and stereo
- **Maximum channels:** Limited only by processing power and memory requirements
- **Real-time effects:** Sample rate, volume, loop offset, priority, pan
- **3D audio:** Renders 3D audio in the 3D world with attenuation and Doppler effect
- **Music formats:** XM (eXtended Module), MIDI

File I/O

X-Forge also provides a virtual file system for storing game data, which includes the following features:

- **Compression and encryption:** Supported transparently, with a plug-in interface for compression and encryption filters
- **Command set:** STDIO-style file I/O command set
- **Plug-ins:** ZLIB, StringXOR

Controls

X-Forge provides an interface to all device buttons and analog controllers that consists of:

- **Virtual control mapping:** Physical button to virtual control mapping
- **Virtual screen button:** Used for touch screens to make virtual buttons that behave exactly like normal buttons
- **Vibration interface:** Access device's vibration and simulate vibration magnitude with 1 bit vibration interface

Network

X-Forge hides network differences behind simple sockets API:

- **Socket interface:** Offers consistent interface to network services offered by the OS
- **Supported networks:** GPRS, WCDMA, WLAN, Bluetooth
- **Packet types:** Guaranteed, non-guaranteed, quick-guaranteed, and recent-state

Math Library

X-Forge's assembler optimized fixed point math library offers the following:

- **Operations supported:** Comprehensive 3D mathematics library, including vectors, 3×3 and 4×4 matrices, quaternions, trigonometrics, logarithmics, procedural smoothing, etc.
- **Fixed point format:** 16.16

Miscellaneous Features

The X-Forge core also provides the following additional features:

- **String handling toolkit:** STDIO-style string manipulation command set
- **Data containers:** Hashtable, linked list, priority list, dynamic array, N-tree
- **Power management API:** Controlling subsystems on/off in order to save battery power
- **Others:** Random number generation, FPS counter, date, time, etc.

X-Forge Engine Features List

The following sections detail the features available in the X-Forge engine.

Game Graph

Through the following, the X-Forge engine provides the fundamental structure of the 3D world:

- **Node types:** Actor, Zone, Object, Group, Sound, Microphone, Camera, Mesh, Sprite, Particle System, Light, Helper, Portal, Various collider types

- **Culling methods:** Zones, Portals, Bounding volume culling trees with cullers for Actors, Zones, Sounds, Lights
- **Bounding volumes:** Axis-aligned box, Sphere
- **Animation players:** PRS animation controller with skin+bone character animation support
- **Lightmapping:** Automatic light map cache and light mapper tool

Loader framework

The X-Forge plug-in interface for game graph loaders provides:

- **Level loading:** Loads the level recursively from several files
- **Customization:** Easy creation of own pluggable node types and loaders
- **Controller framework:** Fundamental way of controlling game entities with controllers
- **Built-in controllers:** PRS-animation, physics controller
- **Parameterized controllers:** Framework enabling mapping of content parameters for interactive functionality

Collisions

The engine offers a collision framework with highly optimized collision culling:

- **Collision types:** Oriented box, Sphere, Height field, Constructive Solid Geometry, Sprite, Line segment
- **Collision info:** Collided objects, Position, Penetration normals, Physics info, Collision materials

Physics

X-Forge supports pluggable physics with rigid body and particle physics:

- **Physics parameters:** Directly adjustable from game content
- **Physics controllers:** Particles, Rigid bodies, Helper trackers, Animation trackers, Constraints, Springs
- **Supported constraints:** Distance constraint, Pin constraint, Angle constraint
- **Global parameters:** Forces, Damping, Angular damping, Material mapping: Static and sliding friction, Restitution
- **Particle parameters:** Mass, Position, Penalty force, Damping
- **Rigid body parameters:** Mass, Position, Orientation, Inertia, Penalty force, Damping, Angular damping, Material
- **Spring parameters:** Length, Spring coefficients, Damping

UI Toolkit

The UI Toolkit offers multiplatform user interfaces with a configurable look'n'feel engine:

- **Support for UI widgets:** Button, Checkbox, Image, Label, Panel, Slider, Text, TextField, Virtual keyboard
- **Particle System:** High-quality particle effects, specially designed for mobile 3D
- **Resource manager:** Full resource management for resources used by the game
- **Game tuning facilities:** Various methods for tuning game play parameters in real time
- **Application remote tuning:** Connect to the device and adjust game parameters on-the-fly
- **Real-time adjustment**: Adjust game parameters during game play in separate window
- **Parameterized controllers:** Give controller parameters (default values) in 3ds max

Debugging Facilities

X-Forge provides various methods for debugging game applications:

- **Wireframes:** All game graph nodes, collisions, custom debug lines
- **Debug dumpers:** Game Graph: XML, Height fields: TGA, Memory-map: BMP
- **Remote debugger:** Connect to the device and adjust and inspect game parameters on-the-fly
- **In-device profiling:** Get accurate execution time profile with low-resolution clocks and minimal performance hit
- **Event debugging:** Simulate mobile device events (incoming call, sms, etc.) in PC
- **Debug logger:** Logging facility for in-device debugging purposes

X-Forge Tools Features List

Finally, the following sections detail the tools included with X-Forge.

3ds max Exporter

X-Forge's 3ds max plug-in supports:

- **Real-time preview:** Freely adjustable dimensions, debug colliders, portals, actor bounding volumes
- **Game graph viewer:** Browse through game graph, all parameters visible
- **X-Forge objects:** Zone, Actor, Object, Group, Portal, Loader, Sprite, Particle system, Microphone, Sound
- **Colliders:** Oriented box, Sphere, Height field, CSG-box

- **Material settings:** Colors, shading: matte, flat, Gouraud, grayscale Gouraud, Blending: alpha, additive, Other: perspective correction, double-sided, Z-bias
- **X-Forge max scripts:** Advanced reset xform, rope creator and pivot point release

Particle Effects Editor

The X-Forge tools include a stand-alone particle systems editor with a real-time preview window.

Content Packager

The content packager allows developers to create virtual file systems with compressed and encrypted data files.

- **Pluggable filters:** Provide for different compression and encryption algorithms
- **Content encryption:** Directory, headers, file content encryption selectable individually per file

Profiling Tools

Also included are various tools for game and content performance optimization tuning:

- **Rendering profiler:** Investigate polygon parameters fed to the GL and their distribution
- **Execution profiler:** Investigate running-time function distribution
- **Game graph profiler:** Investigate game graph culling behavior in various situations

SVG Tools

The tools for editing SVG content include:

- **SVG Filter Editor:** Produce SVG filters in real-time filter editor
- **SVG Binary Compiler:** Compile the SVG XML files to Fathammer proprietary binarized XML format

Supported Platforms

Fathammer is working closely with leading operating system and hardware manufacturers to support their technologies, platforms, and devices in X-Forge. This is an ongoing process and ensures that X-Forge customers always have instant and trouble-free access to all commercially viable mobile platforms.

X-Forge currently supports the following platforms:

Symbian OS™ / N-Gage™

Symbian OS / Series 60

Symbian OS / UIQ

Windows Mobile™/Smartphone

Windows Mobile/Pocket PC

Gizmondo™

Palm OS®/Tapwave™ Zodiac

Mobile Linux/various

X-Forge has been optimized for the most common processor architectures, including Intel® XScale™, Texas Instruments® OMAP™, and Intel® StrongARM™. X-Forge has been successfully used with hardware accelerators from ATI, Intel, NVIDIA, and others. OpenGL ES is the key interface between X-Forge and the underlying hardware-accelerated graphics pipelines.

X-Forge Development Environment

X-Forge basically offers two starting points for game development:

- **X-Forge Engine** offers a complete game framework with portals, object culling, collisions, physics, scene loading, etc. This is the way to go if the game development is started from scratch. Also, if you have a half-ready engine on top of another 3D platform, you may want to restart the development with X-Forge Engine.

- **X-Forge Core** offers a complete mobile 3D gaming platform interface with 3D/2D library, file-i/o, mobile device events, inputs, sound, error handling, etc. This is your option if the game is ported from another platform, which already had a 3D GL built in. The X-Forge Engine is built on top of the X-Forge Core.

In addition to the above, X-Forge is not just a 3D graphics library and game engine, but it also offers versatile and high quality 2D support (image transformations, vector graphics, image loading) and comprehensive audio library. The X-Forge fixed point math library provides an excellent base for mobile 3D game physics and animation.

Besides the game engine, the SDK also contains a collection of tools to support game development with the X-Forge game engine. Among these is a game graph exporter tool that integrates with 3ds max, giving artists full control over 3D content as well as all other aspects of the game graph. Other tools include a particle system editor, content and code profilers, and a content compression, encryption, and packaging tool. The tools are specially designed to optimize the development cycle in terms of time and efficiency.

Documentation and Examples

The X-Forge SDK includes comprehensive documentation for programmers and artists. By following the documentation, it is possible to get started with X-Forge in a matter of days. The documentation is divided into tutorials, a guide, and a full API reference. The tutorial provides step-by-step instructions for how to create a game using X-Forge, guiding the reader from a very simple application to a complex first-person shooter-style game. The guide is a complete description of the X-Forge development system and covers the Core and Engine layers of the game engine, as well as the tools and development environments and specific nuances of each platform. The guide also includes documentation for artists on how to efficiently create optimal content in terms of memory consumption, performance, and visual quality.

Any game SDK would be useless without good examples. The X-Forge SDK includes various examples both for using only the GL or other X-Forge Core features and for building complete game applications with a wide set of functionality. The examples give both programmers and artists a good insight on what is happening under the hood in an X-Forge game, and how they can really start implementing their tasks in their own X-Forge game. All examples are thoroughly documented and commented.

Programmer View to X-Forge

When using the X-Forge Engine, a developer does not need to know almost anything about the underlying GL. Everything is done with the game graph and programming the controllers attached to actors within the game world. However, if a different path is chosen, and the developer wants to develop his own game graph solution on top of the X-Forge GL, that is also supported. The X-Forge GL closely resembles OpenGL and Direct3D interfaces and is familiar to programmers who have previously worked with them.

The developer may choose between different rendering devices, depending on the underlying platform. There are primarily three devices as of this writing;

- Base, which only offers a simple framebuffer device and no 3D functionality
- Default, X-Forge's software 3D pipeline and rasterizer
- Hardware acceleration through OpenGL ES (OpenGL, Direct3D 7+, and D3Dm may also be supported in a future version)

The X-Forge GL hides the major differences between different rendering pipelines in different systems. The majority of all rendering code is exactly the same, regardless of which rendering device is being used. The biggest difference with the X-Forge default software renderer and OpenGL ES is that with hardware rendering, the content has to be exported in triangle mesh form, while with software rendering, content can also be in a more efficient polygon mesh form. Some expensive operations such as multitexturing or fog will only work with hardware rendering. This approach enables optimal performance in both software and hardware rendering systems. The rendering pipeline can be switched at compile time with a single command.

All X-Forge applications are developed in C++. The developer may choose any editor he wishes. However, the X-Forge example project files are delivered in Microsoft Visual C++ Studio project files. The games are mainly developed in desktop PC environments and then compiled and transferred to the mobile devices. Due to different controls and screen resolutions, the user interface configuration is the largest part of porting work between different platforms.

X-Forge offers developers multiple debugging interfaces to ease the game development. Wireframes can be rendered to debug bounding volumes, collisions, etc. The Game graph, rendered height field bitmaps, and the application memory map may be dumped to disk for further inspection. With an application level remote debugger, developers can connect to the game running on the mobile device and adjust and inspect game parameters even during game play. The in-device execution-profiling timer can be used to produce accurate execution profile data even with very low clock resolutions existing in mobile devices today. An event debugging interface is offered that developers may use to test their game reactions to different mobile device events already on the PC.

The X-Forge development environment is shown in Figure 8.11.

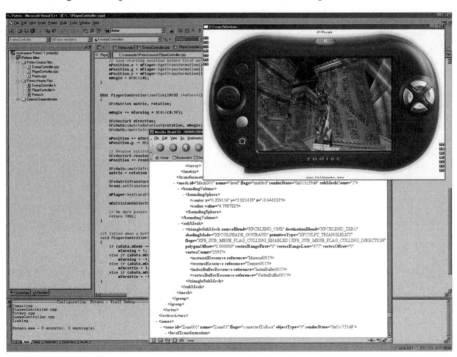

Figure 8.11 The X-Forge development environment.

The developers are exposed to the full X-Forge Engine source code, enabling the full understanding and free customization of the engine code. X-Forge Engine's highly modular structure allows easy customization of the engine. The design philosophy in X-Forge has been that the default implementation should be enough 95% of the time. More important than engine customization is the X-Forge controller architecture. Actors can be added to controllers and controller sets. One actor can have several controllers, which can even form hierarchies of their own. Basically, an X-Forge application consists of the main application with a bunch of controllers taking care of the action in the game scene.

The X-Forge architecture transforms a lot of responsibility from the programmer to the artists, who can define the functionality in the content. This results in a relatively small amount of program code and fast prototyping of interactive content in the beginning of the project.

In addition to the modular and highly efficient game graph solution, X-Forge offers good debugging and profiling tools for programmers and artists. Packaging tools are used to create virtual file systems, which store all the game content in compressed and encrypted form to prevent content ripping and hacking.

Artists' View of X-Forge

Artists are given full control of the X-Forge game engine from within 3ds max using the X-Forge exporter for 3ds max. The exporter supports real-time previewing of 3D content through a previewing window that uses the actual X-Forge 3D renderer. This allows artists to see what their content would look like on the actual target mobile device without going through the lengthy cycle of exporting, uploading, and testing. A tree-view of the scene graph is also provided to see exactly what the equivalent X-Forge scene graph looks like to any given 3D scene in the modeler. All custom X-Forge objects are exposed completely, giving artists freedom to create and edit portals, collision objects, parameterized controllers, materials, lights, zones, actors, helper objects, etc.

The X-Forge 3ds max tools consist of four components: GameGraphViewer, X-Forge Viewport, X-Forge Material, and X-Forge Exporter.

The GameGraphViewer gives you a hierarchical view of the X-Forge scene to be exported. You'll be able to browse the details of the scene right down to details such as PRS values, material assignments, collision settings, etc.

The X-Forge Viewport enables you to view your 3D scene exactly as it would appear on the screen of your target mobile device. This improves the art workflow since there is no need to export to an external application in order to be able to view your scene.

X-Forge includes a material editor for X-Forge compatible materials for use in game production. This new material is available in the normal 3ds max material list, and it provides a more user-friendly access to all the necessary parameters for mobile 3D, such as color parameters, Z-bias, perspective correction settings, blending, etc.

The path of the game object or scene from 3ds max to X-Forge application goes through the X-Forge Exporter. The Exporter has various options for configuring the exported data files. Among these are various filters, data manipulation options, vertex duplication threshold, adaptive sampling settings, export scales, etc. When using OpenGL ES rendering, the content needs to be exported as triangle meshes to be hardware-rendering friendly.

The X-Forge plug-ins can be seen in Figure 8.12.

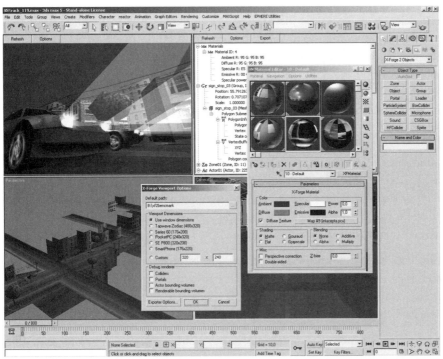

Figure 8.12 The X-Forge plug-ins.

In addition to these, X-Forge is supplied with max scripts that ease artist's work in monotonous tasks. Also, artists are actively sharing their max scripts in the X-Forge developer community to further improve the value of the tools.

Besides the X-Forge 3ds max tools, the SDK offers the X-Forge Particle System Editor, which is used to create X-Forge compatible particle systems that can produce high-quality particle effects such as fire, smoke, explosions with bouncing debris, sparks, lightning, falling snow, and water splashes. The particle system adjustable parameters include emit rate, visible and total number of particles, particle age with noise, velocity with noise, emitter size, colliders, weight, damping, sprite size, rotation and age, textures, various blending parameters, and particle system ticking pace.

All 2D content of the game can be created in any advanced image editor, such as Adobe Photoshop. X-Forge supports PCX, TGA, PNG, and JPG file formats in all 2D and 3D content. Audible assets are constructed in standard sample editors, trackers, and sequencers. X-Forge uses standard WAV files for producing its in-game sounds. AudioProducer, the audio mixing and streaming interface of X-Forge, is able to alter a sample's format, sampling rate, volume, panning, and priority in real time.

X-Forge Licensing

The X-Forge development system is distributed to licensees in the form of an SDK that contains the X-Forge game engine, tools, documentation, and examples. In addition to the SDK, Fathammer provides platform packages for each of the supported platforms. Platform packages contain the X-Forge game engine libraries for a specific platform and enable the developer to deploy and publish a title on the selected platform. Also included in the development system is the developer support package.

The X-Forge licensing model is divided into two parts: development and deployment.

The development license is annual and allows game developers to develop X-Forge-based games on the PC desktop environment using the X-Forge SDK. The development license includes developer support with access to the X-Forge Developer Forum for a 12-month period. The development license does not include rights to publish or deploy any titles either commercially or noncommercially.

Deployment licenses enable developers to deploy and publish a title either commercially or noncommercially on a selected platform. The deployment license is always tied to a game title and a specific platform. Deployment licenses are paid as a single flat fee when the game is released.

Game developers can evaluate the complete X-Forge SDK using a 45-day evaluation license. During the evaluation period, the developer has access to Fathammer's technical developer support. The developers are encouraged to use the evaluation period to create a working prototype of their game to assist in securing a publishing deal.

The X-Forge SDK and a commercial or an evaluation license can be obtained by contacting Fathammer. To start the process, the developer is requested to fill in a short questionnaire about professional background, track record, and the project where X-Forge will be used.

Contact Information

Fathammer Europe

Fredrik Kekäläinen, Vice President, Business Development

E-mail: **fkekalainen@fathammer.com**

Address:

Tammasaarenkatu 7 A

FIN-00180 Helsinki

FINLAND
Fax: +358-9-693-3013
Phone: +358-9-694-4044

Swerve

http://www.superscape.com

Swerve Client is a fast and efficient software 3D engine that, when downloaded to or embedded within the wireless device and driven by application code, generates and manages the interactive 3D scenes on the screen using model description data. Swerve Client abstracts the more complex requirements for building interactive 3D applications, making it both easy and fast for designers and programmers to create content without the need for detailed knowledge of such techniques as 3D rendering. It also provides a low-level immediate mode API for use by expert graphics programmers.

There are two versions of Swerve Client: Swerve Client SR and Swerve Client ES.

Swerve Client SR

This implementation of Swerve Client provides OEMs with the lowest cost bill of materials (BoM) for the delivery of console quality games and other applications on mass-market devices. The Swerve software renderer accommodates the full range of screen sizes and color depths available on today's devices and requires no additional graphics libraries.

Swerve Client ES

Swerve Client ES is an implementation of Swerve that utilizes OpenGL ES to execute many of the rendering functions required in JSR 184. It provides OEMs with the benefits of both the high-level scene tree API necessary to enable downloadable games and low cost development in the wireless environment, together with the power and increased graphic quality delivered by dedicated hardware accelerators. Swerve Client is available as a BREW extension and also for WinCE environments. Figure 8.13 should give you a better idea of the Swerve software layers available.

Recent Swerve Game Titles

The following sections detail recent games developed using Swerve.

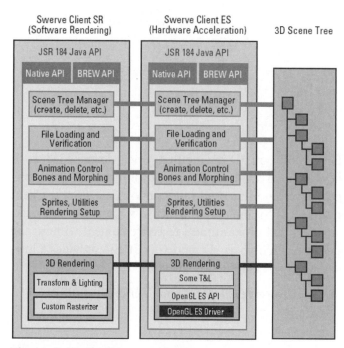

Figure 8.13 The Swerve architecture.

Van Helsing (Universal)

Genre: First-Person Shooter

Players: 1

Release Date: Summer 2004

Based on Universal's blockbuster, this FPS gives the player control of Van Helsing, God-sent mercenary against Evil whose mission is to bring down the infamous Count Dracula. To succeed, he must battle through several increasingly difficult levels of baddies, including wraiths, flying pygmies, Dracula's brides, werewolves, and ultimately Dracula himself. Each level requires exploration, a certain degree of puzzle solving, and lots of combat. Levels are populated with weapons, ammo, defensive enhancements, power-ups, and obviously monsters.

Independence Day (20th Century Fox)

Genre: Action/Flight

Players: 1

Release Date: Summer 2004

Based on the 20th Century Fox blockbuster, *Independence Day* puts you in the cockpit of an F18-Hornet, leading mankind's last attempt to destroy the alien menace hovering over its major cities. The game starts on July 4th, after a computer virus has been uploaded to the alien lead mother ship orbiting Earth, disabling all other alien ships' shields: The free forces of the world can now fight back!

Street Hoops (Activision)

Genre: Sports

Players: 1

Release Date: Summer 2004

Street Hoops, based on the console hit from Activision, emphasizes flashy ball handling, fake-out moves, mad skill moves, and a variety of dazzling slam-dunks. This game is more about betting, winning one game at a time, and continuing to own the court than about the score. The player has the chance to play against some of the best street players in the U.S. As the player wins, he earns cash and the reputation that puts him among the best on the court. The game has a strong cinematic component (slow zooms, replays, etc.).

AMF Xtreme® Bowling (Vir2L)

Genre: Sports

Players: 1

Release Date: Summer 2004

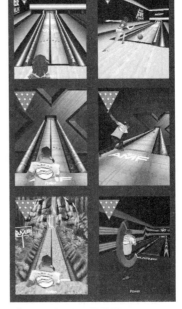

Immerse yourself in the 3D action of wireless *AMF Xtreme Bowling*—packed with vivid graphics and addictive game play! *AMF Xtreme Bowling* includes four different lanes, animated players, four difficulty levels, and Player versus AI and Tournament modes. Bowl your way to the top of the high scorer list in the rich 3D world of AMF Xtreme Bowling!

Screenshots from *AMF Xtreme Bowling* can be seen in Figure 8.14.

Evel Knievel (GWE)

Genre: Stunt/Extreme Sport

Players: 1

Release Date: Summer 2004

Figure 8.14 *AMF Xtreme Bowling.*

Evel Knievel Evel-ution is an extreme sports/stunt game starring Evel Knievel, the world famous daredevil and true American Icon. Play as Evel Knievel through five game levels and re-create five great moments of Evel Knievel's stunt career—jumping over cars, buses, trucks, through flaming hoops, and fountains!!

Screenshots from *Evel Knievel* can be seen in Figure 8.15.

Figure 8.15 *Evel Knievel.*

Additional Screenshots of Swerve in Action

Figure 8.16 shows screenshots from the Swerve-based Ivan Stewart's *Ironman Baja Off-Road*.

Figure 8.16 Ivan Stewart's *Ironman Baja Off-Road*.

Swerve Capabilities

Swerve provides developers of 3D mobile games with a rich feature set spanning the following categories (please see the Swerve Client spec sheet for full details):

Geometry:

- Triangular meshes
- Instanced geometry
- Sprites

Textures:

- PNG—All formats supported by MIDP 2.0 (RGB, RGBA, Alpha, Luminance)
- Swerve Plasma textures
- Instanced textures

Lighting:

- Ambient, parallel, omni, spot lights
- Exclusion list per light
- Attenuation
- Number of light sources supported

Animations:

- Linear and Bézier (spline, squad, slerp and step) controllers
- Multiple animations
- Skinned mesh (bones)
- Morph mesh
- Weighted animations
- Instanced animations

Cameras:

- Multiple cameras
- Perspective and orthographic projections

- Field of view
- Clipping planes
- Zoom
- Aspect ratio

Materials/Appearance:

- Multiple materials per object
- Diffuse, ambient, specular, and emissive colors
- Shininess
- Compositing mode (Alpha, Alpha-add, Modulate, Modulate*2, Replace)
- Flat and smooth shading
- Multiple textures per polygon
- Geometry culling
- Layers
- Object alpha
- Object renderable/nonrenderable
- Perspective correct textures
- Fog (linear and exponential)
- Texture blending modes (Add, Blend, Decal, Modulate, Replace)
- Polygon color—based on object, vertex, or diffuse color

Scene:

- Backgrounds—textured, colored, and tiled
- Clipart objects
- External z buffer—stage set
- Alignment controller (independent alignment of any node in Y/Z axes)

SDK:

- User-defined properties
- Object identification
- Windowless mode
- Multiple worlds
- Multiple views
- Access to rendered view
- Create objects and animations
- Access vertex, normal, and texture coordinate data

The Swerve solution has several benefits:

- OTA delivery of console quality 3D mobile games directly to handsets, thanks to key proprietary features enabling file size reduction (plasmas, stage set)
- Generic 3D engine-enabling high-quality 3D graphics for any kind of mobile applications, from top branded games to UIs, character messaging, screen savers, and location based services
- High-level scene tree for faster development

Supported Platforms

Swerve Client can work on any mobile platform and has already been integrated in all major wireless execution environments, including BREW, Pocket PC, J2ME, Symbian, Linux, and several RTOS.

Toolsets, Development Environment

Developing content for the Swerve solution is most efficiently done using Swerve Studio, Superscape's professional development environment, and the appropriate IDE for the target language.

Built around the industry standard design tool 3ds max, Swerve Studio provides a familiar environment for the design, prototyping, and development of high-quality 3D mobile games and other 3D applications. Its seamless integration into 3ds max addresses all the issues associated with 3D application development by providing a complete, integrated development environment, allowing designers to perform all actions required in the creation of a 3D game prototype (and possibly an entire application) within a single tool.

Designers can rely on the extensive 3D modeling, texturing, lighting, and animation capabilities of 3ds max working hand-in-hand with the powerful on-target preview and behavior scripting features brought by Swerve Studio to build a prototype of a game without calling upon programming resources or switching between several tools.

Swerve Studio easily integrates into existing mobile games development practices and tool chains, enabling the rapid development of high-quality 3D content. Below is a high-level overview of the tool chain required to develop a 3D application. Swerve Studio easily integrates into existing 2D mobile games' development processes and tool chains and provides powerful and efficient tools to tackle the challenges introduced by 3D development. Figure 8.17 gives an overview of the Swerve development environment.

For further information on Swerve Studio, please see the Swerve Studio spec sheet or visit the following page: **http://www.superscape.com/ products/swerve_studio/**

Figures 8.18, 8.19, and 8.20 show the benefits of the Swerve Studio integrated approach.

At the click of a button, the designer can preview his rough 3D model as it would look like on the target platform without leaving Swerve Studio/3ds max.

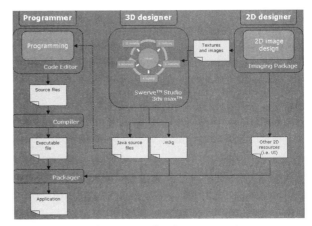

Figure 8.17 The Swerve development environment.

Figure 8.18 The Swerve Preview within 3ds max 5.1.

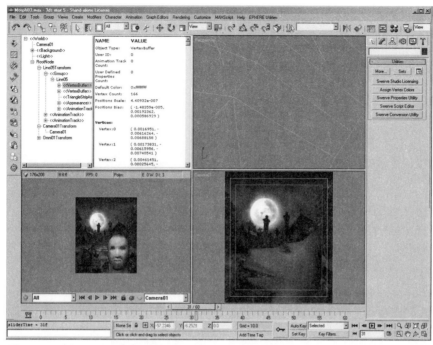

Figure 8.19 Swerve Scene Graph within 3ds max 5.1.

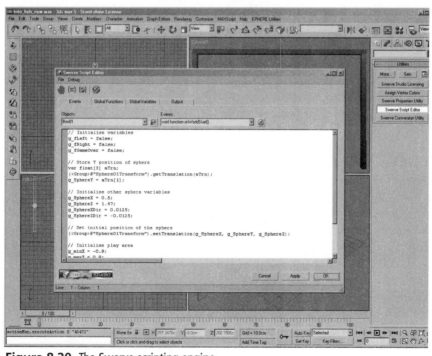

Figure 8.20 The Swerve scripting engine.

With preview and scripting abilities it gives you the following benefits:

- Real-time visual feedback on quality of content
- No preview environment setup time and cost
- No costly transfers of content between tools and/or resources
- Full control of prototype in the hands of one individual (the designer)
- Capability to create a fully functional prototype without the need for programming resources

When the time has come to create a full commercial application, Swerve Preview still enables designers to preview their work quickly and apply any modifications, while programmers develop optimized Java or C/C++ code in parallel. Any content created in Swerve Studio can be exported at the click of a button.

Getting Started with Swerve on BREW

Swerve Client is a BREW extension running on BREW devices with capabilities similar to the QUALCOMM 6100 FFA (BREW 2 or above). As such, it is not necessary to license and embed the engine into an application. This extension is usually provided by the network operator for download to the end-user's handset.

Getting Started with Swerve on WinCE

Please contact Superscape for any enquiries related to the development of 3D applications on the WinCE platform.

Efficiently developing a game taking advantage of Swerve's powerful features (in BREW or WinCE) requires the licensing of Swerve Studio. For further information on licensing Swerve Studio, please contact Superscape.

Contact Information

For further information, please visit **www.superscape.com** and **www.swervepowered.com**.

Please contact Superscape at the following locations:

USA

Superscape, Inc.

131 Calle Iglesia

Suite 200

San Clemente, CA 92672-7542

United States

Phone: +1 800 965 7411 (Toll Free)

Fax: +1 949 940 2841

United Kingdom

Superscape Ltd

Cromwell House

Bartley Wood Business Park

Hook, Hampshire

RG27 9XA

United Kingdom

Phone: +44 (0)1256 745 745

Fax: +44 (0)1256 745 777

Japan

Superscape KK

Level 18

Yebisu Garden Place Tower

4-20-3 Yebisu, Shibuya-ku

Tokyo 150-6018

Japan

Phone: +81 3 5789 5775

Fax: +81 3 5789 5757

Mascot Capsule V4

http://www.hicorp.co.jp

Launched in 2001, the Mascot Capsule Engine Micro3D Edition was the first commercially deployed mobile 3D solution. Developed by HI Corporation of Japan, Mascot Capsule was first implemented as a compact, embedded 3D rendering engine for the Sharp SH-51 handset for J-Phone, now Vodafone KK. J-Phone concurrently launched a downloadable 3D character, screensaver, and virtual pet service utilizing the Mascot Capsule engine. The service was quite successful and soon became a priority not only for J-Phone, but for the other wireless operators in Japan. By 2002, all three carriers in Japan had adopted the Mascot Capsule platform for mobile 3D graphics, and by 2003, more than 20 carriers worldwide had adopted the platform, and more than 30M handsets had a version of the Mascot Capsule Engine embedded.

To maximize rendering performance, HI Corporation worked with handset manufacturers to embed "native" implementations of the engines in handsets, written in C, with Java wrappers to enable Java games and content to access the engines. The feature sets also evolved in these native engines, eventually adding lighting, perspective texture mapping, etc. By Version 3, the Mascot Capsule Engine was capable of delivering Playstation-level performance on ARM9-equivalent handsets. It wasn't until late 2003 and early 2004 that open standards came to mobile 3D graphics as the Khronos Group, an industry standards group with such members as HI, Nokia, Motorola, and 3Dlabs, brought out the low-level, hardware-oriented OpenGL ES API. Shortly thereafter, a group formed through the Java Community Process (JCP) established JSR-184, the higher-level, scene graph-oriented M3G (Mobile 3D Graphics API for J2ME) API standard.

Mascot Capsule Version 4, launched in 2004, bridges the pre- and post-standards world of mobile graphics by providing a validated implementation of the M3G standard and support for the Mascot Capsule V3 API in the same engine. Built either with a pure software renderer for devices with no graphics hardware support or as a layer on top of OpenGL ES for devices with OpenGL ES hardware rendering capability, Mascot Capsule Engine Version 4 provides M3G support for any ARM9-equivalent mobile device. Implemented as a device-independent core, the Mascot Capsule Engine works with any operating environment, be it Java, BREW, Linux, Symbian, or Smartphone.

Capabilities

Given different footprints and different target markets, feature sets and performance vary widely from engine to engine in the Mascot Capsule Platform. Each subsequent version of the Mascot Capsule Micro3D Engine adds capabilities and supports more platforms but also tends to require a higher level of handset performance.

Versions 1 and 2 are typically targeted at ARM7-class handsets and provide full graphics rendering capabilities for screensavers, animated ringtones, and simple 3D games and applications. Version 3 is a much more full-featured graphics engine, better targeted for fully-textured action games, delivering Playstation 1-class rendering. As such, Version 3, while possible to run on an ARM7-class handset, is best served by handsets with ARM9 or better performance. Version 4 is not supported for anything less than ARM9.

These engines all include full 3D rendering engines in software that runs on the handset CPU. For handsets that have additional hardware for 3D graphics rendering, both Version 3 and Version 4 offer optional implementations that layer the V3 and JSR-184 API implementations over the OpenGL ES interface utilized by the processor to tap into graphics hardware rendering capabilities in the handset. Device independent, Mascot Capsule Micro3D Engine can be made available for almost any handset platform or architecture—there is no dependency on any CPU or OS architecture.

Recent V4 Game Titles

Through the course of the four generations of Mascot Capsule engines, more than 300 titles of screensavers, virtual pets, and games have been developed. HI Corporation has worked with Bandai, Namco, Capcom, Taito, Sega, Sony, Square, and other leading game developers and publishers to develop and deploy both new and ported versions of 3D games.

Some of the well-known content ported to mobile using the Mascot Capsule Engine includes:

Screensaver Characters:

- Gundam
- Hello Kitty
- Sylvester the Cat
- Bugs Bunny
- Kermit the Frog
- Woody Woodpecker
- Curious George
- Godzilla
- Dragon Quest
- Winnie the Pooh
- Snoopy
- Popeye
- Micky Mouse
- Wallace & Grommit

Games:

- *Real Tennis* (Sega)
- *Intelligent Qube* (Sony Computer Entertainment)
- *Ridge Racer* (Namco)
- *Energy Airforce* (Taito)
- *Gundam Battle 3D* (Bandai)
- *Monkey Ball* (Sega)
- *Biohazard* (Capcom)

Figures 8.21 through 8.25 show some of the games that have been developed using Mascot Capsule.

Figure 8.21 *Winning Lap* © IT Telecom, Inc.

Figure 8.22 *Commander* © IT Telecom, Inc.

Figure 8.23 *3D Field GOLF* © IT Telecom, Inc.

Figure 8.24 *METALCLAW* © IT Telecom, Inc.

Figure 8.25 *Asonde! Inutomo* © HI & BANDAI NETWORKS 2003.

Feature List

Mascot Capsule supports both Java and a native/C interface. It is currently available on the following platforms:

- BREW
- Java
- Linux
- PalmOS
- Symbian
- Smartphone

Mascot Capsule supports the ARM7 and ARM9 processors, and it offers hardware acceleration via OpenGL ES graphics hardware. It exposes Mascot Capsule V1, V2, V3, and V4 APIs, as well as M3G and OpenGL ES APIs.

Mascot Capsule offers the following high-level rendering features:

- Scenegraph
- Retained Mode Render
- Articulated Bone Figures
- Bone Weighting
- Key Frame Object Animation
- Key Framing Object Properties
- Dynamic Polygon Groups
- Basic Meshes
- Morphing Meshes
- Auto-Alignment of Objects

It also offers the following low-level rendering features:

- 8 bit Texture Mapping
- 24 bit/32-bit Textures
- Multiple Texture Mapping
- Environment Mapping
- Two-sided Polygons
- Transparency

- Flat Shading
- Gouraud/Toon Shading
- Blending
- Ambient/Specular Lighting
- Multiple Light Sources
- Colored Lights
- Directional Lights
- Attenuation
- Parallel Projection
- Perspective Projection
- Lines, Points, Sprites
- Tri-strips
- Z-buffer
- Fog
- Alpha Blending
- OpenGL ES Renderer (optional)

Content Development Tools

Mobile 3D engines are faced with a variety of constraints not shared with their desktop or laptop peers. With no floating point support and limited processing power and memory, mobile content must be vastly more compact and efficient than content aimed at game consoles or PCs. To support this process, HI includes a variety of utilities in the Mascot Capsule Toolkit, diagrammed In Figure 8.26. Largely available from carriers or from the mascotcapsule.com Web site, the toolkit is designed to mesh with game developers' existing tool paths. The tool set includes the following components:

Exporter Plug-ins allow developers to export models/animation from:

- 3ds max
- Maya
- Lightwave
- Softimage
- Animation Master

Polygon Post-Processing Tools enable the modification of polygon and texture attributes to fit the constraints of the mobile environment.

Model Converters convert output models from PC formats to mobile formats.

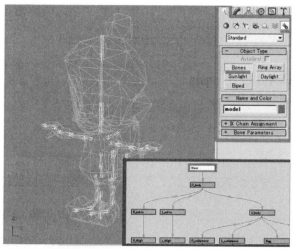

A PC-based Desktop Viewer enables previewing of mobile models, scene graphs, and animations for verification prior to deployment on actual mobile devices. Figure 8.27 shows the desktop viewer.

Figure 8.26 The Mascot Capsule Toolkit.

Figure 8.27 The desktop viewer.

The Path to Mobile Content

Mobile handsets are, unfortunately, widely disparate in their capacities, capabilities, and performance. Typically speaking, architectural differences assure that ports must be verified on each unique handset to assure that any given mobile application runs properly and with sufficient speed.

The following issues are indicative of the difficulties typically encountered when developing mobile games, in contrast to developing PC and console games:

- Limited application size and heap memory
- Comparatively low CPU processing speed

- Inefficient operation
- Screen size is very small
- Color varies from display to display
- Low-quality sound
- Poor I/O devices for user input
- There are many tasks for the handset other than the game application itself
- Short development cycle

Tips and Tricks

To successfully address these constraints, it is critical to follow a few key guidelines. By keeping these in mind, the mobile game developer can avoid many of the pitfalls that can derail a game development project to get the game in on time and with the desired performance.

Memory

Small application and heap sizes can be the cause of difficult problems. These two memory issues can become very challenging to manage, especially with 3D hardware, which can render more complex scenes (i.e. more polygons) than, say, a software rasterizer.

Two methods can help reduce the size of the data and therefore application size for downloads:

- **Compression per file**—This is an effective method for PC/console games that not only reduces the data size, but also enables additional data encryption.
- **Eliminate empty sectors**—The sector size is typically 4K to 8K, depending on the mobile terminal, but actual data files often are not exact multiples of these sizes, resulting in many empty sectors across the total number of files. To reduce the loss due to these empty sectors, the data can be merged into one big file. HI adopted this method for in-house title development and dramatically reduced the resulting application size.

Although there are few good solutions for reducing heap memory usage, performance will suffer if it is not sufficiently reduced. Over time, handset memory heap sizes will grow, and this will become less of an issue.

CPU Speed

Overall hardware speed, particularly in the CPU, has improved substantially in recent mobile handsets, but when compared with consumer game consoles, handsets are still extremely slow. This can be especially seen in the following two key areas:

- The bus to transfer the framebuffer for screen rendering is slow.
- Floating point operation is extremely slow or nonexistent.

In the case of the bus transfer speed, it doesn't matter whether the game is in 3D or 2D, this bus limitation hampers maximum attainable frame rates. Even if the case where the CPU is slow, a game can still effectively be realized if the bus is sufficiently fast. It is extraordinarily difficult to work around a slow bus since it is so core to the handset hardware architecture.

As for the floating point performance, the emergence of 3D games made the need for fractional arithmetic inevitable. The demand for improved floating point capabilities can only increase since it is such a significant factor in various characteristics of sophisticated games, such as enhanced physics. For the 3D rendering, fixed point operation has been adopted to improve the computation speed and to maintain the application performance. Fixed point numbers, however, almost always experience certain cases of underflow or overflow.

For rendering, an alternate solution is to use integer vertex and texture coordinate data together with scale and bias values that map the integers to the real values required. The scale and bias can be folded into a floating point transformation matrix and, with some clever implementation, vertex transformation becomes almost the same as a fixed point operation.

User Interface

Ultimately, what is most important in the game is the "playability," which represents the interface between the user and the game application. In this domain are the characteristics of the game play that determine how comprehensible the user interface is, how the story unfolds, and how the physical UI of the handset ties into the controls of the game. Due to the wide variations in handset design, particularly outside of Japan (where handset layouts are more strictly specified), the operation of any given game could differ substantially based upon how the buttons are laid out. The result of this, unfortunately, is that the difficulty of the game itself will change from handset to handset. These issues must be considered very carefully from the beginning of the planning stage.

When porting a game from one handset to another, game operation is one of the main sources of problems. As an example, diagonal input may have worked on the original handset while it may be unsupported on the handset, to which the game is being ported. Another key issue is that not all handsets recognize when more than one button is being pressed at the same time. These constraints dictate that a careful analysis of handset capabilities be conducted before selecting the target handsets for any given game.

While there is no simple overall solution, here are some examples on how HI has addressed these issues in past game development projects:

- Identify in advance the exact models of handsets to be supported to discern the minimum level of capabilities to be supported and to design in usability alternatives for different devices.

- Allow the player to play at a lower difficulty level when diagonal input is not supported by the handset by keeping a diagonal input flag in the program. When diagonal input is available, the game can switch to its normal level of difficulty.

- Drive the same features, such as "jump" or "attack," to multiple buttons or embed a key-customization feature.

With these countermeasures, the bulk of usability problems can be alleviated to a large extent. Depending upon the type of the game, there may be more efficient ways to solve this problem, so that is left as an exercise for the developer.

Screens and Colors

Handset screens are just now becoming more standardized on a few key resolutions. Even as resolutions rise, however, the sizes remain rather small due to the size constraints of the handsets. Today, the best handsets are offering screens with QVGA resolution (320×240), while the lower-end handsets typically offer QCIF (176×120) resolution. The difference will impact fill rate performance for rendering of triangles, so if any given game is intended to support a higher-end handset, the performance of the game at that resolution must be verified.

Unfortunately, while screen resolutions are beginning to standardize, color representation on different screens can vary dramatically, just as they do on different computer monitors or television sets, due to the wide variety of suppliers providing the LCD panels, color filters, and backlights. There really is no alternative to running the game on each display to check that letters making up words in the UI are readable for any given display quality and resolution. For color validation, use of desktop LCD monitors for development can help significantly in verification prior to deployment to the specific handsets.

Sound

As if these other issues weren't enough, there is an even greater disparity in sound quality among mobile handsets than there is in user interface issues. The best bet is to stick to one unified approach across the range of devices.

1. First, create the BGM and sound effect with the best quality possible.

2. Next, reduce the sound quality on a case-by-case basis for each handset and embed the feature by adjusting the data size.

Depending upon the application size supported by the handset, there is a large amount of sound data that cannot be embedded, resulting in significant degradation of sound quality. The key is to subtract data until the target application size is achieved.

Other Tasks Take Away from Game Cycles

Game consoles are dedicated devices. Turn them on and their only purpose in life is to run the game. Handsets, however, are first and foremost phones, secondarily calendar and phone book management devices, and then, perhaps, they are game machines. Thus, while for a console the player need only turn the console on and off, in the case of mobile handsets, programmers have to build support into the game software to recognize when phone calls or e-mail arrives in the midst of playing the game, or when other applications are running in the background and deal with these other applications appropriately. For a phone call, for instance, the game must suspend itself until the call is complete and then allow the player to restart.

Rather than reinvent the way this is handled on a game-to-game basis, it's possible to create a common library to tackle this issue and embed the game onto this library. The most development time will be required for the first handset because the library needs to be created and tested the first time out. From the second handset on, however, this library can be quickly ported, freeing the programmer from having to program anything but the game itself.

Licensing

HI Corporation licenses the Mascot Capsule Engine to semiconductor and handset manufacturers and, in certain instances, to wireless carriers. Since the engines are typically preloaded in the devices, content developers and publishers rarely have to pay licensing fees to HI Corporation. Licensing is handled by each of HI Corporation's regional offices so as to provide a local resource for the licensee.

Please contact HI Corporation at one of the following locales:

Japan (Head Office)
HI CORPORATION
6F Higashiyama Bldg. 1-4-4
Tokyo, 153-0043
Tel: +81-3-3719-8158
Fax: +81-3-3793-5109

United States
HI CORPORATION America
1300 Crittenden Lane, Suite 105
Mountain View, CA 94043
Tel: (650) 962-0719
Fax: (650) 962-9710

Singapore

HI CORPORATION Singapore Pte. Ltd.

2 International Business Park

#10-01 Tower 1, The Strategy

Singapore 609930

Tel: +65-6267-9870

Fax: +65-6267-8982

China

HI CORPORATION China

Fazhan Center, 19F

No. 5 North Rd.

Dongsanhuan Chaoyang District

Beijing

Tel: 0086-10-6590-9524/28

Korea

Mr. Kim Joonhyung

Tel: +82-11-1726-3632

E-mail: **KIM_Joonhyung@hicorp.co.jp**

Summary

In this chapter, we covered the three most popular mobile 3D game engines. While there are others out there and even ones that will be custom-built by certain developers, the three engines mentioned here are gaining a lot of momentum in the industry. Currently, the phone resources are very limited in terms of file space and memory. With these constraints, there are advantages to using an engine that may be integrated on the phone or available as a highly-optimized downloadable extension. As new phones become available, so will larger memory footprints and storage space to allow developers to extend their games to include more custom effects or features.

This chapter focused on the Fathammer, Superscape, and Hi Corp 3D engines to give the developer a better idea of what is available in the marketplace. We have talked to several game developers that will be porting their games to OpenGL ES as they start working more into the mobile market. But with that said, for new games that are being developed, one should always consider the value and advantages of using a highly-tuned and optimized game engine when development cycles are short and the time to market is very tight. All these engines covered in this chapter take advantage of OpenGL ES and the graphics software and hardware available on various platforms as they evolve into the next generation of graphics for mobile devices.

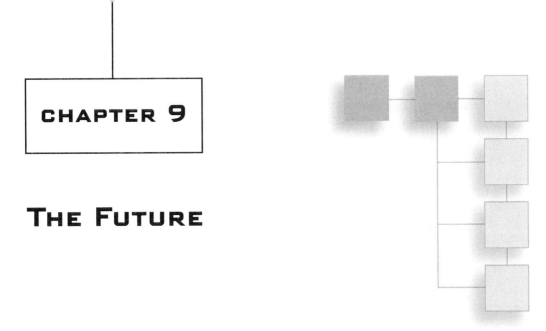

CHAPTER 9

THE FUTURE

At SIGGRAPH 2004, the OpenGL ES 1.1 specification was released. Although support for 1.1 won't be present in commercial products for a little while, it introduces some significant improvements that will be described in this chapter.

When OpenGL ES 1.0 was released, the designers realized that most of the early implementations would be in software, which had a big impact on the design decisions that were made. They also knew that hardware support wouldn't be long in arriving, so one of the intents of OpenGL ES 1.1 was to add features that could both make the hardware more efficient and provide features that weren't practical in software implementations.

OpenGL ES will be sure to evolve beyond 1.1, just as OpenGL continues to evolve. In this chapter, we'll cover the following information:

- What's new in OpenGL ES 1.1
- What features are likely for future versions of OpenGL ES

OpenGL ES 1.1

OpenGL ES 1.0 is based on the OpenGL 1.3 specification, but OpenGL ES 1.1 is based on the OpenGL 1.5 specification. As mentioned in Chapter 3, a number of important and useful features were added in OpenGL 1.4 and 1.5, so all of these were considered for OpenGL ES 1.1. In addition, many features that had been dropped or made optional in 1.0 were reexamined.

This section will detail which features have been added in OpenGL ES 1.1. Where applicable, it will also mention OpenGL 1.4 and 1.5 features that were not included, as well as 1.3 and earlier features for which support has changed. The tables from Chapter 3 have been included here and updated with changes and additions. Changes are marked in bold. Tables that have not changed are not included.

Geometry Specification

Although there have been some new geometry specification features added to OpenGL since 1.3, none of them were included in OpenGL ES 1.1. In fact, the only addition in this area is the restoration of an older function.

In addition to glColor4f(), OpenGL ES 1.1 restores the glColor4ub() and glColor4ubv() functions, since working with unsigned bytes for colors is often more convenient than floats.

OpenGL 1.4 added the ability to specify a secondary color and fog coordinate per vertex. These features are not frequently used, however, so they are not included in OpenGL ES 1.1.

The ability to draw multiple subsets from a set of vertex arrays with a single call was also not included, since the same functionality can easily be implemented by the application, if needed.

Table 9.1 contains updated geometry specification function support in OpenGL ES 1.1. (Again, note that the changes that are new are marked in bold.)

Table 9.1 Geometry Specification Functions

Function	Notes
glBegin()	Not supported.
glEnd()	Not supported.
glEdgeFlag[v]()	Not supported.
glVertex{234}{sifd}[v]()	Not supported.
glNormal3f()	Supported.
glNormal3{bsifd}[v]()	Not supported.
glTexCoord{1234}{sifd}[v]()	Not supported.
glMultiTexCoord4f()	Supported.
glMultiTexCoord{1234}{sifd}[v]()	Not supported.
glColor4f()	Supported.
glColor4ub[v]()	**Supported.**
glColor{34}{bsifd ub us ui}[v]()	Not supported.
glSecondaryColor3{bsifd ub us ui}[v]()	**Not supported.**
glFogCoord{fd}[v]()	**Not supported.**
glIndex{sifd ub}[v]()	Not supported.
glVertexPointer()	Supported. Type cannot be GL_INT or GL_DOUBLE, **but support for GL_BYTE has been added**

continued

glVertexPointer()	Supported. Type cannot be GL_INT or GL_DOUBLE, but support for GL_BYTE has been added.
glNormalPointer()	Supported. Type cannot be GL_INT or GL_DOUBLE, but support for GL_BYTE has been added.
glColorPointer()	Supported. Type cannot be GL_INT or GL_DOUBLE, but support for GL_UNSIGNED_BYTE has been added. In addition, the alpha value must be included with all colors; there is no support for specifying only the RGB values.
glSecondaryColorPointer()	**Not supported.**
glFogCoordPointer()	**Not supported.**
glIndexPointer()	Not supported.
glTexCoordPointer()	Supported. Type cannot be GL_INT or GL_DOUBLE, but support for GL_BYTE has been added. Also, because there is no support for 1D textures, at least 2 texture coordinates must be provided per vertex.
glEdgeFlagPointer()	Not supported.
glInterleavedArrays()	Not supported.
glArrayElement()	Not supported.
glDrawArrays()	GL_POINTS, GL_LINES, GL_LINE_LOOP, GL_LINE_STRIP, GL_TRIANGLES, GL_TRIANGLE_STRIP, and GL_TRIANGLE_FAN are supported. GL_QUADS, GL_QUAD_STRIP, and GL_POLYGON are not supported.
glDrawElements()	GL_POINTS, GL_LINES, GL_LINE_LOOP, GL_LINE_STRIP, GL_TRIANGLES, GL_TRIANGLE_STRIP, and GL_TRIANGLE_FAN are supported. GL_QUADS, GL_QUAD_STRIP, and GL_POLYGON are not supported. Type must either be GL_UNSIGNED_BYTE or GL_UNSIGNED_SHORT (not GL_UNSIGNED_INT).
glDrawRangeElements()	Not supported.
glMultiDrawArrays()	**Not supported.**
glMultiDrawElements()	**Not supported.**
glEnableClientState()	Valid for all supported attributes.
glDisableClientState()	Valid for all supported attributes.

Buffer Objects

Buffer objects are perhaps the most important addition to core OpenGL since 1.3. The benefits they offer are even more important on OpenGL ES devices, so they were a natural inclusion in OpenGL ES 1.1, although they are somewhat restricted.

Since buffer objects aren't covered in any books available at the time of this writing, they'll be covered here in greater detail than other OpenGL ES features have been covered.

To fully understand the benefits of vertex buffer objects—or VBOs as they're often called—let's take a moment to review how vertex arrays work.

With vertex arrays, you declare or allocate an array that is used to store the data representing the object you want to render. When you make a call to one of the `glPointer()` functions, you're telling OpenGL ES where that data is located in memory. Then, when you call `glDrawElements()` or one of the other drawing functions, OpenGL ES retrieves the data from that memory location and processes it.

The important thing to note here is that the array exists in client memory. For OpenGL ES hardware to access that data, it needs to be copied from client memory across a bus and into video memory. Bus speeds tend to be slow, especially on embedded devices, both because of low clock speeds and limited bandwidth. Thus, when rendering even modestly-sized data sets, the overhead involved with transferring data across the bus can become a bottleneck.

Vertex buffer objects solve this problem by allowing you to store frequently-used vertex data in video memory. The APIs associated with vertex buffer objects enable you to manage many different sets of data with fairly detailed control over how they are used.

Creating Buffer Objects

Buffer objects are quite similar to other OpenGL ES objects, such as texture objects. To use them, you must first create the buffer object and associate it with a unique identifier—namely an unsigned integer that acts as a name or a handle. Each buffer object has a set of states and data associated with it.

Just as with texture objects, you can create and manage unique identifiers yourself, or you can have OpenGL ES generate a range of unused identifiers for you. This is done with `glGenBuffers()`:

```
GLvoid glGenBuffers(GLsizei numBuffers, GLuint *buffers);
```

This will store `numBuffers` unique buffer names in `buffers`. The names are guaranteed to be unused, which means they haven't been bound (via `glBindBuffer()`) or generated by `glGenBuffers()` previously.

Calling `glGenBuffers()` doesn't actually do anything other than marking the names as used. The buffer objects associated with these names aren't actually created until a call to `glBindBuffer()` is made:

```
GLvoid glBindBuffer(GLenum target, GLuint buffer);
```

target must be set to `GL_ARRAY_BUFFER`, and `buffer` is the buffer name. Zero can never be used as a buffer name. Calling `glBindBuffer()` on a buffer that has already been created selects it as the currently active buffer, allowing you to make changes to it.

Placing Data in Buffers

A buffer consists of a state vector and a data store. When a buffer is initially created, the data store is empty. To place data in the currently bound buffer, you will use the following API:

```
GLvoid glBufferData(GLenum target, GLsizeiptr size, const GLvoid *data, GLenum usage);
```

target should be set to GL_ARRAY_BUFFER. *size* is the size, in machine units, of the desired data store. *data* points to the client-side memory that you want to have copied into the buffer. *usage* provides a hint to OpenGL as to how you intend for the data to be used, so that it can optimize for performance. Valid values for *usage* and their associated meanings are listed in Table 9.2. Keep in mind that these values are intended only as a hint; nothing (other than a possible performance penalty) will prevent you from using a buffer differently from the specified *usage* value.

Table 9.2 Buffer *usage* Values

Value	Meaning
GL_STATIC_DRAW	The data for the buffer is provided once by the application and will be used frequently by OpenGL drawing commands.
GL_DYNAMIC_DRAW	The data for the buffer is provided repeatedly by the application and will be used frequently by OpenGL drawing commands.

Note

OpenGL 1.5 supports additional buffer *usage* modes (GL_STREAM_DRAW, GL_STREAM_READ, GL_STREAM_COPY, GL_STATIC_READ, GL_STATIC_COPY, GL_DYNAMIC_READ, GL_DYNAMIC_COPY), but these modes aren't supported in OpenGL ES 1.1.

Calling glBufferData() on a buffer object that already contains data will cause the old data to be freed before the new data is copied. If you try to create a data store that is larger than the available video memory, the call will fail, and the GL_OUT_OF_MEMORY error condition will be set.

In addition to being able to update a buffer's entire data store, you can modify a portion of it using the following:

```
GLvoid glBufferSubData(GLenum target, GLintptr offset, GLsizeiptr size, const GLvoid *data);
```

target should again be GL_ARRAY_BUFFER. *offset* and *size* are used to indicate the section of data being updated, and *data* points to the new data.

When changing the entire contents of a data store without changing its size or usage, calling glBufferSubData() will tend to be more efficient than calling glBufferData(), since the latter will require that memory be freed and reallocated.

Destroying Buffers

When you're done with your buffer objects, it's important to tell OpenGL to delete them to prevent a resource leak. This is done with the following:

```
GLvoid glDeleteBuffers(GLsizei numBuffers, GLuint* buffers);
```

buffers is an array containing the *numBuffers* buffer names that you want to delete. After this call is made, each name in *buffers* is marked as unused, and the data associated with it is removed. If *buffers* contains bogus values (such as unused names or zero), they will simply be ignored without generating an error.

Using Buffers with Vertex Arrays

Buffer objects can be used as the data source for any vertex arrays. To do so, the data in the buffer must be of a type and format that is valid for the given vertex array attribute. When a call to one of the gl*Pointer() functions is made and a non-zero buffer is bound to GL_ARRAY_BUFFER, that buffer will be used as the attribute data source, and the pointer parameter will be treated as an offset into the buffer.

Buffer objects can also be used to store the indices for glDrawElements(), though the process for doing so is slightly different. When calling glBindBuffer(), glBufferData(), or glBufferSubData(), GL_ELEMENT_ARRAY_BUFFER is used instead of GL_ARRAY_BUFFER as the *target* parameter. When glDrawElements() is called, if a non-zero buffer is bound to GL_ELEMENT_ARRAY, it will be used for the source of vertex indices, and the *indices* parameter acts as an offset into the indices in the buffer.

The following code snippet shows how to use vertex buffers with vertex arrays to draw a simple triangle.

```
// global
GLuint buffers[3];
...

// during initialization
GLfloat vertices[] = {
   1.0f, -1.0f, 0.0f,
  -1.0f, -1.0f, 0.0f,
   0.0f, 1.0f, 0.0f
};
```

```
GLubyte colors[] = {
  255, 50, 160,
  180, 255, 70,
  90, 10, 255
};

GLuint indices[] = { 0, 1, 2 };

glGenBuffers(3, buffers);

glBindBuffer(GL_ARRAY_BUFFER, buffers[0]);
glBufferData(GL_ARRAY_BUFFER, 9 * sizeof(GLfloat), vertices, GL_STATIC_DRAW);

glBindBuffer(GL_ARRAY_BUFFER, buffers[1]);
glBufferData(GL_ARRAY_BUFFER, 9 * sizeof(GLubyte), colors, GL_STATIC_DRAW);

glBindBuffer(GL_ELEMENT_ARRAY_BUFFER, buffers[2]);
glBufferData(GL_ELEMENT_ARRAY_BUFFER, 3 * sizeof(GLuint),
             indices, GL_STATIC_DRAW);
...

// during rendering
glEnableClientState(GL_VERTEX_ARRAY);
glEnableClientState(GL_COLOR_ARRAY);

glBindBufferARB(GL_ARRAY_BUFFER, buffers[0]);
glVertexPointer(3, GL_FLOAT, 0, 0);

glBindBufferARB(GL_ARRAY_BUFFER, buffers[1]);
glColorPointer(3, GL_UNSIGNED_BYTE, 0, 0);

glBindBufferARB(GL_ELEMENT_ARRAY_BUFFER, buffers[2]);
glDrawElements(GL_TRIANGLES, 3, GL_UNSIGNED_INT, 0);

glDisableClientState(GL_COLOR_ARRAY);
glDisableClientState(GL_VERTEX_ARRAY);
...

// shutdown
glDeleteBuffers(2, buffers);
```

Mapping Buffers

In OpenGL 1.5, it is possible to map the contents of a buffer to client memory. This functionality is not supported in OpenGL ES 1.1, so the functions associated with it (`glMapBuffer()` and `glUnmapBuffer()`) aren't present.

Supported: `glBindBuffer()`, `glDeleteBuffers()`, `glGenBuffers()`, `glBufferData()`, `glBufferSubData()`, `BUFFER_USAGE` = `STATIC_DRAW`, `STATIC_COPY`, `DYNAMIC_DRAW`, `DYNAMIC_COPY`, `GL_BUFFER_USAGE` = `GL_WRITE_ONLY`

Unsupported: `glMapBuffer()`, `glUnmapBuffer()`, `GL_BUFFER_USAGE` = `GL_STREAM_COPY`, `GL_STREAM_READ`, `GL_STATIC_COPY`, `GL_STATIC_READ`, `GL_DYNAMIC_COPY`, `GL_DYNAMIC_READ`

Clipping and Culling

User-defined clip planes have been a part of OpenGL since the beginning, but they were not included in OpenGL ES 1.0 due to their limited usefulness in the types of applications developed for OpenGL ES devices. However, certain visibility determination algorithms make use of a clip plane, so OpenGL ES 1.1 requires that at least one be supported. The number of clip planes can be determined by calling `glGetIntegerv()` with `GL_MAX_CLIP_PLANES`.

These changes are summarized in Table 9.3.

Table 9.3 Clipping and Culling Support

Function	Notes
`glClipPlane()`	Not supported.
`glClipPlanef()`	**Supported for at least one clip plane.**
`glFrontFace()`	Fully supported.
`glCullFace()`	Fully supported.
`glEnable()`/`glDisable()`	Supports `GL_CULL_FACE` and `GL_CLIP_PLANE0`. **Some implementations may support** `GL_CLIP_PLANE{1-5}`.

Points, Lines, and Polygons

The only change that has occurred in this area of OpenGL is the addition of functions that allow greater control over how points are rendered. These controls allow developers to add distance attenuation to points. This feature has been included in OpenGL ES 1.1. This change is reflected in Table 9.4.

Table 9.4 Primitive Rendering Modes

Function	Notes
glPointSize()	Supported, but support for sizes other than 1 is optional.
glPointParameterf[v]()	Fully supported.
glPointParameteri[v]()	Not supported.
glLineWidth()	Supported, but support for widths other than 1 is optional.
glLineStipple()	Not supported.
glPolygonStipple()	Not supported.
glPolygonOffset()	Fully supported.
glPolygonMode()	Not supported.
glEnable()/glDisable()	GL_POINT_SMOOTH and GL_LINE_SMOOTH are supported but have no effect unless point and line sizes other than 1 are supported. GL_POLYGON_OFFSET_FILL is supported, but GL_POLYGON_OFFSET_LINE and GL_POLYGON_OFFSET_POINT are not. GL_LINE_STIPPLE, GL_POLYGON_STIPPLE, GL_POLYGON_SMOOTH are not supported.

Texturing

Texturing support in OpenGL ES 1.1 has changed in a couple of significant ways, especially in regards to multitexturing. Implementations are required to support at least two texture units, making the most common multitexturing operations possible.

In conjunction with this, the GL_COMBINE texture environment mode is supported now as well. All combine operations are included, with the exception of texture crossbar, which allows the color from any texture to be used as an input to a combiner operation, regardless of which texture unit the texture is bound to.

ES 1.1 also adds the ability to have mipmap levels automatically be generated whenever a texture is created or updated. However, the ability to influence how this is done via a hint (GL_GENERATE_MIPMAP_HINT) isn't supported.

There were several other texture-related features added in OpenGL 1.4 and 1.5 that were not included in OpenGL ES 1.1. These include the following:

- Mirrored repeat wrap mode
- LOD bias
- Depth textures and their related shadow mapping operations

The changes to texturing present in OpenGL ES 1.1 are summarized in Table 9.5.

Table 9.5 Texturing Support

Function	Notes
glTexImage1D()	Not supported.
glTexSubImage1D()	Not supported.
glCopyTexImage1D()	Not supported.
glCopyTexSubImage1D()	Not supported.
glTexImage2D()	Supported with restrictions: the internal format and format must match and meet the requirements listed in Table 3.7, the border size must be 0, proxy textures cannot be used, and cube maps cannot be used.
glTexSubImage2D()	Supported with restrictions: The internal format and format must match and meet the requirements listed in Table 3.7.
glCopyTexImage2D()	Supported with restrictions: The color buffer format and texture format must meet the requirements listed in Table 3.8, and the border size must be 0.
glCopyTexSubImage2D()	Supported with restrictions: The color buffer format and texture format must meet the requirements listed in Table 3.8.
glTexImage3D()	Not supported.
glTexSubImage3D()	Not supported.
glCopyTexImage3D()	Not supported.
glCopyTexSubImage3D()	Not supported.
glCompressedTexImage1D()	Not supported.
glCompressedTexSubImage1D()	Not supported.
glCompressedTexImage2D()	Supported, but only with the OES_compressed_paletted_texture format, and subject to the other restrictions on 2D textures.
glCompressedTexSubImage2D()	Supported, but undefined for the paletted texture format, so this will only be useful if the vendor has provided other compressed formats.
glCompressedTexImage3D()	Not supported.
glCompressedTexSubImage3D()	Not supported.
glClientActiveTexture()	**Supported for at least two texture units.**
glActiveTexture()	**Supported for at least two texture units.**
glTexParameter{if}[v]()	**Supports** GL_NEAREST **and** GL_LINEAR **for the magnification filter,** GL_NEAREST, GL_LINEAR, GL_NEAREST_MIPMAP_NEAREST, GL_NEAREST_MIPMAP_LINEAR, GL_LINEAR_MIPMAP_NEAREST, GL_LINEAR_MIPMAP_LINEAR **for the minification filter, and** GL_REPEAT **and** GL_CLAMP_TO_EDGE **for s and t wrap modes. Also supports** GL_GENERATE_MIPMAP. GL_TEXTURE_BORDER_COLOR, GL_TEXTURE_MIN_LOD, GL_TEXTURE_MAX_LOD, GL_TEXTURE_BASE_LEVEL, GL_TEXTURE_MAX_LEVEL, GL_TEXTURE_LOD_BIAS, GL_DEPTH_TEXTURE_MODE, GL_TEXTURE_COMPARE_MODE, GL_TEXTURE_COMPARE_FUNC, GL_TEXTURE_WRAP_R, **and**

continued

	GL_TEXTURE_PRIORITY are not supported. GL_MIRROR, GL_MIRRORED_REPEAT, and GL_CLAMP_TO_BORDER wrap modes are not supported.
glTexEnv{if}[v]()	Fully supported except for texture crossbar.
glGenTextures()	Fully supported.
glDeleteTextures()	Fully supported.
glBindTexture()	Supports GL_TEXTURE_2D, but not GL_TEXTURE_1D, GL_TEXTURE_3D, or GL_TEXTURE_CUBE_MAP.
glIsTexture()	Not supported.
glAreTexturesResident()	Not supported.
glPrioritizeTextures()	Not supported.
glTexGen()	Not supported.
glEnable()/glDisable()	Supports GL_TEXTURE_2D. Does not support GL_TEXTURE_1D, GL_TEXTURE_3D, GL_TEXTURE_CUBE_MAP, GL_TEXTURE_GEN_S, GL_TEXTURE_GEN_T, GL_TEXTURE_GEN_R, or GL_TEXTURE_GEN_Q.

Fog

OpenGL 1.4 gave developers greater control over how the fog factor at each vertex is calculated through the use of fog coordinates. As previously mentioned, this feature was not included in OpenGL 1.1, which has a slight impact on the fog support shown in Table 9.6.

Table 9.6 Fog Support

Functions	Notes
glFogf[v]()	Supported other than GL_FOG_INDEX and GL_FOG_COORD_SRC.
glFogi[v]()	Not supported.
glEnable()/glDisable()	Supports GL_FOG.

Fragment Operations

OpenGL ES 1.1 includes a few minor changes to blending. The ability to change the blend equation, set a blend color, and use blend functions based on a constant color was promoted from optional (as part of the imaging subset) to required in OpenGL 1.4. However, these features were not included in OpenGL ES 1.1, nor was the ability to use separate blend functions for the RGB and alpha components.

OpenGL 1.4 also introduced blend squaring, which was included. This feature allows GL_SRC_COLOR and GL_ONE_MINUS_SRC_COLOR to be used as the source blend factor and GL_DST_COLOR and GL_ONE_MINUS_DST_COLOR to be used as the destination blend factor. The ability to multiply a color by itself in this way is useful in multipass algorithms.

Occlusion queries—introduced in OpenGL 1.5—are not supported in OpenGL ES 1.1, due to the fact that they aren't frequently used and are unlikely to offer much benefit on the platforms on which OpenGL ES is available.

Stencil buffer support itself is still optional and otherwise remains unchanged from 1.0.

All of these changes are summarized in Table 9.7.

Table 9.7 Per-Fragment Features

Functions	Notes
glBlendFunc()	Supported for all modes except GL_CONSTANT_COLOR, GL_ONE_MINUS_CONSTANT_COLOR, GL_CONSTANT_ALPHA, and GL_ONE_MINUS_CONSTANT_ALPHA.
glBlendFuncSeparate()	Not supported.
glBlendEquation()	Not supported.
glBlendColor()	Not supported.
glDepthFunc()	Supported, but implementations aren't required to support a depth buffer (though it's unlikely that they won't).
glDepthMask()	Supported, but see glDepthFunc().
glStencilFunc()	Supported, but implementations aren't required to support a stencil buffer.
glStencilOp()	Supported, but see glStencilFunc().
glStencilMask()	Supported, but see glStencilFunc().
glSampleCoverage()	Supported, but implementations aren't required to support a multisample buffer.
glAlphaTest()	Fully supported.
glScissor()	Fully supported.
glLogicOp()	Fully supported.
glBeginQuery()	Not supported.
glEndQuery()	Not supported.
glDeleteQueries()	Not supported.
glEnable()/glDisable()	Supports GL_MULTISAMPLE, GL_DEPTH_TEST, GL_STENCIL_TEST, GL_MULTISAMPLE, GL_SAMPLE_COVERAGE, GL_SAMPLE_ALPHA_TO_COVERAGE, GL_SAMPLE_ALPHA_TO_ONE, GL_ALPHA_TEST, GL_SCISSOR_TEST, GL_COLOR_LOGIC_OP, GL_DITHER. Does not support GL_INDEX_LOGIC_OP.

Everything Else

OpenGL 1.4 added a function (glWindowPos()) to allow developers to directly specify the raster position in window coordinates. Because glBitmap() and glDrawPixels() aren't supported in OpenGL ES, this function would be meaningless, so it's not supported.

Querying State

The restrictions on querying dynamic state have been greatly improved in OpenGL ES 1.1. Almost all dynamic and static states supported by OpenGL ES can now be queried. This change was necessary to support layered game engines, where it's not possible to track the current state on the application side. The states that can be queried are listed in Table 9.8.

Table 9.8 Queryable States

State	State
GL_ACTIVE_TEXTURE	GL_DEPTH_RANGE
GL_ALIASED_LINE_WIDTH_RANGE	GL_DEPTH_TEST
GL_ALIASED_POINT_SIZE_RANGE	GL_DEPTH_WRITEMASK
GL_ALPHA_BITS	GL_DITHER
GL_ALPHA_SCALE	GL_FOG
GL_ALPHA_TEST	GL_FOG_COLOR
GL_ALPHA_TEST_FUNC	GL_FOG_DENSITY
GL_ALPHA_TEST_REF	GL_FOG_END
GL_BLEND	GL_FOG_HINT
GL_BLEND_DST	GL_FOG_MODE
GL_BLEND_SRC	GL_FOG_START
GL_BLUE_BITS	GL_FRONT_FACE
GL_CLIENT_ACTIVE_TEXTURE	GL_GREEN_BITS
GL_CLIP_PLANE1	GL_LIGHT0
GL_COLOR_ARRAY	GL_LIGHT1
GL_COLOR_ARRAY_POINTER	GL_LIGHT2
GL_COLOR_ARRAY_SIZE	GL_LIGHT3
GL_COLOR_ARRAY_STRIDE	GL_LIGHT4
GL_COLOR_ARRAY_TYPE	GL_LIGHT5
GL_COLOR_CLEAR_VALUE	GL_LIGHT6
GL_COLOR_LOGIC_OP	GL_LIGHT7
GL_COLOR_MATERIAL	GL_LIGHTING
GL_COLOR_WRITEMASK	GL_LIGHT_MODEL_AMBIENT
GL_COMBINE_ALPHA	GL_LIGHT_MODEL_TWO_SIDE
GL_COMBINE_RGB	GL_LINE_SMOOTH
GL_COMPRESSED_TEXTURE_FORMATS	GL_LINE_SMOOTH_HINT
GL_CULL_FACE	GL_LOGIC_OP_MODE
GL_CULL_FACE_MODE	GL_MATRIX_MODE
GL_DEPTH_BITS	GL_MAX_ELEMENTS_INDICES
GL_DEPTH_CLEAR_VALUE	GL_MAX_ELEMENTS_VERTICES
GL_DEPTH_FUNC	GL_MAX_CLIP_PLANES

continued

State	State
GL_MAX_LIGHTS	GL_SCISSOR_TEST
GL_MAX_MODELVIEW_STACK_DEPTH	GL_SHADE_MODEL
GL_MAX_PROJECTION_STACK_DEPTH	**GL_SMOOTH_LINE_WIDTH_GRANULARITY**
GL_MAX_TEXTURE_SIZE	GL_SMOOTH_LINE_WIDTH_RANGE
GL_MAX_TEXTURE_STACK_DEPTH	**GL_SMOOTH_POINT_SIZE_GRANULARITY**
GL_MAX_TEXTURE_UNITS	GL_SMOOTH_POINT_SIZE_RANGE
GL_MAX_VIEWPORT_DIMS	**GL_SRC0_ALPHA**
GL_MODELVIEW_MATRIX	**GL_SRC1_ALPHA**
GL_MODELVIEW_STACK_DEPTH	**GL_SRC2_ALPHA**
GL_NORMAL_ARRAY	**GL_SRC0_RGB**
GL_NORMAL_ARRAY_POINTER	**GL_SRC1_RGB**
GL_NORMAL_ARRAY_STRIDE	**GL_SRC2_RGB**
GL_NORMAL_ARRAY_TYPE	GL_STENCIL_BITS
GL_NORMALIZE	GL_STENCIL_CLEAR_VALUE
GL_NUM_COMPRESSED_TEXTURE_FORMATS	GL_STENCIL_FAIL
GL_PACK_ALIGNMENT	GL_STENCIL_FUNC
GL_PERSPECTIVE_CORRECTION_HINT	GL_STENCIL_PASS_DEPTH_FAIL
GL_OPERAND0_ALPHA	GL_STENCIL_PASS_DEPTH_PASS
GL_OPERAND1_ALPHA	GL_STENCIL_REF
GL_OPERAND2_ALPHA	GL_STENCIL_TEST
GL_OPERAND0_RGB	GL_STENCIL_VALUE_MASK
GL_OPERAND1_RGB	GL_STENCIL_WRITEMASK
GL_OPERAND2_RGB	GL_SUBPIXEL_BITS
GL_POINT_FADE_THRESHOLD_SIZE	GL_TEXTURE_2D
GL_POINT_SIZE_MAX	GL_TEXTURE_BINDING_2D
GL_POINT_SIZE_MIN	GL_TEXTURE_COORD_ARRAY
GL_POINT_SMOOTH	GL_TEXTURE_COORD_ARRAY_POINTER
GL_POINT_SMOOTH_HINT	GL_TEXTURE_COORD_ARRAY_SIZE
GL_POLYGON_OFFSET_FACTOR	GL_TEXTURE_COORD_ARRAY_STRIDE
GL_POLYGON_OFFSET_FILL	GL_TEXTURE_COORD_ARRAY_TYPE
GL_POLYGON_OFFSET_UNITS	GL_TEXTURE_ENV_COLOR
GL_PROJECTION_MATRIX	GL_TEXTURE_ENV_MODE
GL_PROJECTION_STACK_DEPTH	GL_TEXTURE_MATRIX
GL_RED_BITS	GL_TEXTURE_MIN_FILTER
GL_RESCALE_NORMAL	GL_TEXTURE_MAG_FILTER
GL_RGB_SCALE	GL_TEXTURE_WRAP_S
GL_SAMPLES	GL_TEXTURE_WRAP_T
GL_SAMPLE_BUFFERS	GL_TEXTURE_STACK_DEPTH
GL_SCISSOR_BOX	GL_UNPACK_ALIGNMENT

continued

State	State
GL_VERTEX_ARRAY	GL_MATRIX_INDEX_ARRAY_POINTER_OES*
GL_VERTEX_ARRAY_POINTER	GL_MAX_VERTEX_UNITS_OES*
GL_VERTEX_ARRAY_SIZE	GL_MODELVIEW_MATRIX_FLOAT_AS_INT_BITS_OES*
GL_VERTEX_ARRAY_STRIDE	GL_POINT_SPRITE_OES*
GL_VERTEX_ARRAY_TYPE	GL_POINT_SIZE_ARRAY_OES*
GL_VIEWPORT	GL_POINT_SIZE_ARRAY_TYPE_OES*
GL_COORD_REPLACE_OES*	GL_POINT_SIZE_ARRAY_STRIDE_OES*
GL_IMPLEMENTATION_COLOR_READ_FORMAT_OES*	GL_POINT_SIZE_ARRAY_POINTER_OES*
GL_IMPLEMENTATION_COLOR_READ_TYPE_OES*	GL_POINT_SIZE_ARRAY_BUFFER_BINDING_OES*
GL_MATRIX_PALETTE_OES*	GL_PROJECTION_MATRIX_FLOAT_AS_INT_BITS_OES*
GL_MAX_PALETTE_MATRICES_OES*	GL_TEXTURE_MATRIX_FLOAT_AS_INT_BITS_OES*
GL_MATRIX_INDEX_ARRAY_OES*	GL_WEIGHT_ARRAY_OES*
GL_MATRIX_INDEX_ARRAY_BUFFER_BINDING_OES*	GL_WEIGHT_ARRAY_SIZE_OES*
GL_MATRIX_INDEX_ARRAY_SIZE_OES*	GL_WEIGHT_ARRAY_TYPE_OES*
GL_MATRIX_INDEX_ARRAY_TYPE_OES*	GL_WEIGHT_ARRAY_STRIDE_OES*
GL_MATRIX_INDEX_ARRAY_STRIDE_OES*	GL_WEIGHT_ARRAY_POINTER_OES

*—Part of extension state

In order to support querying all of these states, many of the glGet() and related functions are now supported. The complete updated summary of support for these functions is shown in Table 9.9.

Table 9.9 State Query Support

Functions	Notes
glGetString()	Fully supported.
glGetError()	Supported.
glIsEnabled()	**Supported.**
glGetBooleanv()	**Not supported.**
glGetIntegerv()	Supported.
glGetFloatv()	**Supported.**
glGetDoublev()	Not supported.
glGetPointerv()	**Supported.**
glGetClipPlane()	Not supported.
glGetClipPlanef()	**Supported for at least one clip plane.**
glGetLightfv()	**Supported.**
glGetLightiv()	Not supported.

continued

glGetMaterialfv()	**Supported**
glGetMaterialiv()	Not supported.
glGetTexEnvfv()	**Supported.**
glGetTexEnviv()	Supported.
glGetTexGen()	Not supported.
glGetTexParemeter{if}[v]()	**Supported.**
glGetTexLevelParemeter()	Not supported.
glIsTexture()	Supported.
glGetPixelMap()	Not supported.
glGetMap{ifd}()	Not supported.
glGetTexImage()	Not supported.
glGetCompressedTexImage()	Not supported.
glGetPolygonStipple()	Not supported.
glGetColorTable()	Not supported.
glGetColorTableParameter()	Not supported.
glGetConvolutionFilter()	Not supported.
glGetSeparableFilter()	Not supported.
glGetConvolutionParameter()	Not supported.
glGetHistogram()	Not supported.
glGetHistogramParameter()	Not supported.
glGetMinmax()	Not supported.
glGetMinmaxParameter()	Not supported.
glIsQuery()	**Not supported.**
glGetQueryiv()	**Not supported.**
glGetQueryObject[u]iv()	**Not supported.**
glIsBuffer()	**Supported.**
glGetBufferSubData()	**Not supported.**
glGetBufferParameteriv()	**Supported.**
glGetBufferPointer()	**Not supported.**

Finally, the string returned by glGetString(GL_VERSION) should be OpenGL ES-XX 1.1 for OpenGL ES 1.1 implementations, where XX is CM for Common profiles and CL for Common Lite profiles.

OpenGL ES 1.1 Extensions

Just as in OpenGL ES 1.0, 1.1 includes a number of core additions, required extensions, and optional extensions. Some of these are carried over from 1.0, but there are a number of new ones as well.

Core Additions

The OES_byte_coordinate core addition has not changed, but OES_fixed_point and OES_single_precision have experienced some minor updates, and OES_matrix_get has been added as a new core addition.

OES_fixed_point

This core addition was only modified slightly, adding the following functions:

```
GLvoid glClipPlanex(GLenum plane, const GLfixed *equation);
GLvoid glGetClipPlanex(GLenum plane, GLfixed * equation);
GLvoid glPointParameterxv(GLenum pname, const GLfixed * params)
GLvoid glGetFixedv(GLenum pname, GLfixed* params);
GLvoid glGetMaterialx(GLenum face, GLenum pname, T param);
GLvoid glGetLightx(GLenum light, GLenum pname, T * params);
```

OES_single_precision

The only change made to this core addition was that two of the functions it includes—glClipPlanef() and glGetClipPlanef()—are now supported in OpenGL ES.

OES_matrix_get

Games frequently need to read matrix data, and OpenGL 1.1 makes this possible through using glGetFloatv() (for Common profiles) or glGetFixedv() (for Common Lite). A problem arises due to the fact that Common Lite implementations are free to represent matrices as floating point values internally. Since the Common Lite profile does not include support for floating point values at the API level, it's impossible to return an internal floating point representation using glGetFixedv() without losing information.

OpenGL ES 1.0 included the optional OES_query_matrix extension to help address this issue, but in 1.1, this extension has been replaced with a new core addition, OES_matrix_get.

OES_get_matrix introduces several new tokens, which can be used with glGetIntegerv() to read matrices as floating point values encoded into an array of integers. These floating point values are represented using the IEEE 754 floating point bit layout:

Bit 31 is the sign bit

Bits 30–23 are the exponent

Bits 22–0 are the mantissa

The new tokens are listed in Table 9.10.

Table 9.10 OES_get_matrix Tokens

Token	Notes
GL_MODELVIEW_MATRIX_FLOAT_AS_INT_BITS_OES	Modelview matrix
GL_PROJECTION_MATRIX_FLOAT_AS_INT_BITS_OES	Projection matrix
GL_TEXTURE_MATRIX_FLOAT_AS_INT_BITS_OES	Texture matrix

Required Extensions

OES_read_format and OES_compressed_paletted_texture have not changed and are still required extensions. Two new required extensions, OES_point_sprite and OES_point_size_array, have been added.

OES_point_sprite

Particle systems are an important feature in many games. In order to be able to increase the number and quality of effects that can be simulated with particle systems, most particles are rendered as textured quads. However, quads are an inefficient representation due to the fact that they require four times as many vertices as are really needed. In addition, it's necessary to compute the vertex positions every frame to make sure the quad is screen aligned.

Point sprites were introduced several years ago to make particle system rendering more efficient. Using point sprites, developers are able to specify particles using a single point. The graphics engine then takes these points and applies textures to them as if they were quads. This saves both geometry bandwidth and processing time.

Point sprite support is required in OpenGL ES 1.1 through the OES_point_sprite extension, which is similar to the ARB_point_sprite and NV_point_sprite extensions to OpenGL.

To use point sprites, they must first be enabled, as follows:

```
glEnable(GL_POINT_SPRITE_OES);
```

Point sprites are rendered just as if you were rendering GL_POINTS. They are affected by the current point size (glPointSize()) and point attenuation (glPointParameter()), but they are not antialiased (point smoothing is disabled when point sprites are enabled).

Point sprites will automatically have any currently enabled textures applied to them. Normally, points only have one texture coordinate, and this coordinate will be applied to all fragments in the point, no matter how large the point is. In order to have the entire texture applied to the point sprite (which is normally the desired behavior with particles), you need to tell OpenGL ES to generate texture coordinates appropriately. This is done with:

```
glTexEnvf(GL_POINT_SPRITE_OES, GL_COORD_REPLACE_OES, GL_TRUE);
```

This will need to be done for every texture unit you want to use. Point sprite texture coordinate generation can be disabled with:

```
glTexEnvf(GL_POINT_SPRITE_OES, GL_COORD_REPLACE_OES, GL_FALSE);
```

Texture coordinates will be assigned such that the top left corner of the point sprite is (0, 0) and the bottom right corner is (1, 1).

The following code snippet shows how to use point sprites. Assume that particlePositions and particleTexture have been initialized appropriately.

```
void DrawParticles(GLfloat *particlePositions,
                   GLuint particleTexture, GLint numParticles)
{
  glEnable(GL_POINT_SPRITE_OES);
  glEnable(GL_TEXTURE_2D);
  glEnableClientState(GL_VERTEX_ARRAY);
  glVertexPointer(3, GL_FLOAT, 0, particlePositions);

  glPointSize(2.0);

  // set the point size to decrease linearly with distance
  GLfloat attenuation[] = {1.0f, 0.5f, 0.0f};
  glPointParameterfv(GL_POINT_DISTANCE_ATTENUATION, attenuation);

  // set up point sprite texture coordinate replacement
  glTexEnvf(GL_POINT_SPRITE_OES, GL_COORD_REPLACE_OES, GL_TRUE);
  glDrawArrays(GL_POINTS, 0, numParticles);

  // clean up
  glTexEnvf(GL_POINT_SPRITE_OES, GL_COORD_REPLACE_OES, GL_FALSE);
  glDisableClientState(GL_VERTEX_ARRAY);
  glDisable(GL_TEXTURE_2D);
  glDisable(GL_POINT_SPRITE_OES);
}
```

OES_point_size_array

One limitation of the point sprite system as described so far is that it's only possible to change the size of the particles by calling glPointSize(). This is fine if all of your particles are the same size, but in practice, this is often not the case. You could break up your particle data by size and send a few particles at a time, calling glPointSize() between each call to glDrawArrays(), but most OpenGL ES implementations are able to perform better when processing large batches of data at once.

To allow this, OpenGL ES 1.1 includes the mandatory OES_point_size_array extension, which extends the vertex array system to include attributes for point sizes.

Point size arrays are enabled or disabled by passing GL_POINT_SIZE_ARRAY_OES to glEnableClientState() and glDisableClientState(). The point size array is set using:

GLvoid glPointSizePointerOES(GLenum type, GLsizei stride, const GLvoid *pointer);

type is either GL_FLOAT or GL_FIXED, depending on the profile. *stride* has the same meaning as other gl*Pointer() functions. *pointer* points to an array of fixed or floating point values, with one value per vertex.

Distance-based attenuation of point size can be used with this extension as well, in which case the final point size will be determined by using the point size in conjunction with the values passed to glPointParameter().

Note

This extension doesn't just apply to point sprites. It can be used with regular points as well.

Optional Extensions

OpenGL ES 1.1 adds two new optional extensions, OES_matrix_palette and OES_draw_texture, while dropping support for the 1.0 optional extension OES_query_matrix.

OES_query_matrix

Support for this optional extension has been dropped entirely in OpenGL ES 1.1. It has been replaced with support for reading the matrices using glGetFloatv() or glGetFixedv() and the superior OES_matrix_get core addition.

OES_matrix_palette

The optional OES_matrix_palette allows developers to take advantage of OpenGL ES hardware when doing vertex skinning. This extension is a simplified version of ARB_matrix_palette.

To use vertex skinning with OpenGL ES, a palette of matrices is created and loaded. Each vertex includes one or more indices into this palette and a weight for each vertex. When the vertex is transformed, it is multiplied by each entry in the palette that it indexes. The results of these multiplications are then scaled by the weighting factor and summed to obtain the final result. A similar process happens with normals, except that the inverse transpose of the modelview matrices are used instead.

The number of indices that can be used per vertex depends on the total number of *vertex units* supported by the implementation. Vertex units are conceptually similar to texture units. Each represents a single matrix application. The total number of vertex units available can be determined by calling glGetIntegerv() with GL_MAX_VERTEX_UNITS_OES. There is similarly an implementation-dependent limit on the number of matrix palette entries that can be loaded. This value can be determined by passing GL_MAX_PALETTE_MATRICES_OES to glGetIntegerv().

In order to use the matrix palette, it must be enabled and selected instead of the modelview matrix stack. This is done as follows:

```
glEnable(GL_MATRIX_PALETTE_OES);
glMatrixMode(GL_MATRIX_PALETTE_OES);
```

The matrix palette is loaded one entry at a time. To do this, you must first select which entry to load. A new function has been added to support this:

```
GLvoid glCurrentPaletteMatrixOES(GLuint index);
```

index must be a value between 0 and GL_MAX_PALETTE_MATRICES_OES −1, inclusive. After selecting which entry you want to load, the matrix is loaded using the existing glLoadMatrix() function. In fact, all functions that affect the current matrix (e.g. glLoadIdentity(), glRotatef()) will affect the currently-selected entry in the matrix palette when the matrix mode is set to GL_MATRIX_PALETTE_OES. Additionally, the current modelview matrix can be loaded into the currently-selected index with another new function:

```
GLvoid glLoadPaletteFromModelViewMatrixOES();
```

To specify the per-vertex indices and weights, two new functions have been added to the vertex arrays system:

```
GLvoid glMatrixIndexPointerOES(GLint size, GLenum type, GLsizei stride, GLvoid *pointer)
GLvoid glWeightPointerOES(GLint size, GLenum type, GLsizei stride, GLvoid *pointer);
```

The *size* parameter indicates how many indices and weights are being used per vertex. These values must be between 1 and GL_MAX_VERTEX_UNITS_OES, inclusive. *type* must be GL_UNSIGNED_BYTE for matrix indices, and GL_FLOAT or GL_FIXED (depending on the profile) for weights. *stride* is used as in other vertex pointer functions. *pointer* points to an array of indices for glMatrixIndexPointerOES() and an array of weights for glWeightPointerOES(). There should be size indices and weights per vertex.

These arrays can be enabled or disabled by passing GL_MATRIX_INDEX_ARRAY_OES and GL_WEIGHT_ARRAY_OES to glEnableClientState()/glDisableClientState().

The following code shows how to use the matrix palette. This code sample has been borrowed from the extension specification, due to the fact that no OpenGL ES 1.1 implementations were available for testing at the time of writing.

```
/* position viewer */
glMatrixMode(GL_MATRIX_PALETTE_OES);
glCurrentPaletteMatrixOES(0);
glLoadIdentity();
glTranslatef(0.0f, 0.0f, -7.0f);
glRotatef(yrot, 0.0f, 1.0f, 0.0f);

glCurrentPaletteMatrixOES(1);
glLoadIdentity();
glTranslatef(0.0f, 0.0f, -7.0f);

glRotatef(yrot, 0.0f, 1.0f, 0.0f);
glRotatef(zrot, 0.0f, 0.0f, 1.0f);

glEnableClientState(GL_VERTEX_ARRAY);
glEnableClientState(GL_TEXTURE_COORD_ARRAY);
glEnableClientState(GL_MATRIX_INDEX_ARRAY_OES);
glEnableClientState(GL_WEIGHT_ARRAY_OES);

glVertexPointer(3, GL_FLOAT, 7 * sizeof(GLfloat), vertexdata);
glTexCoordPointer(2, GL_FLOAT, 7 * sizeof(GLfloat), vertexdata + 3);
glWeightPointerOES(2, GL_FLOAT, 7 * sizeof(GLfloat),vertexdata + 5);
glMatrixIndexPointerOES(2, GL_UNSIGNED_BYTE, 0, matrixindexdata);

for(int i = 0; i < (numSegments << 2) + 2; i ++)
  glDrawArrays(GL_TRIANGLE_FAN, i << 2, 4);
```

OES_draw_texture

The ability to draw an image directly to the framebuffer is useful for many things in games, such as drawing a static background, bitmapped fonts, and so on. OpenGL ES does not support glDrawPixels() since it requires a separate pipeline that is difficult to implement efficiently. It's possible to draw images using textures, but this approach is somewhat lacking in control or flexibility. Point sprites can be used in some cases, but they too have their limitations.

The OES_draw_texture extension was added as an optional feature to allow for greater control over drawing images, while taking advantage of the existing texturing hardware.

This extension adds a texture crop rectangle, which defines the area of the texture image that will be written to the framebuffer as a screen-aligned rectangle. This region is defined by calling glTexParameteriv() with the *pname* set to GL_TEXTURE_CROP_RECT_OES and *params* set to an array of integers defining the edges of the rectangle.

To draw the texture, two additional functions have been added:

```
GLvoid glDrawTex{sifx}OES(T x, T y, T z, T w, T h);
GLvoid glDrawTex{sifx}vOES(T * coords);
```

Note

The crop rectangle only has an effect during glDrawTex() calls. It does not affect normal texturing operations.

The parameters to these functions define the window region where the texture image will be drawn. The size of the window rectangle does not need to be the same size as the texture crop rectangle, so stretching or shrinking will occur as needed.

z is used to set the depth value of the rectangle in window coordinates. The interpretation of z depends on the depth range near and far values (set by glDepthRange()). If z is less than or equal to 0, it is clamped to the near depth value. If z is greater than or equal to 1, it is clamped to the far depth value. Otherwise, it is calculated using (near + z) $\times$ (far − near). If the near and far depth range values are set to the defaults of 0 and 1, then this is equivalent to clamping the z value to [0, 1]. The z value specified will be constant across the entire surface.

When the call to glDrawTex() is made, fragments are generated for the specified window region, and texels from the textures bound to all currently-enabled texture units are applied to these fragments. The textures are filtered just as they would be normally. In addition, the fragments generated are no different from any other fragments, so all normal fragment operations are applied. These fragments use the current color and have an eye depth of 0 for fog computation unless the EXT_fog_coordinate extension is supported, in which case you can control the fog factor directly.

Texture coordinates are generated automatically such that the texture crop rectangle is sampled across the span of the window rectangle. If mipmapping is enabled, the size of the window rectangle relative to the texture crop rectangle will be used for LOD determination.

Beyond 1.1

OpenGL ES will continue to evolve as the need for high performance, robust graphics libraries on embedded systems grows. Support for programmability will inevitably appear in the near future, at which point the OpenGL ES version number will advance to 2.0, just as has been done with OpenGL. It is not clear at this point whether there will be another OpenGL ES revision between 1.1 and 2.0, but there will almost certainly be many extensions added to implementations during the interim.

To give you an idea of the kind of features that may be added to OpenGL ES devices, this section will provide an overview of future OpenGL ES hardware coming from QUAL-COMM and ATI Technologies.

Shortly after this book is published, QUALCOMM will ship OpenGL ES 1.0-based hardware as part of its MSM6550 chipset, which will be available on a wide range of midrange phones. Additional chipsets will be shipped later with ATI's Imageon 2300 as an external chip. These chips will be available in high-end phones.

QUALCOMM and ATI are currently working together to develop a new chipset with integrated 3D graphics for QUALCOMM's MSM7000 series. In addition to providing full support for OpenGL ES 1.1, this chip will support the following OpenGL features:

- Texture crossbar (`ARB_texture_env_crossbar`)
- Mirrored repeat wrap mode (`ARB_texture_mirrored_repeat`)
- Stencil wrap (`EXT_stencil_wrap`)
- Many additional blending modes (`EXT_blend_minmax`, `EXT_blend_subtract`, `EXT_blend_func_separate`, `EXT_blend_equation_separate`)

This chip will also support an addition extension to allow for a more efficient representation of texture coordinate data. The `ATI_extended_fixed_vertex_data_type` extension allows an application to specify texture coordinates as a 4.4, 8.8, or 4.12 value. The advantage of using these data types for texture coordinates is that developers can keep the texture coordinate data size as bytes or shorts and not have to use a texture matrix. The only way in 1.0 and 1.1 to do this is to specify the texture coordinates as shorts and use an appropriate texture matrix. Since the texture matrix isn't often used otherwise, with this new extension you save an extra matrix operation, which should improve your vertex transformation performance.

This is only one small example of some of the advances that will be made in OpenGL ES, but it should give you an idea of the direction that's being taken.

Summary

In this chapter, you learned about the additions that have been made to OpenGL ES in version 1.1. You've seen the differences between 1.0 and 1.1 and learned about the new features in 1.1 in detail. You've also seen some of the things that are being done in OpenGL ES hardware, paving the way for future revisions.

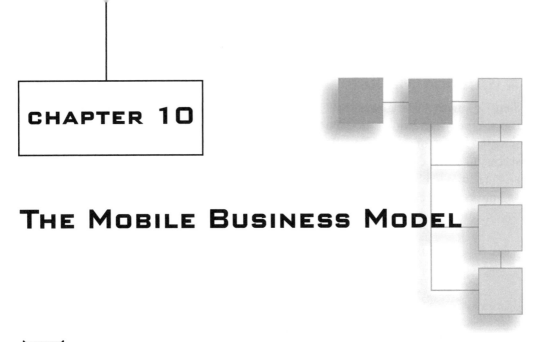

CHAPTER 10

THE MOBILE BUSINESS MODEL

The wireless business model can be a unique challenge for any newcomers to the industry having to confront important questions regarding their market, product, and partnerships. The decisions reached at the onset of a business venture will have a long-lasting effect on its success. The wireless gaming world is no different.

There is a seemingly endless set of forks in the road that wireless game developers must successfully navigate on the path to getting their wares on the catalogs of operators and ultimately in the hands of consumers. However, there is one question that seems settled: It's "game on" for the wireless gaming market.

The vision of many wireless industry leaders is that voice calls and wireless data applications will occupy a significant portion of a user's wireless experience, both in practice and on their monthly bill. No argument needs to be made for the existing value of wireless voice, and as wireless networks continue to improve in both speed and capacity, wireless data applications of all types—video, location-based services, and business and enterprise—will undoubtedly catch up.

Mobile games, meanwhile, have already begun carrying the banner for wireless data. For example, since the launch of Verizon Wireless' Get It Now® service in 2002, as of June 2004 there have been over 70 million games downloaded from this one operator alone. Furthermore, as a general trend, the prices of games have also steadily risen—a positive sign that consumers are willing to pay more as games become more compelling and advanced in nature.

A Growing Market

Sony Computer Entertainment (SCE) announced in January 2004 that cumulatively SCE had shipped worldwide over 70 million units of the PlayStation2 video game consoles since the launch of the system in Japan in March 2000. While the PlayStation 2 is the most successful of the current generation consoles, 70 million units pales in comparison to the existing installed base of mobile phone users globally, a figure well in excess of 1 billion and projected to exceed 2 billion in 2006 (EMC, July 2004). Figure 10.1 shows the worldwide cellular subscribers predicted for 2008.

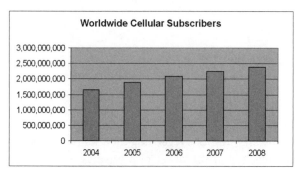

Figure 10.1 Chart showing worldwide cellular subscribers (Source EMC, July 2004)

Moreover, wireless device manufacturers combined will ship over 800 million units in 2008 alone (EMC, July 2004). Due to the sheer size and potential opportunity, it's no wonder that mobile gaming is garnering such widespread attention from industry insiders, as well as the media, analysts, and venture capitalists—investment activity in the latter having noticeably heated up in the last 12 months.

Some industry analysts value the current mobile gaming market in the United States as a $230 million dollar per year industry with about 14.4 million mobile gamers (Zelos Group Inc., July 2004). Worldwide, the numbers are even more impressive, indicating that revenues for mobile gaming could reach $2.3 billion by the end of 2004 (Strategy Analytics, July 2004).

The projections for growth are equally impressive. By 2006, some estimates predict that U.S. wireless subscribers will spend $500 million on wireless games, with European consumers spending about $1 billion and wireless users in Asia spending more than $2 billion. By 2007, those numbers will grow to $800 million in the United States and $1.4 billion in Europe, with the Asian mobile gaming market growing to an astounding $2.8 billion (Yankee Group, September 2003).

Figure 10.2 shows mobile gaming revenue projections in the U.S. through 2008.

And what's good for the industry, naturally, is great for game publishers and developers. While many of them choose to keep dollar amounts close to the vest, some of the more seasoned and successful wireless game specialists are already announcing healthy revenue figures. U.S.-based JAMDAT Mobile, for example, recently announced that the company's BREW-based applications are generating more than $1 million in revenue each month.

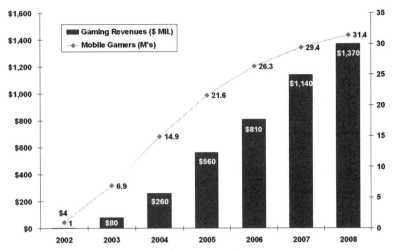

Figure 10.2 Mobile Gaming Adoption Graph
(Zelos Group Inc., July 2004).

Considering the costs to develop wireless games are many orders of magnitude less than developing a traditional video or PC game, it's easy to see that ROIs can be generated today that will continue to fuel the growth of the market.

Big Names, Evolving Convergence

While dollars usually speak for themselves, they're not the only voice lending credibility for a genre quickly gaining acceptance among both casual and competitive gamers.

Stepping up to the plate are some big names from the traditional video game console and PC gaming space like Activision, THQ, Sony Online Entertainment, Capcom Entertainment, Namco, Sega, and Square Enix, as well as international developers who are making the U.S. crossover, such as Com2uS and M-Dream from South Korea, Gameloft and In-Fusio from France, and iFone, Digital Bridges, and Macrospace from the United Kingdom. Also appearing in the wireless scene now are traditional game developers, such as Climax Group and Vicarious Visions, companies previously focused only on console or PC title development.

The evolving convergence of the console/PC and wireless gaming worlds has been prompted not only by the potentially lucrative opportunity that mobile gaming is primed to realize, but also by two other notable factors.

First, there have been great strides made in the quality and capabilities of mobile games. In short, the industry has come a long way since *Snake*.

Major brand owners who initially were worried that a black-and-white handset form-factor would be too limiting are now realizing that their brand representation on phones is not only acceptable, but also is becoming richer and richer all the time. Traditional gaming giants—and in tandem both casual and hard-core gamers—have been drawn in as phone-based games become easier to access and navigate and improved 3D technology makes the experience more compelling.

Within a year or two, 3D-based phones with large color quarter VGA and half VGA displays will be available in the mass market with graphics performance several times the capabilities of the original Sony PlayStation. In addition, 3D surround sound via headphones or external speakers will further enhance the user experience. GPS functionality is yet another technology that will enable more advanced and unique game play. Finally, features such as a "TV out" connector will allow mobile phones to be connected directly to TVs. Phones will also potentially adopt physical form factors and user interfaces that will make them more playable from a gamer's perspective.

All of the above functionalities coupled with high-speed networks will quickly deliver large (several MBs in size), sophisticated games efficiently over the air in sequential fashion based on levels. From a game design standpoint, this framework also easily supports a recurring monthly subscription business model as well. Wireless digital distribution of games will likely become commonplace and make possible a whole new distribution paradigm for traditional game publishers to take advantage of, a paradigm that can potentially even disrupt existing physical retail models. Gone are boxed products on shelves, replaced by digital products being delivered invisibly over the airwaves.

Second, traditional game publishers are seeing the value in cross-promoting their titles across multiple gaming platforms. Many PC and console games now highlight the mobile versions with built-in promotions and incentives. For example, the mobile edition of Gameloft's blockbuster action game *XIII* rewards winners with a special "cheat code" to unlock a secret "big head" mode in the PC version by Ubisoft. This scenario can potentially be a two-way street, allowing PC or console players to be rewarded with mobile phone wallpapers, ringtones, and mobile game cheat codes received, based on success playing the console or PC version. Last, there is also the opportunity for commerce as well—perhaps selling ancillary products like DVDs, CDs, books, magazines, and more.

The experience only improves with advancements in joining together mobile and massively multiplayer online (MMO) gaming. Avid online gamers can use their phones to find out what's going on *right now* in their virtual gaming worlds and make real-time adjustments. Allowing for ubiquitous access for gamers to their online persistent worlds is certainly enabled as mobile networks and devices rapidly advance.

Another example would be the capability for a user to play minigames on a phone that are tangentially related to a MMO game and then insert items won from the phone version, such as a weapon or world currency, back into the MMO game, thus creating an experience that can be played practically anytime. Obviously, there will be the need for proper play, balancing design between the MMO game and the mobile component, but nevertheless, with this example one can see how traditional games can be extended via mobile phones to essentially encourage users to play anytime they're away from the actual MMO game—a pretty enticing user behavior in which publishers would see great value.

In the future, it is also not unimaginable that we will see multiplayer wireless games that are serialized in nature and perhaps even follow a TV show programming paradigm so that players tune in each week to play the game instead of being able to play anytime.

The prospect of a steadily growing mobile gaming market and the entry of established gaming leaders into the mobile space—coupled with the rapidly improving capabilities of wireless devices, networks, and development platforms—creates a winning recipe and indicates that the time is ideal for prospective developers to get in the wireless game.

Game Ecosystem Dynamics and Distribution

A well-defined ecosystem exists within the game business that consists of essentially seven key components: publishers, developers, brands, platforms, distributors, retailers, and consumers.

Publishers are the centerpieces relative to developers in terms of bringing the product to market. They work to build strong brand recognition of their titles as well as the company and will actively undertake consumer and channel marketing activities to achieve this awareness. They also have the financial wherewithal, resources, brand management, and licensing skills to successfully secure brands from professional sports leagues, movie studios, music labels, book/comic publishers, and athletes/celebrities on which games will be based.

Brand licensors actively engage in this activity with publishers because it allows them to extend their brands into interactive media products, generating even more awareness of the brand. They will also provide marketing support upon launch of the publisher's product. The most visible of these tend to revolve around what are known by Hollywood studios as "tent pole" releases of major films. Examples include *Lord of the Rings*, *Spiderman*, or *The Matrix*. It is critical for a publisher to be able to launch their product "day and date" with the movie to maximize sell-through of the game, as well as to piggyback off large marketing spends by the studios. Figure 10.3 shows an overview of the video gaming business.

Publishers have an inherent capacity to scale, since they have the capability to propagate information/custom tools and lessons learned across their developer pool as well as leverage QA and server-side resources across multiple games. They also can minimize risk and adjust to market conditions due to their multititle portfolio approach to the business, where they are not dependent on any single game. Finally, publishers also provide customer support and maintain a knowledge base of known issues.

Figure 10.3 The video game business model.

Examples of traditional console/PC game publishers include Electronic Arts, Activision, THQ, Atari, UbiSoft, and Take 2 Interactive. The wireless business has seen the emergence of pure play wireless-only publishers like JAMDAT Mobile, Mforma, and Sorrent. These wireless publishers perform similar functions as described above for traditional publishers.

Although some publishers also undertake first-party development (i.e., in-house), the majority of work is done by third-party developers. These developers are generally where the true innovation and creativity originate in terms of a new game design or the evolution of an existing genre.

A publisher works with developers via an advance against royalties business model tied to project milestones and deliverables. For example, a publisher may spend a substantial amount of money to secure a major movie license from a Hollywood studio. The publisher will then likely have several targeted developers in mind that will submit game designs based on what type of title they would create with the licensed property (brand) secured by the publisher.

Once a developer has been chosen, the publisher will enter into a contract with the developer. A determination of what platforms (e.g., Sony PlayStation 2, Microsoft Xbox, Nintendo GameCube™) the game will be developed for will also be finalized. Platform providers provide tools, support, developer relations, and other functions to assist publishers and developers with the development of a game. In the wireless space, technology and platform providers include BREW, Java, .NET, and Symbian.

The publisher will advance money to cover the costs of the development and pay this out upon successful completion of certain milestones and deliverables such as "first playable," alpha, beta, "gold master," etc. During this process, the publisher will provide design feedback to the developer and secure the appropriate licensor/brand approvals. Publishers will later spend money marketing the product. Under the standard advance against royalties model, publishers will "earn out" their advance, including recouping their marketing dollars prior to any royalties being paid out to the developer. A similar model is used in both console/PC and wireless gaming.

When the product is completed and ready to go to market, publishers will develop marketing campaigns to support the launch of the game. The marketing mix can include everything from television to radio to print to Internet to channel retail (MDF/co-op) and more. Often, a large component of the marketing mix will be the retail/channel aspect. Publishers will work with retailers like Wal-Mart and Best Buy to ensure their products have the best shelf placement and in-store promotion, as well as external promotion via newspaper circulars and other vehicles to ensure product sell-through to end consumers. In the wireless space, operators like Verizon Wireless, Sprint, T-Mobile, AT&T Wireless, and Cingular take on the role of retailers. Publishers work with these operators regarding game deck placement on a phone as well as the more standard marketing vehicles.

Publishers often take their product to market directly to retailers. However, they may also utilize the services of distributors (e.g., Ingram Micro and Navarre). Smaller publishers will often take this route, and in many cases some of the distributors can even turn out to be other large publishers (e.g., Electronic Arts Distribution (EAD)), companies that tend to have very strong relationships with retail buyers, which is required to get product into the store in the most efficient manner. In these cases, distributors do nothing more than help facilitate sales and delivery of product because the marketing of the product remains the responsibility of the publisher that is utilizing the distributor. Interestingly enough, in the wireless space, the concept of distributors is now starting to appear.

Consumers are the final key component in the game ecosystem. They ultimately decide with their wallets whether or not a product will become a hit, a mega hit, or fail miserably. Strong consumer buzz helps accelerate sales and build pent-up demand for a sequel, which is the first step to building an enduring and profitable franchise like *Tomb Raider*™, *Grand Theft Auto*, or *Madden*—something all publishers want to achieve.

The wireless game business operates under a similar overall framework as the traditional video game business as described above. However, there are some nuances to the business that are discussed in further detail in the section below. Figure 10.4 shows an overview of the wireless gaming business.

Getting Started in Wireless

The labyrinth of choices that need to be made by prospective wireless game developers and the challenges that need to be overcome—on both a business and technical side—are many. So where does one begin?

Perhaps it's best to focus on two initial but critical questions: What type of games do you plan to develop and what target market will your products be geared toward? If your aim is to build a reputation as a strong role-playing game developer, then spending time and resources on sports games won't advance you. Knowing your target demographic—or that of potential wireless operator partners—is critical as well. A wireless cricket game won't be expected to do as well in the United States as it would in India. While these examples are

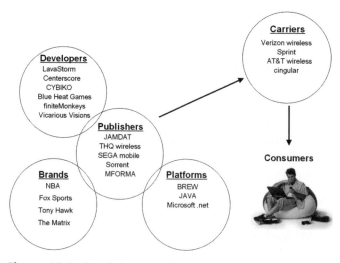

elementary, the importance of identifying a target market and demographic cannot be understated. In turn, knowing who the wireless operators are that most effectively will reach these markets will help solve a number of technical choices you'll be faced with. These choices include the selection of a wireless development and delivery platform and deciding which wireless devices your games need to run on.

Figure 10.4 The wireless game business model.

Selecting the best-suited wireless application development platform often provides a silver bullet for many issues. As mentioned earlier, often it is geography that settles the development platform question outright. Certain technologies simply have a more dominant foothold among wireless operators in certain parts of the world. In the ideal position of having a choice among multiple platforms, many mobile game developers, especially those just getting started, find greatest value in a solution that goes beyond being a simple platform for game development to a complete end-to-end system for taking a game from creation to cash flow. The solution not only helps publishers and developers get their games in front of wireless operators, onto handsets, and in front of consumers, but also includes an efficient structure to enable rapid and consistent payment based on download activity.

Using QUALCOMM's BREW (**www.qualcomm.com/brew**) solution as an example, developers gain access not only to an end-to-end solution for application development but also entry into an ecosystem connecting all members of the wireless data value chain. Publishers and developers create applications in the programming language of their choice on an open, standard, and extendable applications execution platform that resides on the wireless device. Figure 10.5 shows one example of what an end-to-end solution for game developers might look like from start of development to end-sells.

Getting your games on the commercial catalogs of operators poses a separate set of challenges. Operators are similar to the retailers (e.g., Wal-Mart, Best Buy) in the traditional game business. While some developers "go it alone," many find greater success when teaming with branded content providers and publishers that can help bolster those relationships. Getting your game in the door with an operator is one matter, while competing for virtual shelf space with other games is another. This is why many publishers and developers find partnership or licensing deals with well-known brands invaluable. Bank on the fact that *Spider Man* will always be more popular than his generic counterpart.

The work isn't over once your games are in the hands of subscribers. Like any other business, knowing the needs and behavior of the consumers playing your games is critical. Wireless operators utilizing wireless data platforms that

Figure 10.5 The BREW mobile market value chain.

provide insight on application usage offer publishers/developers the best window into how their games are faring, beyond the subscription and download numbers. Insight into who is playing your games and how they are discovering, learning about, and subsequently downloading them provides valuable feedback as to how a publisher or developer can best market them.

Finally, there are financial issues, and many developers will tell you that therein lies their biggest challenge. While the best model for charging for mobile games—whether it is per download or on a subscription basis—remains fluid, developers again find that choosing a wireless development platform that mediates subscriber billing and settlement between them, publishers, and operator partners is the essential, final element for their business model.

In the end, perhaps the best advice for wireless developers is the most basic. Be mobile. Be flexible. And always focus on quality. The wireless industry as a whole is moving at a rapid pace—networks are getting faster, devices are getting better, and the mobile audience is growing and becoming more knowledgeable. While the challenges and choices are great for potential wireless game developers, the opportunities and financial rewards are even greater. Wireless gaming is on the cusp of becoming the next big thing in mobile entertainment, and you don't want to miss it.

Summary

The mobile gaming market is growing and evolving rapidly, providing an excellent opportunity for game developers to expand their business. This chapter is by no means a comprehensive guide for developing your mobile business strategy, but it should at least serve as an introduction to the opportunities available to you.

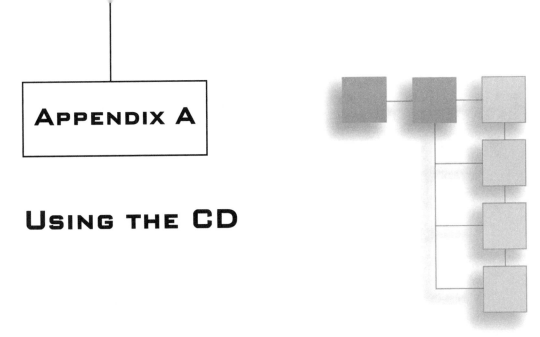

APPENDIX A

USING THE CD

The CD-ROM included with this book contains resources intended to be used in conjunction with the text. It includes an auto-installer, so all you have to do is insert the CD into your CD player and the installer will launch it.

The contents of the CD are detailed in this Appendix.

Sample Code

The sample code provided on the CD includes both WinCE examples and BREW OpenGL ES applications.

BREW OpenGL ES Examples

The following examples will run with the BREW SDK 2.x version. The BREW SDK can be downloaded at **www.brewdeveloper.com**.

A Simple Triangle

The simple triangle example is the most basic OpenGL ES demo that shows how to render a triangle. Figure A.1 is a screenshot from the simple triangle sample.

Textured Cube

The textured cube example is a very basic OpenGL ES application that demonstrates one method of loading and applying textures to a 3D cube.

Figure A.2 shows the textured cube sample running.

Figure A.1 A simple triangle.

Figure A.2 A textured cube.

Figure A.3 A 3D skybox.

Figure A.4 The flying wave.

A 3D Skybox

The 3D skybox example is a basic OpenGL ES application that demonstrates loading textures and using them as a 3D skybox in your game:

The Flying Wave

The flying wave example demonstrates using a fixed point sine function to simulate a wave along a textured surface.

Ffigure A.4 is a screenshot of the flying wave running.

ATI OpenGL ES Examples for Windows

The following examples will only run with the ATI W2300 Dev Kit installed. The demos are already provided as part of the ATI Dev Kit CD, but are provided here for reference. For more information on the ATI OpenGL ES sample code, go to: **www.ati.com/products/imageon2300/index.html**

simple_indexed

This sample will load the model and render it using standard indexed vertex arrays. The texture coordinate and vertex position data are rendered using the GL_FIXED data type. The vertex index data is stored in unsigned shorts.

GL_FIXED was added as a new type to OpenGL ES to make up for the lack of floating point processing on most handheld CPUs. All GL functions that previously used floats as data types have new versions using GL_FIXED instead. GL_FIXED is represented as one sign bit, followed by 15 bits covering $2^{14}..1$, followed by 15 bits covering $2^{-1}..2^{-16}$. In other words, it is (+/-)(15bits)(decimal point)(16bits). GL_FIXED data can be added and subtracted (with other GL_FIXED data) and set to 0 with no extra work. More complex functions like multiplication, division, and square root can be performed efficiently with only integer math using the helper functions provided in the fixed.c/h files.

simple_unindexed

This sample will render the model using non-indexed vertex and texture coordinate arrays. The indexed geometry in the 3ds file is converted to a flat structure in model.c. The texture coordinate and vertex position data is rendered using the GL_FIXED data type.

simple_retained

This sample will preload the vertex array, the texture coordinate array, and the index array into Vertex Buffer Objects using the ARB_vertex_buffer_object extension. The full specification for ARB_vertex_buffer_object can be found in the OpenGL Extension Registry at **http://oss.sgi.com/projects/oglsample/registry/ARB/vertex_buffer_object.txt**.

The texture coordinate and vertex position data is stored as GL_FIXED data. The vertex index data is stored in unsigned shorts.

On a handheld platform, bus bandwidth between the CPU and the graphics chips is often a serious bottleneck. Using a retained vertex buffer object (VBO) for frequently used models can substantially aid performance. The downside of using VBOs is that they occupy video memory, which may be in limited supply.

simple_retained_short

This sample uses VBOs to hold the model data, but it also converts the vertex positions and texture coordinates from floating point values to short values. This requires that the range of data be scaled to a higher range to avoid losing meaningful precision. When the data is rendered, it must be scaled back to its original values using the modelview matrix.

Choosing the target range for the short-based vertex position data is a balancing act. The range must be high enough to represent the model without distortion or collapsing vertices to the same position. But if it is too large, then it will result in an underflow in the modelview matrix when the data is scaled back to its original range. The smallest representable value in GL_FIXED is roughly 1/65536. So using a target range of -1000..+1000 for the shorts will leave only a few extra bits of precision in the matrix for other transformations.

The effect of changing the target range for short data can be seen by changing the SHORT_VTX_RANGE value in model.h and recompiling. It if is set much higher than 1000, then the model will rotate choppily and there will be some distortion to the model since meaningful precision is being truncated in the model matrix. If the value is set much lower than 1,000, then the model will rotate smoothly, but the vertices will begin to collapse into each other.

fog_and_alpha

The geometry is stored and rendered in the same manner as the simple_retained sample, but fog and alpha blending have been added. Linear fog will be applied, to the semi-transparent model. The keys to control the fog and alpha states are written on the screen.

This sample required additional UI to control it, so a distinct copy of the main source file is used. `fog_and_alpha.c` is present in this sample's source directory and is used rather than simple.c in the common source directory.

Sample Audio files

LoudLouderLoudest.com has provided a number of mobile audio samples to accompany the audio chapter. Use any media player (iTunes, Real Audio, Windows Media, WinAmp) to play the MP3 files. The following list outlines the audio examples provided on the CD:

- **`AudioExample1.mp3`:** This is a Simple MIDI File played back on a Nokia 6600. It is an actual recording of a phone "performing" this MIDI file.

- **`AudioExample2.mp3`:** This is the same Simple MIDI File used in `AudioExample1`, except this it is played back on a Motorola V600. Note how different the same MIDI file sounds.

- **`AudioExample3.mp3`:** This is the same Simple MIDI File used in `AudioExample1.mp3`, except this is played back on a Soundblaster Live PC Soundcard. Notice the striking difference between this recording and the recording of the phones is `AudioExample1` and `AudioExample2`.

- **`AudioExample4.mp3`:** This is the same Simple MIDI File used in `AudioExample1.mp3`, except this is played back on a Korg Triton Synthesizer. Notice the striking difference between the recording of this synthesizer and the recording of the phones.

- **`AudioExample5.mp3`:** This is a recording of a General MIDI drum track played back on a General MIDI synthesizer. This is how the file is supposed to sound.

- **`AudioExample6.mp3`:** This is a recording of a General MIDI drum track played back on a non-General MIDI synthesizer. This is the same file as `AudioExample6`, if you can believe it. It is because of problems like this that General MIDI was invented.

- **`AudioExample7.mp3`:** This is the pre-phone adapted title music for the shooting game described in the chapter. Compare this with `AudioExample9a` and `AudioExample9b`, which are versions of this file adapted for specific phones.

- **`AudioExample8.mp3`:** This is a recording of a MIDI gunshot sound effect as described in the audio chapter. Compare it to `AudioExample12b`, which is the MIDI gunshot SFX playing back on a phone.

- **`AudioExample9.mp3`:** This is the WAV source that will be used to create the QCP gunshot sound effect. Compare it to `AudioExample12b`, which is the QCP file playing back on the phone.

- **`AudioExample9a.mp3`:** This is a recording of a Nokia 3650 playing back the Title Music for the shooting game.

- **AudioExample10a.mp3:** This is a recording of a Nokia 3650 playing back Lose Game Music for the shooting game.
- **AudioExample11a.mp3:** This is a recording of a Nokia 3650 playing back Win Game Music for the shooting game.
- **AudioExample12a.mp3:** This is the MIDI Gunshot sound effect playing back on a Nokia 3650.
- **AudioExample13a.mp3:** This is the MIDI Can Hit sound effect playing back on a Nokia 3650.
- **Audio Example14a.mp3:** This is the MIDI Can Hit Bonus sound effect playing back on a Nokia 3650.
- **AudioExample15.mp3:** This is a MIDI file played back at normal pitch and normal tempo.
- **AudioExample16.mp3:** This is a MIDI file played back at half pitch and normal tempo. Pitch can be controlled in the engine in order to get more mileage out of 1 MIDI file.
- **AudioExample17.mp3:** This is a MIDI file played back at normal pitch and double tempo. Tempo can also be controlled in the engine.

INDEX

7593

THOMSON
★
COURSE TECHNOLOGY ™

Professional ■ Trade ■ Reference

GOT GAME?

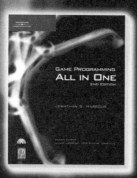

Game Programming All in One,
2nd Edition
1-59200-383-4 ■ $49.99

3D Game Engine Programming
1-59200-351-6 ■ $59.99

Mathematics
for Game Developers
1-59200-038-X ■ $49.99

3D Game Programming
All in One
1-59200-136-X ■ $49.99

Premier
Ⓟ
Press ™
A division of Course Technology

PREMIER PRESS
GAME DEVELOPMENT

Call **1.800.354.9706** to order
Order online at **www.courseptr.com**

Gamedev.net

The most comprehensive game development resource

- The latest news in game development
- The most active forums and chatrooms anywhere, with insights and tips from experienced game developers
- Links to thousands of additional game development resources
- Thorough book and product reviews
- Over 1,000 game development articles!
  Game design
  Graphics
  DirectX
  OpenGL
  AI
  Art
  Music
  Physics
  Source Code
  Sound
  Assembly
  And More!

Gamedev.net

OpenGL is a registered trademark of Silicon Graphics, Inc.
Microsoft, DirectX are registered trademarks of Microsoft Corp. in the United States and/or other countries.

License Agreement/Notice of Limited Warranty

By opening the sealed disc container in this book, you agree to the following terms and conditions. If, upon reading the following license agreement and notice of limited warranty, you cannot agree to the terms and conditions set forth, return the unused book with unopened disc to the place where you purchased it for a refund.

License:

The enclosed software is copyrighted by the copyright holder(s) indicated on the software disc. You are licensed to copy the software onto a single computer for use by a single user and to a backup disc. You may not reproduce, make copies, or distribute copies or rent or lease the software in whole or in part, except with written permission of the copyright holder(s). You may transfer the enclosed disc only together with this license, and only if you destroy all other copies of the software and the transferee agrees to the terms of the license. You may not decompile, reverse assemble, or reverse engineer the software.

Notice of Limited Warranty:

The enclosed disc is warranted by Thomson Course Technology PTR to be free of physical defects in materials and workmanship for a period of sixty (60) days from end user's purchase of the book/disc combination. During the sixty-day term of the limited warranty, Thomson Course Technology PTR will provide a replacement disc upon the return of a defective disc.

Limited Liability:

THE SOLE REMEDY FOR BREACH OF THIS LIMITED WARRANTY SHALL CONSIST ENTIRELY OF REPLACEMENT OF THE DEFECTIVE DISC. IN NO EVENT SHALL THOMSON COURSE TECHNOLOGY PTR OR THE AUTHOR BE LIABLE FOR ANY OTHER DAMAGES, INCLUDING LOSS OR CORRUPTION OF DATA, CHANGES IN THE FUNCTIONAL CHARACTERISTICS OF THE HARDWARE OR OPERATING SYSTEM, DELETERIOUS INTERACTION WITH OTHER SOFTWARE, OR ANY OTHER SPECIAL, INCIDENTAL, OR CONSEQUENTIAL DAMAGES THAT MAY ARISE, EVEN IF THOMSON COURSE TECHNOLOGY PTR AND/OR THE AUTHOR HAS PREVIOUSLY BEEN NOTIFIED THAT THE POSSIBILITY OF SUCH DAMAGES EXISTS.

Disclaimer of Warranties:

THOMSON COURSE TECHNOLOGY PTR AND THE AUTHOR SPECIFICALLY DISCLAIM ANY AND ALL OTHER WARRANTIES, EITHER EXPRESS OR IMPLIED, INCLUDING WARRANTIES OF MERCHANTABILITY, SUITABILITY TO A PARTICULAR TASK OR PURPOSE, OR FREEDOM FROM ERRORS. SOME STATES DO NOT ALLOW FOR EXCLUSION OF IMPLIED WARRANTIES OR LIMITATION OF INCIDENTAL OR CONSEQUENTIAL DAMAGES, SO THESE LIMITATIONS MIGHT NOT APPLY TO YOU.

Other:

This Agreement is governed by the laws of the State of Massachusetts without regard to choice of law principles. The United Convention of Contracts for the International Sale of Goods is specifically disclaimed. This Agreement constitutes the entire agreement between you and Thomson Course Technology PTR regarding use of the software.